GREEK FIRE

To T.H.
'Not back to the Greeks, but forward with the Greeks.'

GREEK FIRE

Oliver Taplin

Atheneum   New York   1990

End papers: An aquatint of a daguerreotype taken in 1839, the year that the process was discovered. The Parthenon looks very different today: all the columns have been re-erected and the mosque inside was long ago demolished. Half-title: A Byzantine manuscript illustrating their secret weapon of 'Greek fire'. Dedication picture: Rehearsal of Tony Harrison's *The Trackers of Oxyrhynchus* in the ancient Stadium at Delphi in June 1988. The spring of Castalia and the crags of the Phaedriades are the backdrop. Chapter openers: Know Thyself: The spring of Castalia (or Castaly), where visitors used to wash before consulting the Delphic oracle. Tragedy: The closing scene of the London National Theatre's *Oresteia* (1981). Athena commands that the Furies should be robed in purple for the final torchlight procession. Aesthetics: Alma-Tadema's vision of Phidias putting the finishing touches to the Parthenon Frieze ('The Elgin Marbles'). It had been demonstrated in the nineteenth century that Greek sculptures were painted in bright colours. Myth: *Orpheus in the Underworld* by Jan Breughel. Aphrodite: *The Judgment of Paris* by Rubens. Paris chooses the blonde! Above a Fury presages the sack of Troy. Physics: Fermilab, the high-energy physics research centre near Chicago. Ideas: Raphael painted the *School of Athens* in the Stanza della Segnatura in the Vatican in 1509–11. Plato and Aristotle are in the centre and various Greek philosophers surround them. Diogenes lounges on the steps. Politics: The Forces of Fascism fly over the Cradle of Democracy. Architecture: A painting by Carl Laubin (1987) to give an impression of Leon Krier's proposed new city of Atlantis on Tenerife. War: *The Greeks and Trojans Struggle for the Body of Patroclus* by Antoine Wiertz (1806–65). A painting of Homeric violence and pathos.
Picture research for *Greek Fire* by Pat Hodgson

Excerpts from *Collected Poems* by Louis MacNeice, *Collected Shorter Poems* by Ezra Pound, *Four Quartets* by T. S. Eliot, and from *Forewords and Afterwords* and *Collected Poems* by W. H. Auden are reproduced by permission of Faber and Faber Ltd. 8 lines from 'Orpheus. Eurydike. Hermes' by Rainer Maria Rilke are from *Twentieth Century German Verse* edited by Patrick Bridgwater (Penguin Books, Revised Edition, 1968), edition copyright © Penguin Books, 1963, 1968. The author would like to thank Tony Harrison for permission to quote at length from his *Lysistrata*, and M. Robertson for permission to quote from his translation of Archilochus' verse.

First published in Great Britain by Jonathan Cape Ltd

Atheneum
Macmillan Publishing Company
866 Third Avenue, New York, N.Y. 10022

Library of Congress Cataloging-in-Publication Data
Taplin, Oliver.
Greek fire / Oliver Taplin.
p. cm.
Includes bibliographical references.
ISBN 0–689–12096–6
1. Civilization, Occidental—Greek influences.   I. Title.
CB245.T33   1990
909'.09821—dc20   89–17617 CIP

Macmillan books are available at special discounts for bulk purchases for sales promotions, premiums, fund-raising, or educational use. For details, contact: Special Sales Director, Macmillan Publishing Company, 866 Third Avenue, New York, N.Y. 10022

10 9 8 7 6 5 4 3 2 1

Printed in the United States of America

FOREWORD

by Revel Guest

R ECENT ADVANCES in modern science and technology have revolutionised our concepts of self and society. In communications, in industry, in education, in medicine and in our attitudes each to the other and to our environment, drastic changes are needed.

Significantly, this bewildering rate and scale of change confronts us at the end of a millennium, inevitably a suggestive time for recollection and reappraisal of the past. Now is surely the moment to look back at our roots and to question why it is that we act and conduct ourselves in the way we do. To fail to do this, to behave as if memory began this morning, would be to change but not to learn. Before we can prepare for the future, we must understand the influences of the past that have made us what we are.

Several years ago, when I was producing a film in the Sinai desert on St Catherine's Monastery, I was fascinated with the continuity and relevance that the monks were able to give to events, concepts and beliefs which were formulated over two thousand years ago. The experience gave me confidence. If the past could be made to feel so close, if coherent and instructive patterns could be teased out of its complexity, then why not investigate the contemporary relevance of the greatest of all influences on the culture of the West – classical Greece?

I discussed the idea with writer and director Roger Parsons of Transatlantic Films. We discovered that, over the centuries, many had 'gone back to Greece', among them some of the world's greatest and most formative thinkers. It was not simply their interest in Greece but the different ways in which they interpreted its influence throughout history which confirmed our belief that a fascinating and significant television series could be made of the subject. But how do you make a film of interpretations, of ideas alone? Surely this is the stuff of the written word.

We took our project to one of the academic world's leading young classicists, Dr Oliver Taplin of Magdalen College, Oxford, who responded to it with characteristic enthusiasm and agreed to be our guiding expert. The three of us worked together for many months before being joined by writer and director Chris Goddard, whose documentaries have been applauded for their treatment of cerebral subjects with powerful visual appeal. Yet before our ten films were in the can, it was clear to us all that the series should be accompanied by a book. Presented on television around the world, 'Greek Fire' will reach many millions of viewers, provoking some of them to ask questions, stimulating their curiosity. Oliver Taplin's book takes those questions to greater depth and brilliantly explores the answers with a weight and substance that only the written word can accomplish. His book is not a transcript of the television series, nor is the series a film of the book; they complement each other.

If there is one quality that typifies the ancient Greeks and accounts for their extraordinary achievements, it is inquisitiveness. Here then is a book for the inquisitive, for those who like to investigate ideas. It is written by a scholar who wears his astonishing breadth of knowledge lightly and who has a gift for inspiring those in his company, whether erudite in the classics or not, with his vision of what Greek culture has meant to people of all kinds for more than 2,000 years – and especially its significance in the uncertain mood in which we live today.

PREFACE

THIS BOOK IS ABOUT what has been *made out of* ancient Greece and about how the modern world has been inspired by, reacted against, imitated, transformed, parodied, recycled, subverted or received 'classical' Greece. The subject is huge, a life's work or several lives' works. This is a fragmentary compilation, like the bits and pieces recovered from an emergency excavation. I have not been able, for instance, to consider the Hebraic tradition and its relation with Greece – Christianity is, of course, the product of both. There is not much about the first great inflammation of Greek Fire, in ancient Rome, and hence about the place of Greece in the momentous rediscovery of Rome, the Renaissance. Most of the book is given to the period from 1750 to the present, and there is a special emphasis on the last twenty-five years, the time I myself have been an adult – the present is, after all, the standpoint of our perspective. There is also more to be said about the Greek influence of athletics, comedy, Aristotle's philosophy, rhetoric, education, law, Alexander the Great, Plutarch's *Lives*, history, religion. Whole books might be made of each of these: I am indeed producing a book about one topic neglected here, Odysseus and the *Odyssey*, to accompany a series of programmes which I am presenting on BBC Radio 4.

Greek Fire arose in the first instance out of a series of television documentaries made for Channel 4 by Transatlantic Films. The ten chapters expand on the themes explored in the corresponding films: but they are not intended merely as an academic documentation of what is essentially a televisual experience. The book sets out to explore the ideas for itself without getting bogged down in footnotes and references – though it is hoped that the bibliography given at the end will lead many on to further exploration.

I owe much to the close collaboration I have enjoyed with the producer Revel Guest, the director Roger Parsons, and the researchers Nancy Van Den Bergh, Fiona Wailes-Fairbairn, and, most of all, Jonathan Stamp. Their ideas and discoveries are scattered throughout. I have also plundered the interviews recorded for the films, and hope that I have acknowledged the quotations I have selected. I should like to thank Mary Beard, Allan Bloom, Sir Terence Conran, Sir Kenneth Dover, Chris Hill, Richard Jenkyns, Lindsay Judson, Raymond Klibansky, Leon Krier, Leon Lederman, Oswyn Murray, Enoch Powell, Anthony Storr and Jonathan Walters. It will be evident that I am especially indebted to two contributors, Bernard Knox and George Steiner.

I have others to thank for making contributions, answering questions and reading drafts. They include Jim Burge, Rosemary Burton, Tony Harrison, Pontus Hellström, Geoffrey Lloyd, Joe Mordaunt Crook, David Norbrook, Catherine Osborne, Richard Rutherford, Andy Szegedy-Maszak, Kim Taplin, Marion True and Michael Vickers. Above all, Robin Osborne has been prompt and generous with large suggestions and small improvements alike. I should also like to mention the patient word-processing of Rachel Woodrow and Janet Randell. Tony Colwell has been my discreet and helpful editor at Cape, and Pat Hodgson has searched untiringly for the illustrations I have wanted.

The original 'Greek fire' (illustrated on the half-title page) was strictly speaking nothing to do with ancient Greece. It was an inflammable substance developed by the Greeks of the later Byzantine era, which they used with a kind of flame-thrower to destroy enemy ships. It was alleged that it could stay alight even under water, submerged in a contrary element. Despite the anachronism *Greek Fire* is an apt title: ancient Greece can stay alight submerged in alien cultures, it has the capacity to benefit and to harm, it can be obvious on the surface or latent below. And, as with the half-legendary stuff, it is not the 'correct' version of Greece that matters for these purposes, it is what has been productively believed.

Oxford   Oliver Taplin
February 1989

CONTENTS

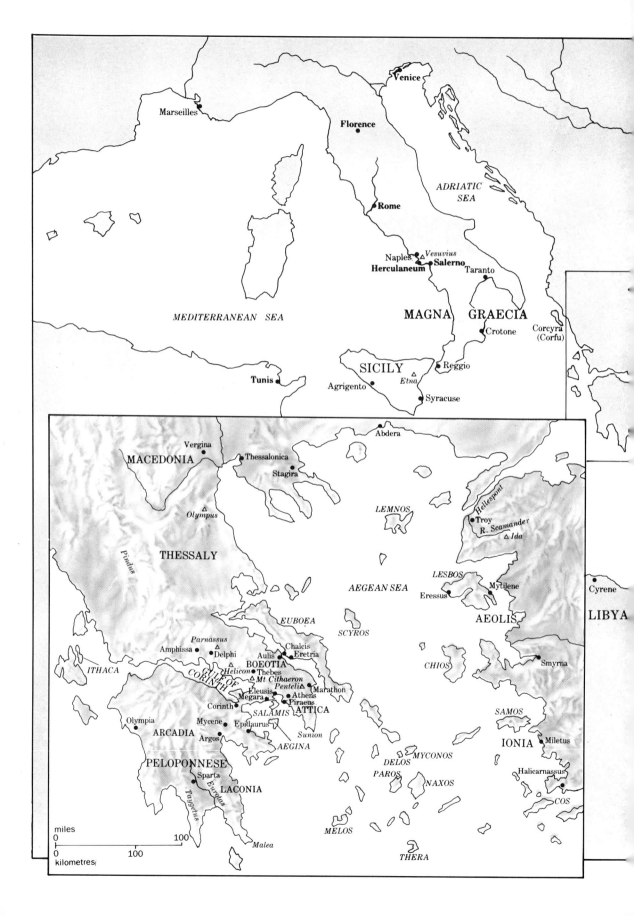

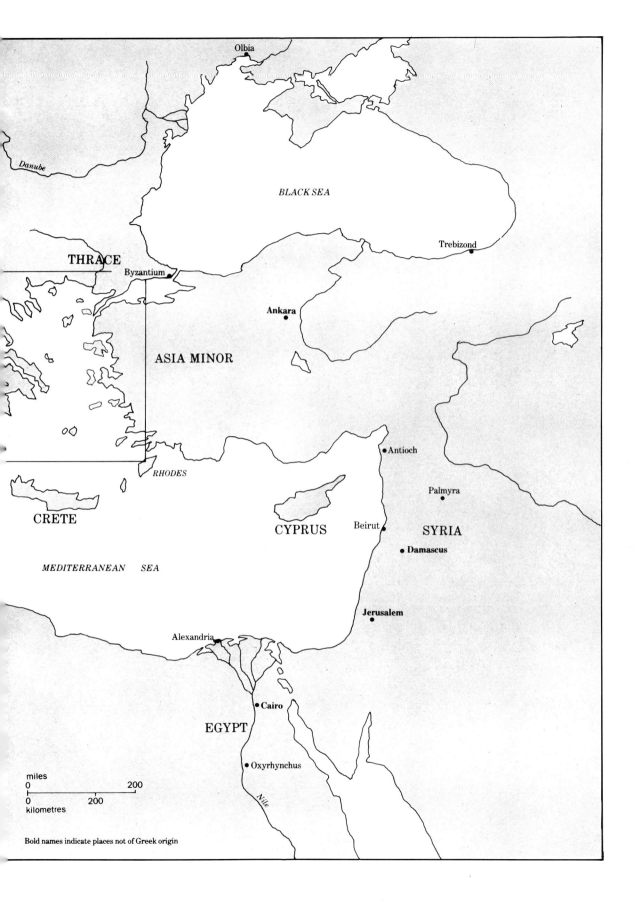

Olbia

Danube

BLACK SEA

Trebizond

THRACE

Byzantium

Ankara

ASIA MINOR

Antioch

Palmyra

RHODES

CRETE

CYPRUS

Beirut

SYRIA

Damascus

MEDITERRANEAN   SEA

Jerusalem

Alexandria

Cairo

EGYPT

Oxyrhynchus

Nile

miles
0   200
0   200
kilometres

Bold names indicate places not of Greek origin

Know Thyself

THE SOURCE OF THE WEST

Had Greek civilization never existed . . . we would never
have become fully conscious, which is to say that we would
never have become, for better or worse, fully human.

W. H. Auden

The thought of what America would be like
If the classics had a wide circulation
Troubles my sleep.

Ezra Pound

KING ZAHIR OF AFGHANISTAN was out hunting near the village of Aï
Khanoum on the Darya (or Oxus) River in 1961. By 1979, when the
Russians came from the other bank to support the regime in Kabul, the days of
the cultured monarchy were over. When Zahir saw the remains of a stone
column sticking out of the sand, decorated with overlapping acanthus leaves, he
recognised that this was a Corinthian column, here over 1,500 miles away from
Greece. Excavations by the French uncovered a Greek city of the third and
second centuries B.C., with a huge gymnasium, a theatre, an administrative
centre (*agora*), and even fragments of a philosophical text in Greek. There was
also an inscription proudly telling how someone called Clearchus went all the
way to Delphi to copy with his own hand the words of wisdom which were
inscribed around the great temple of Apollo's oracle there, so that he could take
them back to his fellow-citizens. Clearchus went to the source.

The most famous of the Delphic proverbs was:

ΓΝΩΘΙ ΣΕΑΥΤΟΝ
KNOW THYSELF

Scholars agree that in early Greece this meant 'know that you are mortal, know
that you are not a god', but its significance has not been static. Socrates in the
late fifth century B.C. was said by the oracle to be the wisest man in the world:
he would more likely have taken the words to be close to his motto 'The
unexamined life is not worth living'. Friedrich Nietzsche, that disturbing
precursor of twentieth-century preoccupations, said: 'The oracle proclaims to
you at the beginning of your wanderings Know Thyself. It is a hard saying, for
"the lord of Delphi neither speaks out nor conceals, he offers signs", as

2

Greek remains at Aï Khanoum with the River Oxus and the Russian bank in the background

Heraclitus said.' For Nietzsche the signs pointed to the liberation of the self. In the age of Freud 'Know Thyself' has meant primarily the introspective search below the surface for the real self, the search for our own deep motivations. Towards the end of our century, in the 'post-modern' era, it has also come to mean 'know where you have come from, since the past cannot be destroyed and should be known'. Rather as Freud said that childhood must be studied in order to understand the adult, so we look to 'the childhood of man', as Marx called Greece, in an attempt to clarify the present. So the ancient Greek message – its original stone long since fragmented – has meant different things to different ages; and many interpretations have been 'right' for different times and places. It is monumental and eternal, yet broken up and open to reformations.

Beneath the mental landscape

The Greeks posed and explored many of the questions that still keep the ground insecure beneath our feet. Why be good? What is the best organisation of society? Are international relations ultimately selfish? Should doctors always preserve life? How did the world begin? Is the universe made of some basic stuff? Do the gains of victory ever outweigh the losses? Do men and women inevitably have conflicting interests? How can we face the apparent shapelessness and unfairness of life? When such questions are raised in the following chapters, they will not be answered, of course – not even the Greeks could answer them! But it may be a good time to consult them, to go to the source. The late twentieth century shares with the Greeks, of the high classical period at least, a sense of losing touch with fixed points of reference; we also share a sense of power over social structures and over the environment combined with a growing fear of the consequences of those powers. Through their failures as well as their successes, they may give us contemporary insights.

Whether we like it or not – 'for better or worse' as Auden says – Greece is the geology underlying the mental landscape of Western civilisation. The Greeks marked out the map of our conceptual geography and set the categories by which

The 'Temple of the Gods' at the Museum of the Moving Image in London. This monument to the stars of the silent screen parodies the Caryatid porch on the Acropolis in Athens.

Ageing modern Caryatids photographed in Athens in 1953 by Henri Cartier-Bresson

we order our perceptions. That is significantly true however much such huge generalisations sweep aside some qualifications. The tendency, for example, to analyse by cause and effect, to make distinctions of levels of causation and to order by sequential explanation – all this goes back even to Homer. When Aristotle formalised logic – the assumption that we should, as a rule, try to order our thoughts and inferences in a systematic and consistent way – he was analysing a Greek way of thinking. The openness of the question whether we act through free will or under external compulsion, and the desire to find a way for both to coexist, while deeply coloured by Christianity, is at root a Greek way of trying to make sense of responsibility, crime, guilt, credit, praise and all that problematic yet essential area of human experience.

Our tendency to arrange issues by pairs and to set them against each other in dialectic, although not exclusively of Greek background, is highly characteristic of it. Examples of such basic polarities might be illusion versus reality, ends versus means, words versus actions. As fundamental as any is the very Greek opposition of convention and nature, or relative and absolute. Is everything a

5

matter of how you see it, of opinion, presentation and persuasion? Or are there ultimate and essential truths, standards fixed beyond our fallible interpretations? How far is ancient Greece a reality and how far a shifting collage of the perspectives of later ages? We shall return to that question before long.

It is characteristic of the magnetism of Greek ways of thinking that assertions should become pulled round into questions, as in the previous paragraph. Ancient Greece was a world of processes rather than products, questions rather than answers. There was no monolithic culture, no final orthodoxy or ultimate authority. Anything whatsoever that the mind could get a grip on was up for question, open to enquiry; nothing should be – or at least nothing need be – taken for granted. Socrates was at first baffled when an admirer reported from Delphi that he was the wisest of men; but he began to look for some enigmatic interpretation of the signs, since that is the way of oracles. Then he realised (with his typical irritating perversity) that, while everyone else believed that they possessed at least some knowledge, he was the only man wise enough to realise that he knew absolutely nothing for sure.

If we consult ancient Greece we find that, like Apollo, it neither speaks out nor conceals, but gives signs, in a way that is at once fascinating and frustrating. In many ways the ancient Greeks are so different, alien, dead, with their absurd gods, weird rituals, endless civil wars, slavery, indifference to technology –

> it was all so unimaginably different
> and all so long ago

as the poet and classical scholar Louis MacNeice complained. At the same time there is so much that is similar, close and alive. Enoch Powell tells how he was recently reading to friends from the *Odyssey* when the emotional immediacy became too much to bear: 'This is what happens when we, by this incredible privilege which we've been accorded, are spoken to heart-to-heart by other men, so unlike ourselves'. Far yet near, past yet present, it is important to keep both sides of the paradox if we are to benefit at all. In Richard Jenkyns's words, 'They are so modern and so remote. If we can hold these two things together and play one off against the other, we can learn something about the past and about ourselves.'

The alphabet, like it or not

No-one should underestimate the importance of *language* for our whole way of thinking about the world. Yet few realise how pervasive Greek is in modern

English. 'It's all Greek to me.' In Shakespeare's *Julius Caesar* Cassius is asking Casca for news:

Cassius Did Cicero say anything?
Casca Ay, he spoke Greek.
Cassius To what effect?
Casca Nay, an I tell you that, I'll ne'er look you i' the face again; but those that understood him smiled at one another and shook their heads; but, for mine own part, it was Greek to me.

A high proportion of the Greek words in modern languages have been introduced in the last two hundred years; Greek is not as remote as it was in Shakespeare's day. It supplies much of the language of medicine and the life sciences, the elements and processes of chemistry, most of the technical terms of astronomy, of geography and philosophy. Indeed many of the words which lie at the heart of the greatest achievements and the most deep-seated problems of our times are derived from Greek. An alphabetical selection can sound like a semi-parodic roll-call of the twentieth century:

analysis	*cybernetics*	*genetics*	*psychology*
astronaut	*democracy*	*holocaust*	*strategy*
carcinogenic	*economics*	*hydrogen*	*syndrome*
critical theory	*euthanasia*	*pornography*	*technology*

Most of these, for all their reverberations, have that polysyllabic feel which one might associate with Greek; but it has subtly infiltrated more everyday speech as well. Take *bible, character, Christ, cinema, disc, drama, fantasy, hygiene, logic, music, mystery, phone, planet, poetry, rhythm, telly, type, xerox*. Against 'It's all Greek to me' set 'The Greeks had a word for it'.

The Greeks established literacy at the core of Western civilisation. So it is appropriate that 'alphabet' is Greek, simply the first two letters of the ABC, *alpha, beta* (in large letters *AB*, in small *αβ*). At first glance the Greek alphabet may seem to be one of the great barriers between us and that 'dead' world. Yet, while it will always retain a touch of the exotic, anyone who has made the effort will have found the Greek alphabet easy to conquer. It does, after all, underlie our own which is simply the Roman adaptation to Latin (which is why the letter Yy, which was the Greek *Yυ*, but was not a letter in Latin, is still called in French *y grec*). The Russian or 'Cyrillic' alphabet is also an adaptation of the Greek, which was invented by the Greek missionary St Cyril in the ninth century to transcribe the Slavic languages. So from *alpha* to *omega*, from gamma rays to river deltas, from *phi beta kappa* to πr^2 Greek is the ABC of Western literate culture.

Phi beta kappa, dating from 1776, is the most prestigious of the American university fraternities; and when the fraternity system became established in the 1830s it adopted Greek labels which have been maintained ever since. While Greek letters may thus symbolise the intellectual heritage, Greek Fire has had a chequered and controversial history in the United States. Though some founding fathers, such as John Quincy Adams and Thomas Jefferson, were admirers of ancient Greece, there were many who would have been happy for the new world to cast off this burden of the old (as has been shown in detail by Meyer Reinhold in *Classica Americana*). 'Do not men', complained Benjamin

Two scenes from Sparta, Wisconsin. Note the Grecian columns behind Lt Harr's police car.

Rush in 1789, 'use Latin and Greek as the cuttlefish emit their ink, on purpose to conceal themselves from an intercourse with the common people?' I have heard from two separate sources an anecdote that in the early days Congress defeated by only one vote a proposal to make ancient Greek the official language of the United States. This is far from the truth – in fact a majority might well have voted to abolish the language entirely. The nineteenth-century poet Walt Whitman epitomises the ambivalence. While he resolved to have no classical allusions whatsoever in his *Leaves of Grass*, he was none the less given to riding up and down Broadway on the top of a bus, hair and beard flying in the wind, declaiming Homer. We owe this anecdote to Henry David Thoreau, a great enthusiast for ancient Greece, yet also a significantly subversive figure.

In the nineteenth century, Greek revival architecture swept through America in both public and domestic building. Cities were given Greek names. The most

left A coin from Syracuse in Sicily: the nymph Arethusa on one side and a victory chariot on the other   *right* An American dollar of 1794 – again the head and the symbol

extraordinary must be Eureka on the North California coast – the word, meaning 'Found it!', with which Archimedes proclaimed a scientific discovery. Others range from Ithaca, New York, home of Cornell University, to Sparta, Wisconsin, an agricultural town of some 7,000 inhabitants, where the first settlers were persuaded by 'Grandma Pettit' in 1852 so to name their town 'because they were as brave and suffered as many hardships as the Spartans of Greece'. Police Lt Francis C. Harr has proudly collected the police badges of the eight Spartas in the United States (six of them have an Athens in the same state!).

Whether people like it or not the surface of everyday life and culture in the West is littered with recognised and unrecognised symbols, fragments and labels which go back to ancient Greece, though sometimes by devious routes. From the columns of a portico or key-pattern decoration to athletics, drama or democracy, most people are probably aware that these in some way originated in ancient Greece. They are less likely to appreciate that the statues in parks reflect the way that the Greeks used to dedicate statues and plant trees in their sacred places; or that the coins in their pocket or purse are mostly round metal discs with a head on one side and some sort of national symbol on the other because the Greeks minted that way 2,500 years ago.

The road past Castalia

There has recently been a series of commercials on American television for Olympic Airways, in which celebrities from a variety of ethnic origins – Irish, Polish, Swedish, African – say that for their holiday this year they are going home, 'home to Greece'. In a sense Greece is home for every child in Western civilisation. The Englishman Lawrence Durrell writes in *The Greek Islands* of this sense on arrival in Greece; so does the American Henry Miller in *The Colossus of Maroussi*; so does the German Christa Wolf in the 'Travel Report' which accompanies her novel *Cassandra* (1983). Many know this *nostalgia* – not just the whimsical twinge of the modern word, but an *algos*, 'pain', for *nostos*, 'homecoming', a deep ache like that of Odysseus for Ithaca. To go to Greece is to arrive at our source, to satisfy a craving for a self-knowledge that was not there on departure – in T. S. Eliot's words:

> to arrive where we started
> and know the place for the first time . . .

Or, as the psychologist James Hillman puts it, 'we return to Greece in order to rediscover the archetypes of our mind and of our culture'.

'Home to Greece.' What is or was Greece? How solid? A monumental massif or an elusive sequence of metamorphoses? Shelley wrote in his *Hellas* (1822):

> Greece and her foundations are
> Built below the tide of war
> Based on the crystalline sea
> Of thought and its eternity.
> Her citizens, imperial spirits,
> Rule the present from the past . . .

This was an attempt, fired by the struggle for Greek independence from the Turks, to eternalise the ever-changing. Even the map changes. When modern Greece first became a political entity it was much smaller than the Greece of today. This is, in its turn, very different from ancient Hellas, which was in effect all those places inhabited by Hellenes (the Greek word as opposed to Latin *Graeci*). In 600 B.C. Hellenes were to be found not only on the mainland but round much of the coast of the Aegean, including Asia Minor, in the best coastal plains of Sicily and South Italy, and in smaller scattered states from Marseilles (*Massilia*) to Cyrene (now in Libya) and Olbia on the Russian Black Sea coast at the estuary of the Bug. In 300 B.C., after the conquests of Alexander the Great, Greece included Egypt, Syria and places as far as the Indus and Aï Khanoum.

Ancient Hellas had no official entity, however, no core; it was the sum of several hundred parts. States flourished and declined – Argos, Corinth, Lesbos, Athens, Sparta, Syracuse, Thebes, Rhodes, Pergamum, Alexandria – but there was no capital. There was, however, a particular place which claimed to be the *omphalos*, the 'navel of the world'. The story was that Zeus sent two eagles flying round the earth in opposite directions, and that where they met he founded the great sanctuary and oracle of his son Apollo – Delphi.

Greece has looked very different across the centuries, both on the ground and as perceived from distant lands. Delphi will make a good centre, an *omphalos*, while following these journeys through time and place, and intellectual history.

The modern route from Athens to Delphi is flat and unexciting as far as Thebes and beyond to Levadia, until, for the last 50 kilometres, it takes to the wild passes between the two great mountains, Helicon and Parnassus. Since this road was opened up to traffic for military purposes in the 1940s it has been much improved, and high up, near the turn to Dhistomo, one can still see where the old road used to run some miles to the north. I followed the old way recently to find a T-junction with a home-made blue signpost which said DAULIS 8. It is hard to convey the frisson that this nondescript place gave me. In Sophocles' tragedy *Oedipus the King* Jocasta recalls how her husband Laius was killed by a stranger on his way from Thebes to Delphi, 'where there is the meeting of three roads, one way from Delphi, the other from Daulis'. I was standing on the very spot where Oedipus killed his father – yet in a landscape of my imagination. For even if there was ever such a man as Oedipus, and even if he killed his father, it is as good as certain that it did not happen here. The place is significant because of Sophocles' play, and because Sigmund Freud turned to it when he was mapping the way that the twentieth-century self would think of itself. Whatever we now make of his analysis, Freud's motto was undeniably 'Know Thyself'.

After the fine mountain town of Arachova, some 15 kilometres further on, the road starts a long descent towards the distant 'sea' of olives in the plain of Amphissa. It turns a corner and suddenly, without warning, the archaeological site of the sanctuary of Apollo is there on the hillside ahead, thronged with tourists now as it was 2,500 years ago, though it will have been nothing remotely like the incredible 485,321 who visited Delphi in 1988. Above loom the crags of the Phaedriades, the shining cliffs, changing from pink to orange and from mauve to purple in different lights. The air-conditioned coaches hurry past a group of plane trees at the cleft between the two Phaedriades, making for the car parks and the modern tourist town of Delphi. Some people fill their plastic water bottles at a spout by the road, but few venture up under the planes to the spring of Castalia. In ancient times all visitors to Apollo's sanctuary had first to wash

A view of Delphi taken from high up the Phaedriades. The Sacred Way leads up to the Temple of Apollo. Above that the theatre can be seen.

their face and hands in its water. It cleared the heads of those who wished to know themselves.

At a glance Castalia is not impressive. The rock face is covered with various niches, and a stream of water, clogged with cress, runs down a channel which contains an old metal pipe. Yet Castalia's planes are still when gusts stir the rest of Delphi, and there are cool breezes when everywhere else bakes. This is a special place, and Delphi surely originated here. Before Apollo there was a cult of the Earth goddess, Gaia or *Ge*; and the great cleft where the life-giving water issues seems to be the right spot for her. Anyone who has read Jim Lovelock's book on environmental science, *Gaia*, will know that she is in a real sense still alive; and that we offend her at our peril. It may be no coincidence that stones falling from the Phaedriades are making Castalia a dangerous place.

A chance observation in 1988 brought home to me how much the outward appearance of Castalia has changed over the centuries, and how different it must have been only a hundred years ago. Turning my back on the spring and looking through the wire fence which runs round the archaeological zone I found unmistakable traces of a stepped, paved road, suitable for animals but not for wheeled traffic, going up through the scrub towards the temple of Apollo. This,

The ancient road-junction where Oedipus killed his father, seen from the modern road
to Delphi

The sign to Daulis – Oedipus took the road to Thebes

The Castalian spring engraved in the mid-nineteenth century, photographed in the early twentieth century, and in 1988

I realised, was the road to Arachova from the old village of Delphi, passing by the village fountain on its way.

The long Roman afternoon

It seems to have been in the eighth century B.C. that Apollo's sanctuary on Gaia's ground established itself as a centre for all Hellas. They would gather there for festivals, and would consult the oracle on all sorts of matters – advice about founding new cities, for example – and would make rich offerings. By the fifth century B.C. it was a centre of such artistic richness that it is hard to think of any modern equivalent – except, perhaps, the centre of Florence. One went up through the sanctuary by the Z-shaped Sacred Way, which was lined with the treasure-houses and dedications of various cities, some near, some far distant. There were hundreds of statues, among them the 13 bronzes by the master Phidias, dedicated by the Athenians to commemorate their great victory over the Persian invaders at Marathon in 490 B.C. Further up near the temple was a bowl on top of a high pillar made of three intertwined snakes on which were inscribed the names of 31 Greek cities which fought against the Persians at Plataea in 479 B.C., and so repelled their second invasion. Still higher up the clubhouse of the Cnidians was decorated with Polygnotus' murals depicting the sack of Troy, perhaps the most celebrated of all Greek paintings (long ago decayed of course). The Athenian women who make up the chorus of Euripides' play *Ion* have to concede that Delphi rivals even Athens for the magnificence of its art.

By 300 B.C. Delphi was past its noon. The second century saw Rome grow from a minor state in Italy to the greatest power in the Mediterranean world, and Delphi, like the rest of Hellas, became part of the Roman Empire. Greek culture and language (the language of the New Testament) continued in a fairly stable and prosperous state for another 500 years, but without real power or development any more. To some extent Greece was expected to be a kind of living museum of its great past, but now under the patronage of Rome – 'a sentimentalization of history', in Oswyn Murray's phrase. The centre of gravity had moved west; and Rome, with little high culture of her own, took over the intellectual and artistic heritage she had conquered, and was in turn conquered by it, as the poet Horace observed. Rome and the Latin language left their mark on everything they touched; but Rome's high culture was derivatively Greek. There is some analogy with the United States in relation to Europe. In Rome, as in America, this produced a tension, since in almost every sphere except culture the Romans were fundamentally dissimilar to the Greeks.

Delphi remained a tourist attraction throughout these centuries, depleted but still a marvel. The Roman general Sulla plundered the art in 86 B.C., and the Emperor Nero later took 500 statues in a fit of pique. It is quite possible that the two amazing bronze statues found in the sea off the toe of Italy in 1972 (see pages 86–7) are from the Delphi Battle of Marathon dedication, sunk on their way to Rome. Constantine the Great (proclaimed Emperor at York in 306 A.D.) declared the Roman Empire Christian, and made his new Eastern capital at Byzantium, renamed Constantinople. As one ornament he moved the snake column from Delphi to the Hippodrome, where it still stands in what is now

The bronze column of snakes from Delphi (without the tripod on top) in Istanbul

Istanbul. The bronze horses of St Mark's in Venice may have got there via the same route.

The Emperor Julian (361–3 A.D.) tried to restore classical, pagan Greece; but, when he consulted Delphi, he is said to have received this oracle:

> Tell the emperor this: the ornate temple is fallen to the ground,
> Apollo no longer has a sanctuary, no prophetic laurel,
> No talkative fountain – even the talking water has dried up.

In about 395 A.D. Theodosius officially closed the oracle.

Magnificent dilapidation

After Alaric the Visigoth sacked Rome in 410 A.D., the next century saw the collapse of the world of classical Rome. The fire of ancient Greece was all but extinguished in the western half of Europe. It is immeasurably brighter in 1989 A.D. than it was in 989 A.D. Stories of Troy and of Alexander the Great continued to be told, but they were exotic romances of medieval chivalry without any sense of the world from which they derived. When the Fourth Crusade in 1204 was diverted from Jerusalem, and ended up taking Constantinople instead, far from appreciating the remains of a great civilisation, the Francs destroyed many works of art and literature which had been preserved so long. Famous statues, 1,500 years old, were melted down for coins.

Not that the pagan Greece of the past had meant a lot in the eastern Greek-speaking Mediterranean, except in the metropolis of Byzantium itself. The dominant cultural force was the Orthodox church, which on the whole repudiated ancient Greece. At Delphi two churches stood at the site of the oracle of Apollo and another by Castalia. The Sacred Way became the village street. Below, where there had once been a sanctuary of Athena, stood a monastery, and the area became known as the 'Marble Quarry'! Delphi remained a prosperous town for a while, but debris and landslides, dungheaps and cultivation gradually covered the remains of the sanctuary of Apollo. By the seventh century Delphi had been reduced to a village on a hillside, which took its name, Kastri, from the ancient walls used for fortification (as in Latin *castra*), though they were often inadequate protection against the raids of passing Vandals, Ostrogoths, Huns and Avars. From the Fourth Crusade until 1460 A.D. Kastri belonged to the Dukes of Salona (the first Duke was Thomas d'Autremencourt). Salona was the name of the town on the site of ancient Amphissa some 20 kilometres away.

Besides the depredations of the Fourth Crusade, Byzantine Greece had long

The view of the plain of Amphissa, the 'Sea of Olives', from Delphi. The town of Amphissa is out of sight at the right edge of the picture.

been under pressure from hostile forces, especially the Arabs, who were repulsed with the help of the literal Greek fire. Eventually the Turks proved irresistible, and after Constantinople fell on Black Tuesday (29 May 1453), Salona, Kastri and the rest soon followed. Yet, by one of the most fascinating overlaps of intellectual history, the West had begun before then to rediscover Greece. The Renaissance, the New Age which marked the end of the Middle Age, found ancient Rome afresh, and through Rome inevitably Greece. Educated men realised that to know Rome they must also find and understand the literature, philosophy, science, and all the other achievements of Greece. In the middle of the fourteenth century Petrarch's desire to learn Greek could not be satisfied, but in 1397 the first proper Greek teaching in the West was given in Florence by the diplomat Manuel Chrysoloras – though it was nearly 100 more years before the teaching of Greek permeated as far north as Oxford.

Greeks came to Italy with remains of their past, and Italians went east, especially in search of manuscripts, realising that their survival was in danger in the crumbling world of Byzantium. I know of only one, however, who found his way to Delphi. Ciriaco de' Pizzicolli, usually known as Cyriac of Ancona, was a merchant who developed an absorbing interest in the buildings and monuments of ancient Greece. In 1437 he came to Kastri where he reports: 'The villagers have no idea where ancient Delphi was. I saw magnificent walls in dilapidation . . . broken statues here and there . . . and within as well as out in the fields huge marbles.' It was to be 250 years before anyone else (so far as I know) visited Delphi because it was Delphi – one tourist in 250 years compared with 25,000 on some days in 1988!

17

Meanwhile, in Western Europe, ancient Greece became part of the educated man's mental baggage. Greek texts were printed and translated; Erasmus produced his Greek Bible in 1516; Henry VIII created a Regius Professor at Oxford in 1546. None the less Renaissance humanism was built through and through on Rome. Greece was always at one remove, mediated through Rome; and on the whole the Greek world was perceived as a more primitive and uncouth world than that of Rome. Palladio's architecture and Corneille's tragedies are only Greek in the same sense as those hundreds of paintings of Greek myths based on the Latin of Ovid's *Metamorphoses*. The names say it all: Jove for Zeus, Mercury for Hermes, Ulysses for Odysseus, above all Greece (*Graecia*) for Hellas. Few went to 'Turkey in Europe', a poor land ruled by infidels; they wanted a Greece of the mind.

> The climate's delicate, the air most sweet,
> Fertile the isle . . .

In *The Winter's Tale* the oracle of Delphos is on an island: Shakespeare followed the usual equation of Delphi with Apollo's sanctuary on the island of Delos.

The second Renaissance

It was a new desire for some more direct contact with Greece that inspired the French doctor Jacques Spon and the English gentleman George Wheler in their travels. In January 1676 they arrived at Salona, which was said to be Delphi, but soon found an inscription showing that it was Amphissa. They called next at Kastri, and found an inscribed stone outside the church which showed that this was indeed Delphi. Spon wrote, 'What I found stranger still was that the most famous place in the world should have suffered such a reversal of fortune that we were obliged to look for Delphi in Delphi itself, and inquire about the whereabouts of Apollo's temple even as we stood on its foundations.'

By a hundred years later, things had changed: 1789 was far closer to ancient Greece than was 1689. In the mid-eighteenth century, even while the admiration of Rome as a model went into decline, a new interest in Greece began to grow, both as an ideal and in reality. What had been thought of as primitive and tasteless was now seen as sublimely plain and free, a rejection of moral hypocrisy and superficial ornament. Stuart and Revett, who changed the history of architecture with their drawings of Athens (see pages 227–8), visited Delphi in June 1751. Stuart wrote, 'Kastri, the ancient Delphi, is a most romantic spot.' 'Romantic' – the same word fits the response in 1764 from Richard Chandler (a predecessor of mine at Magdalen College, Oxford): 'The

Castalian fountain, the picturesque and immense rocks . . . a *coup d'oeil* that I think I have not seen equalled anywhere.' John Sibthorp, the botanist from Oxford, was more scientific and down-to-earth when he visited in 1795: 'On the rock of Delphi I observed a new species of Daphne, which I have called *Daphne Castaliensis*. Having dined in a monastery, and drunk some meagre wine whose flavour was not heightened by a large admixture of tar [Retsina!], we left Delphi.'

Edward Lear's sketch (1849) of the village of Kastri on top of ancient Delphi. The viewpoint is from near the edge of the modern town.

The period of, say, 1770 to 1830 – the 'Romantic' or 'Revolutionary' era – was, in effect, a second Renaissance, and it drew inspiration from the rediscovery of Greece direct. The prospect of the liberation of the land from Turkey further inspired the image of Greece as the fountain of freedom and of the arts. Byron died for this image. Yet reality still refused to fit the idealisation. Hugh William Williams visited Delphi in 1817: 'The Castalian spring being quite close at hand, we were led to it first . . . in which we immediately saw the Pythia [Apollo's priestess] in imagination lave her streaming hair. Our classic dreams, however, were soon dismissed by the appearance of a dirty washerwoman trailing a piece of cloth in the sacred stream – the stream of Castaly.' Even so, for all its squalor and its subjection to the Turks, many found themselves in the promised land. Byron recorded his visit to Delphi in his diary for 1809: 'Going to the fountain of Kastri, I saw a flight of 12 eagles (Hobhouse says they were

The young Byron being served in 'Turkey in Europe', by David Allen

vultures) On the day before had I composed the lines to Parnassus, and, on beholding the birds, had a hope that Apollo had accepted my homage.' There is no deflation in the lines which eventually appeared in *Childe Harold* (1812):

> Yet there I've wander'd by the vaunted rill;
> Yes! Sigh'd o'er Delphi's long-deserted shrine,
> Where, save that feeble fountain, all is still . . .

And it is less than 100 miles to Mesalonghi where Byron died of a fever as a freedom fighter in April 1824.

> Where'er we tread 'tis haunted, holy ground;
> No earth of thine is lost in vulgar mould
> But one vast plain of wonder spreads around,
> And all the Muse's tales seem truly told,
> Till the sense aches with gazing to behold
> The scenes our earliest dreams have dwelt upon . . .

A dream, but still full of meaning.

The crucial point about the influence of Greece in this 'revolutionary' period is that it was fresh. As W. H. Auden saw, every country made its own Greece: 'The historical discontinuity between Greek culture and our own, the disappearance for many centuries of any direct influence, made it all the easier, when it was rediscovered, for each nation to fashion a classical Greece in its own image.' But it was not a matter of mere adulation or imitation, it was a creative and independent confrontation. The German poet Hölderlin expressed the challenge well: 'We seem really to have almost no other option: either to be crushed beneath the weight of the received and the positive, or, with a violent presumption, to pit one's self as a living force against everything learned, given and positive.'

As the nineteenth century went on, however, the general approach did become more and more one of imitation and adulation. In many ways this was the great age of Greece; never (since Rome) has her influence been more pervasive and explicit. 'Classics' dominated education; scholarship and archaeology prospered; it went without saying that Greece was admirable. This phenomenon in Britain, ranging from Prime Ministers to Decadents, has been excellently studied in different ways by Richard Jenkyns and Frank M. Turner. Both show how the Victorians believed that they knew Greece well, and that it was in the ways that mattered a world very like their own. Yet it was also an ideal, unspoilt by industrialisation or commerce or what Matthew Arnold dubbed 'philistinism'.

What happened at Delphi is again illustrative. In 1811 the Dane Brøndsted was already complaining: 'The wretched little village of Kastri in many ways

RESTAVRATION DV TEMPLE DS D'APOLLON

Albert Tournaire's reconstruction of ancient Delphi (1894)

renders it difficult to survey the whole site; and to be able to get a satisfactory plan of Delphi, one would have to begin by pulling down many of its huts.' It was not, however, until 80 years later that the French government voted a million francs to Greece in return for the appropriation of the village ('On fait de nous des chercheurs de truffes,' complained a marquis in the Senate). The inhabitants of Kastri were compulsorily resettled on the present site of Delphi town, where there was no natural water supply. The present carriage road replaced the old paved, stepped road I found leading from the temple of Apollo to Castalia. The villagers resisted at first, and the military had to be called in to protect the excavations. These still went ahead with amazing energy between 1892 and 1900, and laid bare the site more or less as it is today – though the tattered columns on the temple were not reconstructed until 1950.

In 1894 Albert Tournaire, who went on to become a distinguished establishment architect, spent his student year abroad working on plans and reconstructions based on the excavations in progress. His 'Restauration perspective du sanctuaire, d'après les ruines actuelles et les textes anciens' is a magnificent picture of the Greece of the nineteenth-century imagination, an ideal world reconstructed without flaw.

Yet beneath the official self-confidence and often banal imitation, Greece remained a subversive, provocative presence. Only consider the three men who are sometimes called 'the founding fathers of the modern mind': Karl Marx wrote his doctoral dissertation (1841) on the materialist and anti-metaphysical philosophers Democritus and Epicurus; Friedrich Nietzsche became a professor of Classics in 1869 before he was 30; and Sigmund Freud was fascinated by many aspects of Greek culture, for example Platonic love and catharsis, long before he coined the 'Oedipus complex' in 1900.

A close-up of Tournaire's reconstruction of the Marathon bronzes by Phidias

Modernism to post-modernism

Modernism, futurism and the other '-isms' that brought in the twentieth century generally rejected all the flaccid complacency of the Victorian era, including the admiration of ancient Greece. All the same, ancient Greece re-emerged in new, less comfortable, less establishment forms, from James Joyce's *Ulysses* to Le Corbusier's architectural theory to Heidegger's philosophy. The pendulum has swung towards and away from Greece at different times and at different places during this turbulent century. Generally speaking those in the vanguard of cultural, political and scientific thought have deprecated Greece and the classics as part of a reactionary establishment which should be consigned to the past.

In the final quarter of the century, however, there seems to be a new sense of the present in the perspective of the past, a new self-consciousness within time. This attitude, which rejects the modernist belief that we can and should break free and create from scratch, is sometimes labelled 'post-modernism' ('new historicism' and 'reception studies' are related academic movements). Umberto Eco has put it thus: 'The post-modern reply to the modern consists of recognising that the past, since it cannot fully be destroyed, because its destruction leads to silence, must be revisited: but with irony, not innocently.' A new return to ancient Greece is all part of this. Instead of trying to reconstruct or imitate Greece as a whole, the new return recognises the vast differences between now and then, in tension with the similarities, and the fragmentariness of the evidence and of our knowledge; and recognises how any picture of ancient Greece must be selective, prejudiced, not innocent. It not only asks what is timelessly 'right', it also seeks what can be made out of Greece now.

The rejection of the old view of Greece as balanced, harmonious, and rational typifies this shift. Now it is seen as more of a seething fusion of the sublime and the sordid, the human and bestial, the light and the dark. At the start of *The Greeks and the Irrational* (1951), one of the greatest works of classical scholarship, E. R. Dodds tells how a young man accosted him in front of the Elgin marbles. 'I know it's an awful thing to confess, but this Greek stuff doesn't move me one bit . . . it's all so terribly rational, if you know what I mean.' Dodds goes on to explore the Greek preoccupations with madness, ecstasy, the paranormal and other irrationalities. They combined rationality and irrationality in a way that intrigues the twentieth century.

In modern Greece too the age of innocence is past. Byron's dream of 'haunted, holy ground' has become somewhat overlaid by a world of industry, commerce and mass tourism. In a series of commercials the television celebrity Alan Whicker claims that Barclaycard is more acceptable in the world's holiday

A mid-nineteenth-century photograph of the Acropolis from the south-east by the American William Stillman

resorts than its rivals, for example in 'the land of Greece, where Homer sang and men worshipped the gods. Now', he adds, 'we all worship the sun, and Sharon flies in from Luton Airport.' Sharon and the other 8½ million tourists each year (as many as the native population) find a land very different from Byron's reality, let alone his reveries. This is particularly true of Athens, which was then a large village called 'Setines': the dust, the jerry building, the porno shows, the shouting and hooting, the graffiti . . . Aristotle attributed the range of great achievements of Athens to the clarity of the Attic air: now Athens is all too often oppressed by the *nefos*, a black-grey-yellow 'lake' of polluted air, mainly from vehicle exhaust. Odysseus crossed the wine-dark sea; the ferries of today cross oil and sewage littered with plastic debris. There were even plans recently for an aluminium works at Delphi.

On the coast about 25 kilometres west of Athens lies Eleusis. In ancient times the temple of Demeter there held a strange ritual which was open to everyone in Athens, including women and slaves, but which they had to keep secret. The Eleusinian Mysteries promised a new serenity and a blessed afterlife. The secret was well kept, but we know that torches blazing in a huge dark hall were somehow important. Every modern tourist who goes from Athens to the Peloponnese follows the 'Sacred Way' by which the worshippers used to process to Eleusis. The only torches they will find when the crowded dual-carriageway reaches the coast are the great red burn-off flames of the oil refineries. Though it has been limited in recent years, it was ironically the pollution from the industries of Eleusis, driven back up the Sacred Way by the wind, which did much of the damage to the marble remains of ancient Athens, and which drove the Caryatids, after 2,400 years out on the Acropolis, indoors into controlled atmospheric conditions (except for the one stolen by Lord Elgin which went indoors sooner!).

This contrast of Byron and Sharon is too facile, however. It is as patronising a distortion of modern Greece as it is a romantic idealisation of ancient Greece. There was no shortage of violence, pornography, corruption and squalor – and graffiti – in the Greece of old. The picture of calm philosophers in white swanning round groves while naked youths exercise against a background of sparkling clear-cut cities is a Greece of the imagination, a nineteenth-century imagination which now seems naive. The Eleusinian cult, like most other religious occasions, must have been awash in the blood and dung of sacrificial animals; as the procession passed over a certain bridge on the Sacred Way the bystanders used to hurl verbal obscenities – and perhaps some turds as well. In the temple of Aphrodite at Corinth there were official prostitutes (*porne* in Greek); after the sublime tragedies the same playwright would put on a play with a chorus of satyrs, part-men part-animals, who sported outsize erections. The twentieth century has come to see ancient Greece as a much less pure, less stable, less rational place.

Fragmentary completion

Two twentieth-century events at Delphi may give a better perspective. In 1927 the Greek poet Angelos Sikelianos and his American wife Eva Palmer mounted a great festival in the ancient theatre excavated from beneath the houses of Kastri. There were displays of sport, folk-dancing, weaving, and the culminating event was a production of *Prometheus Bound* (a few minutes are preserved on film). At the end eagles flew out from the Phaedriades and wheeled above Prometheus as he defied Zeus' power – some say they heard thunder! Sikelianos wanted Delphi, the *omphalos*, to become a spiritual centre, a counterweight to

Sikelianos's production of *Prometheus* at Delphi. The choreography and costumes of the chorus of ocean-nymphs were the work of Eva Sikelianou.

the materialism and war-mongering of the twentieth century. His events were not scholarly, combining weird ideas about the origin of tragedy and the Eleusinian mysteries with oriental mysticism and a feminism connected with Isadora Duncan's dancing. Yet, for all its selectivity and confusion, Sikelianos's festival reverberated throughout the world, and inspired a new cultural self-confidence in modern Greece which led, among other things, to the foundation of the Greek National Theatre and to the first ever modern performance in the theatre at Epidaurus in 1938.

The festivals of ancient drama put on by the European Cultural Centre of Delphi since 1985 are staged in the ancient Stadium, yet higher up than the main sanctuary, where the ancient Pythian Games used to be held. This is not inappropriate since those games used to include competitions in poetry and music which were held on a stage erected in the Stadium. Two of the winning scores have been discovered inscribed on stone and are in the museum at Delphi. Here on 12 July 1988 the World Première of Tony Harrison's play *The Trackers of Oxyrhynchus* was mounted, a single performance at which all filming was forbidden – though it now looks likely that the National Theatre in London will revive it and take it on a world tour in 1990. The core of the play is Harrison's free translation of Sophocles' *The Satyr Trackers* which was found on

The Trackers of Oxyrhynchus, with Barrie Rutter as Silenus, the father of the satyrs. The tatters of the Oxyrhynchus papyrus form a backcloth.

The papyrus found at Oxyrhynchus in 1907 with the fragmentary text of *The Satyr Trackers* (*Ichneutai*) of Sophocles

tattered fragments of papyrus in the sands of Egypt in 1907. This excavation by two Oxford papyrologists, searching for lost texts and for their missing words, takes up the first third of the play. The middle part, the Sophocles, has the chorus of dancing, phallic satyrs searching for the lost cattle of Apollo by trying to reconstruct their confused tracks. In the last part the satyrs, who are refused access to high art by Apollo, go on the rampage as British football hooligans, and end up burning the papyrus that they come from.

So *Trackers* combined such incongruities as ancient Greek, ghetto blasters, papyrology, lager swilling, lyre-playing and clog-dancing (which echoed splendidly off the Phaedriades). It was directly inspired by Sophocles and made possible by classical scholarship; and yet it was Sophocles and scholarship subverted, ironised, anachronised, and turned into a contemporary play. It is significant, I think, that the play was made out of *fragments* of an ancient Greek play. Instead of regretting the incompleteness of the text, Harrison turned that into an essential feature of his production.

There is a contemporary painting by Lisa Milroy, actually called *Fragments*, which makes the same point. The picture, rectangular but unframed, is a sort of display of fragments of Greek pottery decorated with figures and ornament. Milroy explains: 'It's as if the world depicted by the shards doesn't have its boundaries at the edge of the canvas; all those scenes of Greek life, painted on the fragments, can't be contained by the work.' Andrew Graham-Dixon added the comment (the *Independent*, 5 April 1988): 'The composition, leaking off the picture's edges, tells you not about Greek culture but about your inevitable ignorance of it.' The critic puts negatively the point which the artist treats positively. It is true that we do not know Greece whole, it cannot be reconstructed completely and definitively: at the same time its very fragmentation is inexhaustibly suggestive and resilient against final containment. So in Delphi,

29

Lisa Milroy's *Fragments* (1987)

the fallen jumbled stones, the broken inscriptions, the paraphernalia of archaeology and the clutter of tourism are all part of the place as it is now. Ancient Delphi cannot be rebuilt, but the receptive mind can always make a new pattern out of the pieces, and can seek self-knowledge.

The devious road from Marathon

The athletic events held in the Stadium at Delphi in honour of Apollo were much the same as those even more famous games held every four years at Olympia in honour of Zeus. Both were open to all Greeks, wherever they came from, and victory was a great honour for the man and his city. Neither included the event which is now most of all increasing in popularity, The Marathon.

The plain of Marathon is about an hour's drive north-east out of Athens. In *Don Juan* Byron recalled his visit there in 1810:

> The mountains look on Marathon –
>   And Marathon looks on the sea;
> And musing there an hour alone
>   I dream'd that Greece might still be free.

30

Fragments of
ancient Greece in
the museum at
Eleusis

For him Marathon meant the Athenian rout of the Persian invasion in 490 B.C. – 'Even as an event in English history, it is more important than the battle of Hastings', said John Stuart Mill. After the battle a nameless Athenian (not Phidippides, as is often said) ran all the way to the city with the good news. At the games in Athens in 1896, which are regarded as the first official modern Olympic Games, 'The Marathon' was invented to be the climactic event.

Captain Robert Dover had organised Cotswold Olympic Games, open to all comers, in the seventeenth century; and the Olympic Club of San Francisco was founded in 1860. In 1870 the ancient Stadium in Athens, where the Panathenaic Games used to be held every four years, was excavated and cleared. Unheard-of events such as discus and javelin throwing were revived. For the 1896 games, however, organised by Baron Pierre de Coubertin, the Stadium was rebuilt (at Greek expense) with marble from nearby Mount Pendeli, where the quarries were specially reopened. The Greeks themselves were disappointed of prizes, most of which went to college men (who 'looked like Greek gods') from Princeton and Harvard.

The long-distance race was to the Stadium from the village of Marathon, not actually the site of the battle. This was 24 miles and 1,500 yards. The distance was later changed to 26 miles and 385 yards, the length at the London Olympics of 1908; and it became established that the race should be on the flat. That was far from the case in 1896. The course was relatively level for about half the distance along the coast, but then came a long gruelling climb over the pass between Pendeli and Hymettus before descending to Athens. None of the competitors had ever practised over anything like this distance. Most started too fast and dropped out on the climb. By Chalandri, about five miles from the finish, two men were well in front, an Australian called Flack, and a shepherd from the local village of Maroussi, Spiridon Louis. At Ampelokipi, Flack fainted from exhaustion. Rumour reached the crowd of over 50,000 in the Stadium that a Greek was winning. A contemporary account conjures a vivid picture: 'A roar came flowing down Herodes Atticus Street and burst into the Stadium, and with it came its source, a tiny figure dressed in a jersey of blue and white, sunburnt and covered with dust.' There is a less jubilant postscript: at the Berlin Olympics forty years later, old Louis was wheeled out to shake hands with Hitler.

When the black Jesse Owens began winning events, Hitler stayed away and would not congratulate the winners. Baron de Coubertin himself, who had been inspired by British public schools, had exclusive ideas of race and class: that is the real reason for his obsession with amateur competitors. Jim Thorpe, a Red-Indian American who won the pentathlon and decathlon at Stockholm in 1912, was disqualified when he was discovered to have played professional baseball. His confiscated medals were not given to his descendants until 1983. This has nothing to do with the facts about the ancient Olympic Games; they were used to authorise de Coubertin's preconceptions. It has been none the less a vision of

Spiridon Louis, the shepherd from Maroussi, at the victor's ceremony in the Stadium at Athens in 1896

ancient Greece which has kindled the modern imagination. In a fragmented, distorted way the 9,000 Athenians who charged as a body across the plain of Marathon in 490 B.C. survive behind the loneliness of the long-distance runner.

Restless striving

The Olympic Games and the Pythian Games were only two of the many occasions when Greeks competed openly and assertively. These formal contests were a manifestation of the competitive spirit that infused every aspect of Greek life, male life at least, provoking the great tragedies, the magnificent rivalry of dedications at Delphi, or driving Alexander the Great to Aï Khanoum. It was this same competitiveness that led to continual political struggles and made so much of the history of Greece the history of wars between the fiercely independent states, Greek killing Greek.

'Man is the measure of all things,' proclaimed the philosopher Protagoras in the fifth century B.C. This confidence in humanity and human endeavour, combined with competitiveness, led to a restless urge for progress, for change. It was the Greeks, and above all the Athenians, who implanted what Bernard Knox called 'this innovative, revolutionary spirit . . . the salient characteristic of western civilisation since the Renaissance'. This spirit has not been characteristic of most civilisations, and is indeed contrary to the conservatism of most (other) ancient near-Eastern civilisations. Such constant enquiry and endeavour is not comfortable, it refuses to relax and simply be secure: at the same time it has inspired many of the great developments of Western culture. 'Overall,' Knox concludes, 'the most important influence Greece has had on western civilisation is not a permanent influence, but a recurrent one. Time and time again Greek texts, Greek art, Greek philosophy are rediscovered or reinterpreted. And the effect is revolutionary.'

It is important that the great age of Greece came before Christ. The stimulating, even subversive, place of Greece comes from belonging within a Western world fundamentally based on Christianity. Christianity was so secure that it was not shaken by the Renaissance reopening of Rome; but, as Oswyn Murray points out, 'Greece has never been a *dominant* influence in the way that Rome and Christianity have been, so it is always available to be used as a means of questioning the current values of society.' Greek Fire is a paradox, dead yet alive, submerged yet burning, the preserve of the educated establishment, yet a challenging, provocative presence accessible to anyone with an open mind.

Tragedy

OUTSTARING THE GORGON

> It may be that there are demonic forces within us, and outside, set to destroy us; it may be that we will finish in darkness and despair and suicide. And it is of the eminent dignity of a man and a woman to look this possibility in the face: to know at least this may be. The greatest Greek tragedies are a constant education in that nightmare possibility.
>
> George Steiner (interviewed for 'Greek Fire')

WE LIVE IN AN ERA of horrors. Some of them are age-old – natural disasters, unpredictable violence, political instability, family conflict. Others are of more recent origin. There are the bombs that can unleash unimaginable destruction and death within minutes. There is AIDS – and who can say what still more virulent diseases may yet develop? Not least, there is the ever-increasing damage to the environment, to Gaia, damage which will take decades to reverse, if it is not already too late. Decimation of forests, pollution of oceans, breakdown of the stratosphere, indiscriminate spreading of agro-chemicals – these violations may well have engendered monsters which are on the point of awakening to inflict unthinkable suffering and carnage.

Our world is full of things that do not bear thinking about. If someone we love, or even someone we know, is killed in a car crash or contracts leukaemia, we find this hard enough to face. Life seems so unreasonable, chaotic, so unfair. Why him? Why me? If we were to try to *feel fully*, we would be reduced to blind incomprehension, or go mad. While television brings the disasters and atrocities into everyone's home, the only possible way to live through them is to turn one's heart to stone. Television news is Medusa, the Gorgon's head. Confronted with reality we turn our faces away, we are lost for words.

What is the connection of all this with tragedy? Greek tragedy puts the worst into words and expresses the full human response. A. W. von Schlegel said of Aeschylus, 'He holds up the head of Medusa.' Tony Harrison has recently settled on the same image to express his affinity with Greek tragedy:

This dismay and despair of our age is the terror that tragedy allows us to gaze into . . . *yet*, and this is a very important yet, without being turned into

36

stone by the vision. And in an age when the spirit of affirmation has almost been burned out of us, more than ever we need what Nietzsche called 'the highest art to say yes to life'.

Through facing up to older, closer, primal terrors, tragedy shows us how terrors can be confronted and perhaps survived, even those of the late twentieth century. In the theatre we not only stare without averting our eyes and listen without blocking our ears, we actually want the sufferers to go on expressing their terrible experiences and we want to feel their agonising emotions with them. And at the end of the play, we discover that we have not been turned into stone. We get up, leave, and return to life, whether in the fifth century B.C. or the twentieth A.D. We return with the experience as part of ourselves.

This may help to explain why, as George Steiner says, 'The twentieth century has produced more versions of the great Greek tragedies in film, opera, theatre, novels, adaptations than even the Renaissance or the eighteenth century in their forms.' Moreover, the most recent years, say the ten or twelve up to 1989, may well have produced as many as, or more than, any other such period since ancient times. The revival is by no means a phenomenon restricted to the West, or to countries culturally descended from Greece and Rome. It extends from the Far East to Eastern Europe, even to Latin America. Festivals of Greek drama held at Delphi since 1985 have hosted productions from the Chinese, the Venezuelans and the Yup'ik (Eskimo from Alaska) as well as many from more obvious nationalities. The variety of leading directors who have turned to Greek tragedy is also intriguing, from Andrei Serban and Peter Sellars in America to Vittorio Gassman and Walter Pagliaro in Italy, from Yukio Ninagawa and Tadashi Suzuki in Japan to Eugenio Barba in Norway and Ingmar Bergman in Sweden (where he is currently adapting Euripides' *Bacchae* for opera). The range of plays is also broadening from the old 'classics' of *Bacchae*, *Oedipus*, *Antigone* (four in Germany in 1978) and *Medea* (three in London in 1986) towards the whole repertoire of the thirty-two tragedies which have survived the attrition of the centuries.

Of course the range of relationships between these modern productions and their Greek originals is also very wide, all the way from new plays with a Greek inspirational spark to 'straight' productions of the text intact. Robert Wilson's *Overture to the Fourth Act of Deafman Glance* recognises an explicit debt to Euripides' *Medea*, but in the entire hour not one word is spoken: in very slow-motion mime a woman regretfully kills her child, and in parallel a man does exactly the same, always a couple of minutes behind her. In Germany between 1968 and 1984 there were at least 15 productions of *Philoktetes*, but none of Sophocles'. They were all of the play by the East German 'son of Brecht', Heiner

Mount Cithaeron is still covered in pine trees

Agave and the head of Pentheus. Agave is played by Shiraishi Kayoko in the 1981 production by Tadashi Suzuki.

Müller. Müller's work has a complex relation with the original, even quoting it in places; but he also carefully controls the many differences which culminate in the sordid death of Philoctetes, who in Sophocles survives with glory. It is extraordinary, however, to see how many of these revivals at a professional level have been of the Greek play itself, either directly translated or only lightly adapted. They are not done in a pious or antiquarian spirit: these are live, contemporary plays.

A good look at the severed head

Tragedy enables us to live through the unbearable. Greek tragedies, at least all the great ones, are concerned with large, distressing issues, with disruption, conflict, things going very wrong, turning dark. They incarnate the worst

38

horrors, particularly within the family, such as betrayal, incest, murder – killing of mother by son, children by father, husband by wife, every unthinkable combination. Tragedy not only acts out these deep terrors, it makes its audience confront them. As we, the audience, sit in our seats, faces towards the play, voluntarily trapped and helpless, we are forced to live vicariously through the terrible story played out before us.

There is a scene, near the end of *Bacchae*, which emblemises this experience of staring at things which we otherwise could not face. Euripides' last play, first performed after his death in 406 B.C., presents surely one of the most harrowing moments in all tragedy. The god Dionysus has come back to his birthplace, Thebes, but the inhabitants, including his own mother's sisters, do not accept his divinity. He sends them mad and drives them out as bacchants onto Cithaeron, the mountain between Thebes and Athens. There Agave tears her son Pentheus to pieces in her ecstatic madness. She returns to Thebes in triumph with Pentheus' head, under the delusion that it is the head of a lion she has hunted on the mountain. Meanwhile her old father Cadmus (Dionysus' maternal grandfather) has collected the other parts of Pentheus' body. Gradually, patiently, he coaxes her out of her trance ('he talks her down' as it is called in drug therapy), and prevails on her to face reality – a reality so horrible that she will have to leave her home and happiness behind her for ever.

Cadmus	What house did you join on your wedding day?
Agave	You gave me to Echion, so they say.
Cadmus	And what child was borne to your husband in his home?
Agave	Pentheus, fruit of my union with his father.
Cadmus	Whose head, then, are you holding in your arms?
Agave	A lion's – at least so the huntresses said.
Cadmus	Now see straight. Looking takes little trouble.
Agave	Ah, what do I see? What is this I am carrying?
Cadmus	Look hard at it and understand more clearly.
Agave	What I see is deep grief and misery for me.
Cadmus	It doesn't seem to resemble a lion?
Agave	No, but it is Pentheus' head I am holding.

The mother has to face her own son's head, a head wrenched from its trunk by her own hands. She is not spared the pain – 'look hard at it' – she is not cushioned from the truth, she is not hurried off under sedation.

'Now see straight. Looking takes little trouble.' This is the invitation to the spectator also, offered a few hours off work and a spectacular event. Yet, once lured into the theatre, we have to look at the most terrible things we can think of. Imagine hearing one's mother curse with her dying breath, or feeling the

Suzuki's *Clytemnestra* (1983): the dummy represents the body of Agamemnon and her fan symbolises the murder weapon

dismembered head of one's own child – the imagination revolts. Yet in Greek theatre we see such things played out, and our eyes are fascinated. Not to block ears, not to turn away: tragedy demands that we see and hear the worst. *Yet* we are not traumatised for life by the experience, we do not go mad with horror. We live through it and survive. At the end of the play we leave the theatre and go on with real life. The special significance of Greek tragedy for our times lies in the experience of survival.

Four Oresteias

To try to give some substance to these generalisations, I shall look at the *Oresteia*, the set of three tragedies first put on by Aeschylus in the spring of 458 B.C. They have a connected plot which thus forms a trilogy (unlike the annual sets of three plays by Sophocles and Euripides which were unconnected). The trilogy traces a blood-feud of murder and revenge over three generations of the royal house at Argos to its final resolution by the constitution of trial by jury at Athens. Though often regarded as the greatest achievement of Greek tragedy, the *Oresteia*'s scale has perhaps inhibited its staging in modern times, though there have been notable productions such as those directed by Barrault in 1955 and by Gassman with Pasolini in 1960. There were, however, four interestingly various major productions between 1980 and 1983.

The one furthest from Aeschylus was the *Clytemnestra* adapted by the Japanese Tadashi Suzuki for his own company, first put on in 1983. It is, in fact, a composite made of brief scenes from the *Oresteia* and from the *Electra* plays of Sophocles and Euripides. Suzuki disciplines his company rigorously to produce highly expressive body-language and group choreography, based, as he says, 'on analysis of patterns of bodily expression on stage'. He alludes to the ancient Japanese traditions of *Nō* and *Kabuki* which have some striking analogies with Greek tragedy, including masks, male actors, poetic language, and, not least, their setting in the heroic past. At the same time Suzuki alludes directly to the contemporary world, for example by use of incongruous costume and of pop music. He sees his *Clytemnestra* as a study in the increasing spiritual isolation of contemporary man, not least through the disintegration of the family.

In Greece itself the trilogy was put on in 1981–2 by Karolos Koun's Art Theatre. Koun, who died in 1986, was the most vigorous and enterprising Greek director of his day. The Sikelianos festivals at Delphi in 1927 and 1930 (see page 27) inspired a great era in the production of tragedy in Greece in the 1930s, carried on in the 1950s and early 1960s, especially in the vast auditorium at Epidaurus. There was then a period of stagnation and antiquarianism, and Koun's *Oresteia* has been important for encouraging a more intelligent and innovative period. He set it in a primeval world, accentuated by the sombre primitivist masks and costumes designed by Dionysis Fotopoulos, and by the alarming Clytemnestra of Melina Mercouri. The impression was one of a seething complex of dark deeds and thoughts, intermittently illuminated by flares of flame, as human society struggled towards some kind of enlightenment.

Peter Stein's production opened at the Schaubühne am Halleschen Ufer in

Electra at the tomb of Agamemnon, from the second play of Karolos Koun's *Oresteia* (1981). The actress is Reni Pittaki.

Berlin in October 1980, and went on to tour the world. It lasted from 2 pm until 11 pm, including two intervals of an hour. The audience sat on the floor; yet it was agreed that the production was so gripping that all discomfort was dispelled by the overwhelming experience, especially in the first play, *Agamemnon*, which was dominated by Edith Clever's Clytemnestra. The costume and design were eclectic and unspectacular, and the translation was put into plain prose by Stein himself. There was no music, but Stein found an effective device for bringing out the multiple and elusive significance of the choral parts: key concepts, especially those to do with vengeance and society, were expressed, not by one selected word, but were tried out in several near-synonymous words by different members of the chorus. In this way ideas were probed, held up at various angles, so reflecting the way in which the trilogy stumbles towards understanding and justice.

Fourthly, there was Peter Hall's production, created for the National Theatre's Olivier auditorium (which was based on Epidaurus by its architect, Denys Lasdun). It opened in November 1981 and was seen by over 70,000 people before finishing in June 1982 at Epidaurus, the first ever non-Greek production of a Greek tragedy in that unique space. Hall coordinated a troupe of fifteen men who performed the chorus and between them took all the roles,

Athena, played by Jutta Lampe, tries to placate the Furies in the third play of Peter Stein's *Oresteia* (1980)

Clytemnestra (Pip Donaghy) and Orestes (Greg Hicks) in the second play of Peter Hall's *Oresteia* (1981). The costumes and masks were the work of Jocelyn Herbert.

orchestrating a patterned sequence of scenes and tableaux. Jocelyn Herbert's masks and costumes were at once austere and expressive, rather as Harrison Birtwistle's music had a compulsive pulse yet a wide range of tone. The most extraordinary feature of all was the translation by the poet Tony Harrison. Some, including at first many of the press critics, hated it; but most found it at the same time unfamiliar and strangely accessible. Harrison pressed his native Yorkshire phonemes and the alliterative word-building of Anglo-Saxon into a basically trochaic verse (like and unlike *Hiawatha*) to forge a new language which insisted on being listened to with full attention. Through this the thematic complexities, especially those of the conflict between male and female, accumulated: he-child, she-child, blood-bond, bed-bond, blood-price, grudge-hound and so on. This is one reason why, in reverse of every other production I have known, this trilogy became progressively more powerful instead of diminishing. On the other hand this verbal and rhythmical core made for an experience that was emotionally less gripping than that produced by Stein.

What is there, then, about the *Oresteia* to make modern productions on such a scale and in such different styles? Great theatre, for a start. The watchman looking out for the beacon at the start of *Agamemnon* is a dramatic opening unrivalled until the sentinels on the castle walls in *Hamlet*. Agamemnon's progress into his palace trampling on delicate purple cloth, Clytemnestra's appeal to her son by the breast at which he sucked as a baby, the jurors of Athens voting one by one while Orestes and the Furies await the verdict – these are theatrical coups to stand with the greatest.

The theatre would not, however, live on by itself, without the issues it raises. The issues at stake in the trilogy are not remote or parochial. Revenge is still the instinctive response of those who have been wronged, especially those whose close kin have been murdered. How far can or should people take revenge into their own hands? Where does vendetta stop? What claims does the family have, regardless of the law of the state? How far does the greater good of society override even the claims of blood? In the *Oresteia* it takes *persuasion* to untie some of these knots. Is persuasion anything other than rhetoric and manipulation? Yet how can people ever find solutions to their dilemmas without it?

There can be conflict between the family and society outside, but all too often there is conflict even within that closest bonding. How is it that the fiercest, most harrowing struggles are between those nearest by blood? British Home Office records show that some forty per cent of all homicides occur within the family, and that four per cent are, like Orestes and Clytemnestra, the murder of parent by child. Above all, there is the conflict of male and female, wife and husband. Clytemnestra, the mere woman, brings the supreme male conqueror low. He goes to his death in ignorance and humiliation, while the slave Cassandra sees her fate and accepts it bravely. To avenge his father Orestes plunges his sword into his mother's breast; and she with her dying curse summons the old female goddesses the Curses (or Furies or Erinyes), daughters of Night without a father; they confront Apollo, who belongs to the new Olympian family of Father Zeus. At the trial of Orestes Apollo makes the claim that the father alone is the true parent and that the mother is a mere incubator for his seed. This claim is not so outlandish as it may sound at first, and in both the Stein and Hall productions it provoked a strong reaction in the audience. There are, after all, in the closing years of the twentieth century, salesmen of wombs who go around marketing 'surrogate mothers', in other words an incubator for another's seed.

Tragedy as shape and containment

What did tragedy mean in practice, what does it mean? 'Tragedy' is a Greek word meaning originally 'song for the prize of a goat', or 'at the sacrifice of a goat'. It was one place, Athens, that turned it into a great art form. In 550 B.C. it did not exist, or only in some very rudimentary form; and by 400 B.C. its great age – the age of Aeschylus, Sophocles and Euripides – was over, though the next 750 years continued to imitate and reproduce that great age.

'Tragedy' is still a common word in English, of course, especially with journalists, but it is important to understand that this use today is a contradiction of the Athenian invention. Any unpredictable misfortune, especially one involving untimely death, is a tragedy. 'Tragedy struck in Neasden last night . . .' James Joyce's autobiographical character Stephen Dedalus complains in *A Portrait of the Artist as a Young Man* (1916):

> A girl got into a hansom a few days ago . . . in London. She was on her way to meet her mother whom she had not seen for many years. At the corner of the street the shaft of a lorry shivered the window of the hansom in the shape of a star. A long fine needle of the shivered glass pierced her heart. She died on the instant. The reporter called it a tragic death. It is not . . .

We use 'tragic' of the inexplicable disasters of life in all its unpredictability, its unfair shapelessness: what the Athenians developed was, on the contrary, a highly shaped, formalised, articulated event, experienced under certain fixed conditions.

They set aside a specific *place* (the *theatron*) for their drama (another Greek word), and so established a precedent for almost all drama ever since, though it has been rejected on occasion in recent times. Throughout the great era of the fifth century this place was the rocky slope beneath the south cliff of the Acropolis, a large area above the temple of Dionysus, which might have seated some 20,000 people (the 30,000 mentioned in Plato's *Symposium* is probably only a large round figure). In any case, it was a huge auditorium and a huge audience compared with even the largest of modern theatres and opera houses. Any one who has been in an audience at Epidaurus will know the powerful experience of the 'funnelling' of the concentration of so many people.

The level acting space set aside for the players (the *orchestra*) was on a similar scale, a circle (probably) about 20 metres in diameter, almost large enough to contain the whole auditorium of Shakespeare's Globe. (We cannot stand on a specific spot in Southwark and say, '*Hamlet* was performed precisely here', as we can with the *Oresteia* in Athens.) The acting space, with the scene building

45

The Theatre of Dionysus in Athens, photographed in 1988 from the Acropolis

(*skene*) on the far side and with a road to either side, was specific and fixed; and it was an essential element in the invention of tragedy that the playwright could make it become somewhere else in the captive imagination of his audience. In *Bacchae*, for instance, the *skene* represents the royal palace of Thebes, the great household which is destroyed by Dionysus. The road to one side leads to the city, the centre of civic order, the other to the mountain where the women of Thebes are sleeping in the wooded glens instead of under their domestic roofs.

There was also a specific *time* set aside for this gathering. Unlike our runs or seasons or repertoires, this time was three whole days once a year, part of the great spring festival of Dionysus. The plays, performed in his sanctuary, were in his honour, rather as the Olympic Games were in honour of Zeus. The playwright created for this one occasion; and that single performance was a cultural highspot, experienced together by a huge public. It is important that the audience did not sit in the privacy of the dark, illumined only by EXIT lights: they were in the open air in broad daylight, sharing the same light as the actors, and as their fellow citizens all around.

The actors were, however, marked off from the audience not only by the

46

spatial division of *theatron* and *orchestra*, but also by their elaborate woven costumes, much grander than ordinary clothes, and by their whole-head masks. These masks had their practical advantages, for they enabled the three male actors to double parts, and in such a huge theatre a well-defined image is better than an indistinct face. It is interesting that many of the modern productions have begun to use masks even though the auditoria are smaller, and even though, encouraged by Freud and by film, we have come to expect nuances of facial expression to be a key to what is really going on in the characters. So why should this fixture suit late twentieth-century tragedy? For one thing, it may suggest that each character is defined by words, actions and relationships rather than by inward psychology. They are the *sort* of people to do what they do, and that makes for a drama of social and relational issues rather than of the soul. Actors too find that, rather than searching for a psychology within themselves, the mask gives them their role. Tony Harrison also makes a rather different point about the ever-open eyes and mouth of the mask: 'If a mask gazes at the horrors, the terrors, it has to keep on looking . . . What does a mask do when it suffers or contemplates suffering? Words don't fail it, it goes on speaking. It's created with an open mouth to go on speaking.' Harrison also observed during the production of his *Oresteia* that masks have the peculiar ability of looking lots of people in the eye at one time, and 'if you think that you're being looked at, you listen'. So the masks face the audience, and the audience has to attend to them.

Like the masks, the chorus is a feature of Greek tragedy that has generally been regarded as an alien encumbrance, and yet it has been positively embraced in many of the most recent productions. What does the modern theatre find in this curious group of people without individual identities which happens to be hanging around during the great tragic events? First it should be appreciated

A collection of masks which decorates the studio of the leading Greek theatre-designer Dionysis Fotopoulos

A vase painted in Athens in about 480 B.C. showing six chorus members costumed as young soldiers. They are clearly singing and dancing in unison. The figure on the left may be a ghost which the chorus is summoning from the underworld.

that Greek tragedy characteristically alternated two very different kinds of poetry: speeches or dialogues in the easily speakable iambic metre with songs or 'odes' in highly-wrought lyric metres to be accompanied by music and dance. It was the primary function of the chorus to perform these songs. They do not advance the plot as the spoken scenes do, and they are not reasoned, but move on by association, sweeping freely through time and place, linking the events of the play with the gods, myths and ethics. The American dramatist Timberlake Wertenbaker uses a Greek-style chorus in her play, based on the Greek myth of Philomela, *The Love of the Nightingale* (1988); and she explains, 'I was attracted to the idea of the chorus because it enables you to embody thoughts on the stage without having to put them inside a character.' Each Greek choral ode has a unique and unpredictable relationship to its context, but there is nearly always an element of broadening, of universalisation, moving outwards in thought from the particulars of the play towards all times and all places.

Unlike the chorus of Japanese *Nō* drama, which is entirely detached from the plot of the play (and from its playing space), the Greek chorus has a role within the world of the play, and is concerned with the events, often through a sympathetic attachment to one of the main suffering characters. So the chorus is emotionally involved, often deeply distressed. Yet it can do nothing (there are a few exceptions, most notably in *Eumenides*, the third play of the *Oresteia*). This helplessness is often brought out by their identity as weak old men or as slave women. The group witnesses and responds, but it cannot prevent or cure; it can only join in the grieving. In some important ways, then, the chorus is in a position like that of the audience – and this, I think, has to do with its modern revival. The audience is also caught up in the drama, moved by it, and helpless; it must see it but not prevent it. We, the audience, know that we must not cry out or intervene but must sit still (unlike the rustic in seventeenth-century China who leapt up onto the stage of some travelling players and stabbed the villain!). The response of the chorus, instead of finding expression in physical action, is sublimated into thoughts that are both emotional and abstract, both particular to this play and universal. Above all the chorus does not turn away or switch off or become reduced to silence. When Oedipus in Sophocles' play is first revealed with his bloody, jabbed-out eyes the chorus chants:

> I cannot bear to look at you,
> yet there is much to ask, much to find out,
> much to stare at . . .

They do continue to look at him and to respond to his anguish. They are a model of how to survive, how to keep looking and feeling and thinking without being turned into stone.

The approach to the total art-form

Ancient Greek tragedy was formal and patterned, and to put it mildly, not naturalistic. As well as the masks and costumes, the stage action was bold and economical, so that even such actions as embracing or handing over an object became fraught with significance. The chorus brought in lyric poetry, song, dance and group movement. Even the spoken lines were in a poetic language far from everyday conversation: characters make long set-piece speeches, dialogues are often conducted in exchanges of one line each (stichomythia). Indeed the combination of the separable arts of poetry, acting, costume, scene painting, speech, song, music and dance takes Greek tragedy far beyond what we would normally mean now by 'theatre' and 'drama'. All these models of presentation were combined into a single integrated art-form, a 'total art-work' to translate the German term *Gesamtkunstwerk*.

This has been a recurrent inspiration. The most significant of all came early

Part of the auditorium at Epidaurus. Ancient plays are performed every weekend throughout the summer and attract audiences of over 15,000.

for Greek Fire. There was already considerable interest in Greek tragedy in Italy in the second half of the sixteenth century; and when Palladio's inspired reconstruction of an ancient Roman theatre, the Teatro Olimpico in Vicenza, opened on 3 March 1585 the production was of Sophocles' *Oedipus*. Otherwise, however, the interest was mainly academic; and from the 1570s a kind of discussion group known as the *Camerata* used to meet in Florence to discuss the evidence concerning ancient tragedy. Though many of their ideas were mistaken, they did lay special emphasis on the combination of speech, music, song, dance and chorus, and on the way that tragedy was emotionally heightened and yet clearly audible. This led to experiments in reconstruction in practice, and these in their turn soon inspired the first masterpiece of what we now call opera, Claudio Monteverdi's *La favola d'Orfeo* of 1607. The genre spread and developed rapidly. Within 50 years opera-houses had been built all over Italy, and the spark fanned by the academic *Camerata* still blazes.

Later composers of opera, down to the present day, have recycled Greek myths in hundreds of versions. More important, some have turned to Greek drama for new artistic impetus – for example Gluck and Weber. Weber's

50

interest, and the excitement of the Greek struggle for independence from the Turks, were two factors which moved Richard Wagner (1813–83) towards what became something of an obsession with ancient Greek culture, especially the sublime and celebratory combination of music, dance and poetry. The recurrent imagery of the *Oresteia* was formative in his development of the *Leitmotif*; and while working in the mornings on *Der Ring des Nibelungen* (a kind of trilogy with prelude), he used to read Greek tragedies in his garden after lunch. He wrote in his memoirs:

> I would bring before my imagination the intoxicating effect of the production of an Athenian tragedy, so that I could see the *Oresteia* with my mind's eye, as though it were actually being performed; and its effect on me was indescribable . . . My ideas about the whole significance of drama were without a doubt decisively moulded by these impressions.

Bayreuth probably still offers the nearest modern equivalent to the ancient festivals of Dionysus at Athens.

In the earlier part of the twentieth century the theatre was dominated by a number of great directors. Perhaps the most influential, Max Reinhardt (1873–1943), a formative influence on Piscator and Brecht, was much taken with the idea of the *Gesamtkunstwerk*. He made a great impact with his 1910 production of Sophocles' *Oedipus* in the Zirkus Schumann in Berlin, where the audience was able to sit more than halfway round the acting area, as in the Greek theatre. For this setting Reinhardt developed his own special uses of lighting, music, dance and crowd scenes – he had an overwhelming opening with more than 100

The opening scene of Max Reinhardt's *Oedipus* in Berlin. The crowd of Theban supplicants was played by a vast number of extras.

The London version of Reinhardt's *Oedipus* (1912), starring Martin-Harvey

citizens of Thebes! This revolutionary production was remounted all over the world, beginning in Moscow in 1911, and London in 1912, with the great Martin-Harvey in the leading role. When he took over the Grosses Schauspielhaus in 1919 (opening with the *Oresteia*) Reinhardt pointed to the Greek model for 'a theatre of the people, a festival playhouse, a rite of worship, of purification and of joy . . .' 'The stage', it was claimed, 'has gone back to its beginnings. It is a space for dances, for games, for theatrical action and pageants.'

One of the very best presentations of Greek tragedy I have ever seen was clearly a kind of *Gesamtkunstwerk*, which also drew on the Japanese traditions: Yukio Ninagawa's *Medea*, which was first put on in Tokyo in 1978 (I saw it in London in 1987). Its intensity owes much to the highly formalised use of spectacle, costume, music and dance. All these elements are inseparably integrated by Ninagawa, and the result is something which the audience, for all its horror, cannot but watch and hear.

A final example of the range of Greek tragedy's art-forms is its influence on dance in modern times. It was above all the American Isadora Duncan who brought Greek choreography and drapery off the monuments and into life. Many girls' schools and colleges in Britain and the United States held classes in 'Greek dance' in her style until quite recently. In modern dance, Merce Cunningham has drawn on Greek material; and the first American film of a Greek tragedy will be the dance-film of *Antigone* by Amy Greenfield (to be released in 1990). The most articulate proponent of Greek tragedy in dance has been Martha Graham in, for example, *Night Journey, Care of the Heart*, and

52

Dancers arranged in Grecian robes and poses by Isadora Duncan

The American dancer and choreographer Martha Graham

Yukio Ninagawa's *Medea* with Tokusaburo Arashi in the title role, one of the great modern productions of a Greek tragedy. The chorus of women of Corinth was in fact played by men.

Clytemnestra (1958). She has said, 'Modern man is timid; but the Greeks were realists. We hide from the truth; the Greeks stared life in the face.' My qualification of this would be that they stared life in the face once it was shaped and contained by poetry, dance and the other forms of the theatre.

Transplantation to Northern Europe

The persistence of tragedy has to do with a combination of the quality of its theatricality with the quality, depth, reach and freshness of the issues it dramatises. It is enthrallingly particular yet universal, concrete yet abstract, the questions are open, unanswered and unanswerable. It seems to me that Georg Lukács was utterly wrong when he said, 'The Greek recognises only answers, not questions.' The tragic questions all arise out of conflict, within the family, within society, between family and society, conflict between integrity and compromise, between justice and humanity, between human will and superhuman forces, between freedom and fate. Greek tragedy questions with an immediacy and particularity that can still be extended across centuries and continents. The issues and the terrors they arouse cannot be answered or dismissed; they should be faced, if we are not to be annihilated.

Greek tragedy's openness to various approaches and interpretations is directly related to its resilience. Different ages, and different interpreters within an age, put quite different concerns in the foreground. Some have emphasised ritual, an important notion in much modern theatre. Others have been primarily psychological, like Olivier's celebrated *Oedipus* in London in 1945, or Judith Anderson's *Medea* on Broadway in 1947. Yet others, like John Barton's *The Greeks* in 1980, have made the most of the story-telling potential. Most often, perhaps, the approach has been in various ways political, taking tragedy as a way of asking questions about society, power, responsibility, class conflict, and war. Some of the various approaches are, no doubt, closer to ancient Greece than others; the point is that Greek tragedy has been indefatigably lively because so many different concerns can be drawn out of it.

Such openness must account in part for the broad time-span across which Greek tragedy has been recycled. It was already influential in the sixteenth century, though primarily through the Latin imitations of Seneca (first century A.D.). I am persuaded that Shakespeare read Greek tragedy in Latin translation, and that the influence can be felt especially in the early Histories. It is fortunate that Shakespeare resisted the theorists who, canonising Aristotle's *Poetics*, were laying down the law about what could and could not be done in proper tragedy.

Orestes' vision of the Furies in Goethe's *Iphigenie*   Sarah Bernhardt in Racine's *Phèdre*

Their rules, especially those of the 'Unities' of time, place and action – which were far more rigid than Greek practice – though they now seem sterile, did evidently contribute to the great age of French classical tragedy in the seventeenth century. Corneille was predominantly influenced by Seneca. Racine studied Euripides in Greek, yet his tragedies, with their claustrophobic tension and passion, are very different. In some ways the heroic conflict and defiance of Milton's *Samson Agonistes* (1671) is closer, for all its untheatricality and its redemptive optimism.

It was not until the 'Romantic' release from the artificiality of neo-Classicism that Greek tragedy really came alive again. The way was prepared on a theoretical level by figures such as Herder, Lessing and the Schlegel brothers. (Through them words such as 'catharsis', 'hubris' and 'nemesis' have become part of English vocabulary, though often in senses rather different from the Greek.) The poets and playwrights who drew heat from Greek tragedy in this period include Alfieri in Italy and Shelley in England (he was reading Sophocles at the time of his death). In Germany Hölderlin wrote Grecian dramas and strange haunting translations of Sophocles which have been much performed in this century. Goethe's verse drama *Iphigenie* (1787 – Goethe himself played Orestes) is directly indebted, even though it ends with anti-tragic redemption. In the third act of *Faust* II, completed just before Goethe's death in 1832, Helen of

55

Troy is rescued from Menelaus at Sparta and transferred to Faust's Gothic castle: this symbolised the transplantation of Greek poetry and drama into the more recently tilled soil of Northern Europe.

There were all too many pastiches of Greek tragedy in the nineteenth century, epitomised by John Todhunter's *Helen in Troas* which swept the London aesthete scene in 1885. None is performed today. On the other hand the academic tradition of performing tragedies in ancient Greek has been more lasting: this began at Oxford in 1880, followed by Harvard in 1881, Cambridge and Bradfield College in Berkshire in 1882. The creative influence of Greek tragedy in this period is to be found in the novel. Its absorption by George Eliot has been well brought out by Richard Jenkyns, and Jeanette King has traced its presence beneath Henry James and Thomas Hardy. Hardy also worked for thirty years on *The Dynasts* (published 1904–8), 'an epic-drama of the War with Napoleon in three parts, nineteen acts and one hundred and thirty scenes'. *The Dynasts* owes much to Greek tragedy, both in its use of choral universalising poetry and in the determined way it faces the horrors of human life. Hardy explicitly and characteristically draws on Sophocles' *Women of Trachis*. 'The Spirit of the Pities' speaks:

> A life there was
> Among these self-same frail ones – Sophocles –
> Who visioned it too clearly, even the while
> He dubbed the Will 'the gods'. Truly said he
> 'Such gross injustice to their own creation
> Burdens the time with mournfulness for us,
> And for themselves with shame . . .'

The Furies of World War

As in so many spheres, the nineteenth-century imitation – verging on adulation – of ancient Greece tended towards lifeless conformity, and this is then caught up in the revolt that comes towards the end of the century. Yet the new 'modern' era, even while rejecting the Greeks, finds a new, though sometimes subversive, way of making something out of them. The last ninety years have produced an extraordinary number of plays which are in some way based on or inspired by Greek tragedy. They are often, however, parodies to some extent, or ironic fragmentations.

One thinks of France above all, where the reworking of Greek material has been one of the chief dramatic traditions. André Gide was formative, opening the way for important figures whose careers span the Second World War – Cocteau, Giraudoux, Anouilh and Sartre. Sartre's *Les Mouches* (1942), his first play, transforms the Furies who pursue Orestes into fat blood-sucking flies. Anouilh's *Antigone* was also first produced in German-occupied Paris (1944). The sense that Antigone and Creon are living out pre-ordained parts depends on a foreknowledge of Sophocles' play; yet this sophisticated fatalism has already dated in a way that Sophoclean insolubility has not.

In Germany Hugo von Hofmannsthal's *Elektra* was first put on by Max Reinhardt in 1903, and made into an opera – considered very shocking at the time – by Richard Strauss in 1909. At the end of his long life Gerhart Hauptmann turned to Greek tragedy to face the despair of the Second World War, in his 'verse epic' *Die Atriden-Tetralogie.* Even Brecht, who regarded himself as in opposition to Greek tragedy, especially to what he regarded as Aristotelian emotional empathy (though Stanislavsky is the real opponent), reworked *Antigone* in Hölderlin's translation in 1948. It is an illustration of the irrepressibility of Greek tragedy that Brecht's leading follower, Heiner Müller, has turned to it repeatedly, from his *Philoktetes* (1965) to *Medea* plays in 1974 and 1982 and a *Prometheus* still (so far as I know) in preparation.

W. B. Yeats and Ezra Pound both made their very different versions of Sophocles (Pound's *Electra* was only rediscovered and put on in 1988); but both

Anouilh's *Antigone* performed at the Old Vic in London in 1949, with Vivien Leigh as Antigone

used Greek tragedy eclectically as a channel for fancy rather than a means of expression. Eugene O'Neill's trilogy *Mourning Becomes Electra* (1931), which transplants the *Oresteia* to puritan New England, is a more significant and deeper reworking. T. S. Eliot's long and unsuccessful attempt to accommodate Greek tragedy to his plays is fascinating. The poetry and the chorus work well in the overtly Christian setting of *Murder in the Cathedral*; but the attempt to bring the Furies from *Eumenides* into *The Family Reunion* (1939) was a notorious failure: 'We tried every manner of presenting them . . .' confessed Eliot, 'they looked like uninvited guests who had strayed in from a fancy dress ball . . . they never succeeded in being either Greek goddesses or modern spooks.' The poet himself had to point out eventually that Euripides' *Alcestis* underlies *The Cocktail Party* (1949), though the critics, once alerted, were able to find for themselves Sophocles' *Oedipus at Colonus* under *The Elder Statesman* (1958). Eliot never broke out of the naturalistic and conversational mode that is so alien to Greek tragedy; even more important, his redemptive religion prevented him from facing up to horror in the Greek way.

Eddy and his family in Steve Berkoff's *Greek*

Deborah Warner's production of Sophocles' *Electra* at the Barbican in 1988–9. Fiona Shaw's Electra was a virtuoso performance.

'And through art – life'

It may be the cold wind of a post-Christian era that has produced the recent explosion of productions and recyclings of Greek tragedy with which I opened this chapter. If so, it has produced a wide variety of responses. At an extreme of the disillusioned and anti-spiritual we might put Steve Berkoff's *Greek*, first produced in 1980 and successfully turned into an opera with post-modern music by Mark-Anthony Turnage in 1988. This vigorously profane metamorphosis of *Oedipus the King* is set in Tufnell Park in London and is the story of Eddy. When Eddy discovers that he has been sleeping with his own mother, he responds:

> Why should I tear my eyes out, Greek style?
> Why should you hang yourself?
> Does it really matter that you're my mum?

He rejects the age-old taboo with subversion of Freud: 'Yeah, I wanna climb back inside my mum.'

Lee Breuer's *Gospel at Colonus* is based on Sophocles' other later *Oedipus* play '*at Colonus*', and could hardly be more different from Berkoff in spirit. Breuer sets the play in all the fervour and colour of a black Pentecostal church, where the minister uses the story of *Oedipus'* wonderful death after years of sightless

Declan Donnellan's Cheek by Jowl production of Sophocles' *Philoctetes* (1988). Keith Bartlett plays the outcast Philoctetes who has the magic bow of Heracles, with members of the chorus of sailors.

wandering to preach redemption through suffering. The sense of congregational community and the use of choirs have contributed much to the huge success of *Gospel at Colonus* in America since its first production in Brooklyn in 1983; and furthermore they are in many ways close to the spirit of the Greek original. Lee Breuer has said of it, 'Push pity and fear far enough and, mysteriously, they turn into joy.' We are sorely in need of joy these days; but is that the product of Greek tragedy? In other ways *Gospel at Colonus* is deeply subversive of the Sophocles, which is set at the grove of the primeval terrifying Furies, not in the hallelujah-filled Church. And Oedipus does not go to heaven: he becomes a powerful spirit of Colonus, and his children go to grim deaths in accordance with his curse.

The contemporary playwright who in my experience has turned most directly to Greek tragedy, not for joy, but for the will to survive, is Tony Harrison (born 1937). He claims that the Greek theatre, especially its chorus, has pervaded all his theatre works, such as *The Mysteries*, and not only those with explicit Greek connections. These range from his *Oresteia*, discussed earlier, to *Medea: a sex-war opera* (1985) which, while it actually quotes Euripides in ancient Greek, is in no sense a translation of it. His *Trojan Women*, to be published in 1990, stands somewhere between the two. It is set at the fence of the US nuclear missile base at Greenham Common. The women outside the wire put on the play for the guards inside. While much of the play is close to Euripides, it is constantly interrupted or interfused with anachronistic allusions and details. In Euripides Troy is set alight; in Harrison's version the convoy of missiles drives out of the gate, lights blazing. The last stage-direction sums up Greek tragedy's ability to survive the worst: 'Hecuba rises to her feet, slowly, painfully, but unassisted', and her words are:

> Come on, old girl, up. Totter towards the ships
> and life as a slave. But slavery's a life.

Friedrich Nietzsche published his first book, *The Birth of Tragedy*, in 1872 when he was still under 30 but already a professor of Classics at Basel. It is full of wild generalisations and even errors, but it also contains insights and prophesies. Nietzsche reckoned that the Dionysiac experience led the ancient Greeks to come face to face with the essential horror and absurdity of life; this, he claimed, would have induced a nauseous lethargy, a negation of the will, had it not been counteracted by art, especially tragedy, art which shapes and contains. 'The Greek, uniquely susceptible to the tenderest and deepest suffering, comforts himself, having looked boldly right into the terrible destructiveness of so-called World History, as well as the cruelty of nature . . . Art saves him, and through art – life.'

Aesthetics

COLD BEAUTY FOR EVER WARM

O those Greeks! They knew how to live. What is required
for that is to stop courageously at the surface, the fold, the
skin, to adore appearance, to believe in forms, tones,
words, the whole Olympus of appearance. Those Greeks
were superficial – *out of profundity.*

Nietzsche

'BEAUTY IS TRUTH, TRUTH BEAUTY' – John Keats concluded on his Grecian
urn. Yet presumably true art does not *have* to be beautiful. Much
primitive art and much modern art is certainly not beautiful, and does not
attempt to be. The powerful and persistent expectation of beauty and proportion
in art, especially in the portrayal of the human body, is fundamentally derived
from the Greeks. They sought with unprecedented innovative energy to conquer
the techniques for portraying the body both ideally and naturalistically. Their
world was full of these objects of beauty, and they devoted enormous trouble and
expense to them. They are a constant challenge to us to ask what art is for, what
it has to do with life.

For the Greeks art was very much part of life. At the same time it was highly
idealised, remote from the flaws of reality. There is a deep paradox here. With
one hand we want art to be perfect, pure, untouchable; with the other we long to
touch perfect beauty, to hold it for ourselves, even to possess it in love. We need
to have it now, quickly, because beauty is fleeting, like a rose, like the flush on a
girl's cheek. In that case, however, it is paradoxical to imitate beauty in art, to fix
the uniqueness and movement of the evanescent. The Greek kind of art is in
some strange way both cold stone or paint and yet warm with life, takeable and
yet still intact – the 'still unravish'd bride' of Keats. The fact that so much Greek
art is now fragmentary or faded increases this sense of paradox. The beauty for
us of the Athenian pottery painted on a white background lies in its fleeting
delicacy; the *Venus de Milo* has been found more desirable because she lacks the
tawdry completeness of reality.

The story of Pygmalion, King of Cyprus, reflects this tension between art and
life, the ideal and the real. He fell so deeply in love with a statue (in some

versions he had sculpted it himself) that Aphrodite brought the delectable image to life. The trouble with this tale is that if he had the statue alive in his bed, then she was no longer a work of art, ideal and unravished. Outside myth the statues are locked up at night in cold museums, where they remain unageing and unassailable, surrounded with notices saying 'Do Not Touch'. Museums are 'to preserve beauty'. Yet beauty is perishable, so museums are also caught up in the paradox of art and aesthetics.

Europa carried off to California

The Louvre, the British Museum, the Metropolitan, the Hermitage, Museo Vaticano, the Ashmolean, the Museum of Fine Arts, Staatliche Museen – in all of them Greek art is prominent, indeed central. The newest museum to bid for inclusion among the great collections of the world is the J. Paul Getty Museum at Malibu (surfing capital of California), opened in 1974. There the exhibits are mounted on special fittings which will hold safe the fragile *objet d'art* even during an earthquake. This is a striking symbol of the purpose of a museum: to preserve intact amid the turmoil and destruction of human life. Los Angeles may become a disaster area, but Getty's masterpieces will remain serene. Marion True, the curator of antiquities, has a huge annual budget, and the Getty steadily

left *The Soul Attains*, the fourth in a series of Pygmalion pictures by Burne-Jones (painted 1869–79)
right *Pygmalion and Galatea*, painted by Ernest Normand in 1886

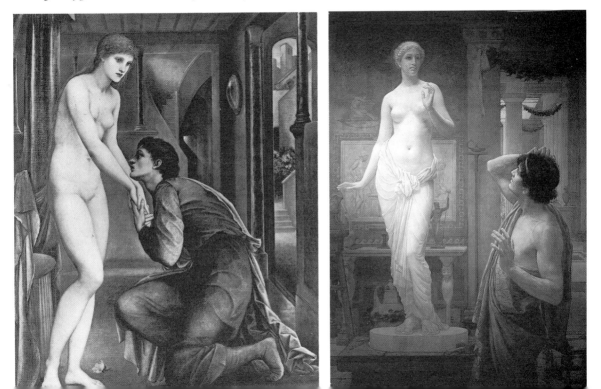

Asteas of Paestum painted his Europa with 'Desire' fluttering above in about 340 B.C.
Europa carved in stone, from the early sixth-century temple at Selinounta in Sicily

opposite A sedate early eighteenth-century Europa by Pierre Gobert
below A more dynamic bull in ink by Henry Fuseli

accumulates ancient Greek art. The statue of an athlete, acquired in 1979, is one of few life-size bronzes in the world, and must have cost millions. At the same time, she also buys painted pottery, even though there are literally thousands of pots in the world's great collections, 5–6,000 in the British Museum alone. There is still a steady supply of high-quality vases in good condition coming onto the market from the illegal plundering of ancient cemeteries in Italy. The Mafia is said to run this big business. A good piece will fetch over $200,000. Indeed, the great bowl of Euphronius acquired (amid controversy) by the Metropolitan in New York cost a million dollars in 1972.

The Getty, which has attracted more than its fair share of controversy, has acquired some vase-paintings which undeniably stand out from the many thousands. These are as varied as the stark, vigorous scenes of the sack of Troy painted in Athens in about 500 B.C. (now published, see page 258), and the ornate Europa painted in Paestum, in Southern Italy, some 150 years later and signed by their leading artist, Asteas (this was acquired in 1981). While the scenes of Troy have a terrible beauty, the Europa, so poised despite being abducted by Zeus in the form of a bull, is the focus of a pretty tableau. She takes

Parthenon sculptures which are not 'Elgin marbles' still *in situ* in Athens, viewed between columns

her place, however, among the many representations ranging from an archaic sixth-century sculpture in Sicily to a Roman villa in rural Kent, from Dürer, Titian, Veronese and Stephen McKenna to a 1984 postage stamp celebrating European parliamentary elections. These representations vary from a rape by a brute male to a placid donkey-ride. Could it be that behind them lies the suggestion that Europe is a combination of the animal male with the sensitive female, a sexist myth underlying a continent?

The Parthenon carried off to Park Lane

Although there is much to be enjoyed in the Getty collection, it is noticeable that many visitors to the museum are more interested in Getty's private life and in the alleged fakes and the scandals surrounding a previous curator, than in the exhibits for which the place exists. I cannot pretend that I always enjoy museums: sometimes they can seem tiring and boring in an especially depressing way. Faced with rows of objects which one is expected to admire, the response can become an uncomprehending stare. I have witnessed many such blank faces in the most prestigious room in the British Museum and have felt not a little sympathy.

The Parthenon frieze reproduced in Wedgwood blue and white on the Athenaeum in London

The Duveen Gallery houses the marbles sculpted in the 430s B.C. under the supervision of the great Phidias to decorate the outside of the Parthenon in Athens, marbles which keep undeservedly celebrated the name of Thomas Bruce, seventh Earl of Elgin. This bleak, institutional gallery was completed in 1938, bombed in 1940 – when the marbles were safely in a station on the London Underground – and finally opened in 1961. The grey London light glowers through the skylight on the frieze that is lined up along the two long walls. Originally it went round all four sides of Athena's temple, and had to be viewed by looking up between the Doric columns that surrounded them. My colleague Robin Osborne points out that they are now displayed 'outside in', for they were designed to face outwards. They were also meant to be seen in the light of Athens – and so they might be again, by many more people than in London, if they were returned there. Somehow their time in London has run out. They are mortified. In a sense they are more alive today in the replicas which can be seen at Hyde Park Corner, at the Athenaeum in Pall Mall, and at the Royal College of Surgeons in Lincoln's Inn Fields.

The marbles were alive when they first came to London. Byron cursed Elgin's 'hated name', but there were many who blessed the opportunity to see them without peril. They were displayed from the summer of 1807, without any reference to subject or original position, in a large shed in the garden of Elgin's

A slab of the south frieze in the Duveen Gallery – the inspiration for 'that heifer lowing at the skies'?

house on the corner of Park Lane and Piccadilly. The painter Benjamin Robert Haydon was overwhelmed, especially by the attention to anatomy in relation to movement and repose. He saw an elbow, for example, 'with the outer condyle visibly affecting the shape . . . the arm in repose and the soft parts in relaxation'. He rushed to fetch Henry Fuseli, born in Zürich and trained in Rome, who had become keeper of the Royal Academy: 'By Gode!' he exclaimed. 'De Greeks vere Gods!' When Antonio Canova, the leading Italian sculptor who in the 1780s had pioneered a new severe Greek style, saw them, he looked back: 'O, that I had but to begin again, to unlearn all that I have learned! I now at last see what ought to form the real school of sculpture.'

The nation paid Elgin £35,000 for his plundered marbles (he had asked for £75,000), and in 1817 they were moved to the temporary Elgin Room at the British Museum. Haydon had befriended young John Keats and took him along there. Keats returned again and again, and sent Haydon his sonnet 'On Seeing the Elgin Marbles'. But it is of course the 'Ode on a Grecian Urn', written in 1819, that epitomises Keats's attitude to art and gives the finest expression to our initial paradox in terms of what might be called 'dynamic stillness'. The painted vase shows a cold pastoral, and yet the love scene on it is 'for ever warm and still to be enjoyed'.

> Bold Lover, never, never canst thou kiss,
> Though winning near the goal – yet do not grieve:
> She cannot fade, though thou hast not thy bliss,
> For ever wilt thou love, and she be fair!

Keats was describing an imaginative composite, not one particular urn. 'That heifer lowing at the skies' might well have been inspired by the work of Phidias.

Discus Thrower carried off to Munich

The parliamentary enquiry set up to decide how much to pay Elgin asked expert witnesses, among other questions, 'Are they good or acknowledged masterpieces, like the *Apollo* and *Torso Belvedere*, and the *Laocoön*?' These three were all in the Belvedere garden of the Vatican by 1511 and have been there ever since, except for a brief interval between 1797 and 1816 when they were removed to Paris by Napoleon. The *Laocoön* became the test case in the great debate on the limits of artistic and literary representation which went on in the second half of the eighteenth century, and is now most recalled by Lessing's *Laokoon* of 1766. The piece was well enough known in 1843 for Dickens to allude to it in Scrooge's final conversion in *A Christmas Carol*: ' "I don't know what to do," cried Scrooge, laughing and crying in the same breath; and making a perfect Laocoön of himself with his stockings.'

The story of the ninety or so classics of ancient sculpture, nearly all of them in Rome and enormously admired and copied from the sixteenth to the nineteenth centuries, is admirably told by Francis Haskell and Nicholas Penny in *Taste and the Antique*. Most of their 'classics' had become completely disregarded in the course of the nineteenth century, but there are still three statues so celebrated as to be represented in human form in the slave market in *Asterix and the Laurel Wreath*, and in various recent advertisements for British Rail and TNT couriers. One is *Laocoön*; a second is *The Thinker*, which is not Greek at all but by Rodin (who was under Greek influence of course). The third is the *Discus Thrower* or *Discobolus*, first rediscovered on 14 March 1781. Walter Pater thought of Oxford undergraduates, claiming that it embodied 'all one had ever fancied or seen in old Greece, or on Thames' side, of the unspoiled body of youth'. At the start of her breath-taking film of the Berlin Olympics of 1936 – which employed 100 cameramen, consumed 1,300,000 feet of film, and took two years in the editing – Leni Riefenstahl reincarnated the *Discobolus* in the form of flesh and blood

left The *Laocoön* in Rome, one of the most famous sculptures of all time
right The *Discobolus*. There have been endless disputes about the reconstruction of the position of the head.

Aryan manhood. Hitler himself became obsessed with the statue, bought it in 1938 for 5 million lire, and put it on display in Munich. It was returned to Rome in 1948.

This *Discobolus* is a Roman marble copy of a bronze statue by the fifth-century Greek Myron, older contemporary of Phidias and the Parthenon. Nearly all those antique works so admired for three centuries are Roman copies, and poor superficial copies at that, of Greek originals, some of the classical age, some – most notably *Laocoön* – of the later Hellenistic era which produced more sensational work. One man above all was responsible for mapping out the history of Greek art, and for insisting on distinguishing between the genuine Greek article and the Roman copies: Johann Joachim Winckelmann (1717–68), a key figure in the late eighteenth-century Hellenic Renaissance which we encounter in chapter after chapter of this story. When Goethe looked back in 1805, he dubbed the whole era 'The Century of Winckelmann'.

The son of a Prussian cobbler, Winckelmann spent his last ten years in Rome, where he was regarded as such an authority that he even rivalled the local oracle, Piranesi. He was making plans to visit what we call Greece when he met his untimely end after being mugged in a tavern in Trieste. So he never got further than the Greek temples of Paestum, one of the many ancient Greek cities in Southern Italy. His *Thoughts on the Imitation of Greek Works*, published in 1755 before he ventured south, was translated into English by the young Fuseli in 1765. In the book, he enthused about how he found in Greek art an idealised pagan soul, counteracting the frustrations of Northern Europe, and a vision of the perfect forms of physical beauty. He coined the famous phrase '*eine edle Einfalt und eine stille Grösse*', that noble simplicity and calm grandeur which he also attributes to Raphael. It seems strange to us now, however, that he should choose *Laocoön* to exemplify this quality.

'The Greeks alone seem to have thrown forth beauty as a potter makes his pot,' Winckelmann wrote with warmth and passion. He felt Greek art with his body and soul, and his sensual response barely conceals his homosexuality, as in this rapturous admiration of the *Apollo Belvedere* in his *History of Ancient Art* (1764): 'An eternal spring . . . clothes with the charms of youth the graceful manliness of ripened years, and plays with soft tenderness about the proud shape of his limbs . . . My breast seems to enlarge and swell with reverence . . . for my image seems to receive life and motion, like the beautiful creation of Pygmalion.'

Winckelmann was technically wrong over many dates and attributions; he thought that Greek statues were all pure white when in fact they were brightly coloured; he makes it all sound far too cool and serene. None the less, as Goethe rightly saw, 'we may learn nothing from reading Winckelmann, but we become something'. This 'Grecomania' (Schiller's word), which he did so much to inspire, was not a matter of mere imitation: it was a liberating inspiration. 'What the Greeks should teach us,' wrote Hölderlin in a letter of 1801, 'is how to come to a free use of our talents.'

The Hellenic apotheosis

The neo-Hellenic era in sculpture and painting, from about 1770 to 1820, is characterised by austerity of ornament, frieze-like composition, sculptural surfaces, especially of naked flesh, whiteness – in a phrase 'noble simplicity and calm grandeur'. A central figure was Canova (1757–1822), much admired throughout Europe, especially by Napoleon (though since dubbed 'the erotic frigidaire' by Mario Praz). Angelica Kauffmann, a friend of his and of Winckelmann, painted pretty pictures in the new Grecian manner. When Goethe visited her in Rome in 1787, he described her as 'very sensitive towards all that is beautiful, true and tender, and also incredibly modest'. Someone else who arrived in Rome in 1787 was the Englishman John Flaxman (1755–1828).

When he returned to England in 1794, much influenced by Canova, he quickly became the most admired sculptor of the day (casts of his work still adorn the lobby of University College, London). He was the most dedicated Grecian of all and his work is the most severely simple. Even his huge crowded silver-gilt *Shield of Achilles*, based on the description in *Iliad* 18, remains calm. He was especially austere in his line-drawing illustrations to Homer and others (their sharp lines had, incidentally, been only recently made possible by the invention of steel pen nibs). They may strike modern taste as pretty lifeless.

Flaxman's work was, however, much admired in its day, and by no less ardent a creator than William Blake, who himself re-engraved some of it, especially his *Iliad*. In his earlier years Blake was an admirer of the Hellenic, and in 1799 claimed that he wanted 'to renew the lost art of the Greeks'; but as he grew more and more visionary and biblical, he became positively hostile to the rationality of that unHebraic world. Another curious figure in this gallery is Henry Fuseli

The Queen's 'top copy' of Flaxman's *Shield of Achilles*. The sun and heavenly bodies in the centre are surrounded by various scenes of human life taken from Homer's description of the shield made by the god Hephaestus.

(1741–1827), who was at one time in love with Angelica Kauffmann. Blake wrote of him:

> The only man that e'er I knew
> Who did not make me almost spew
> Was Fuseli . . .

While he is best known now for his more fantastical work, such as *The Nightmare*, he had a lifelong passion for ancient Greece, and produced pictures which, while still Grecian, are full of vigour and feeling compared with those of Flaxman.

So the Hellenic Renaissance was far from uniform or merely imitative. It interacted with the Romantic, with the *Sturm und Drang* movement, and with the political allegory of the age of Revolution. This is nowhere more true than in France, where it touched at least two major painters. Jacques-Louis David owed more to Rome and to the neo-classical tradition of Poussin; and this includes his most famous Greek work, *The Death of Socrates* (1787). Later, influenced by Flaxman and by the new interest in Greek vases towards the end of the century, his style underwent a kind of purification. In 1799 he wrote: 'I want to make something which is pure Greek, I feed my eyes on antique statues.' *Leonidas at Thermopylae* (1814) is an example. A generation later, the first work of Jean-August Ingres (1780–1867) to make a mark was *The Ambassadors of Agamemnon at the Tent of Achilles* of 1801. When he painted *Napoleon on the Imperial Throne* in 1806 he clearly echoed the archaeological reconstructions of the great statue of Zeus at Olympia by Phidias. The colossal semi-nude statue of Washington commissioned by Congress in 1833 was also modelled on Zeus – 'not *our* Washington', protested one senator! Ingres' *The Apotheosis of Homer* (1827) is a particularly revealing painting, for as well as acknowledging Homer as the great hero of the Greek Renaissance, it pays homage to the great master, Raphael, by imitating his *School of Athens*. Even so, while Raphael's Plato and Aristotle walk beneath a Roman triumphal arch, Ingres' setting is an Ionic temple. Raphael, whose hand is held by the Greek painter Apelles, is the only modern who stands full-length. In 1840 Ingres planned another version to include Winckelmann, Flaxman, David and himself.

Hypocrisy and passéisme

By the 1830s, when Hellas herself was liberated, the Hellenic Renaissance was past its prime. Yet later in the same century artists all over the world would be

Ingres' *The Apotheosis of Homer*. Raphael, on the left, is the only 'modern' among the standing figures. Compare Raphael's *School of Athens* on pages 168–9.

A Sleeping Nymph by Canova, 'the erotic frigidaire'

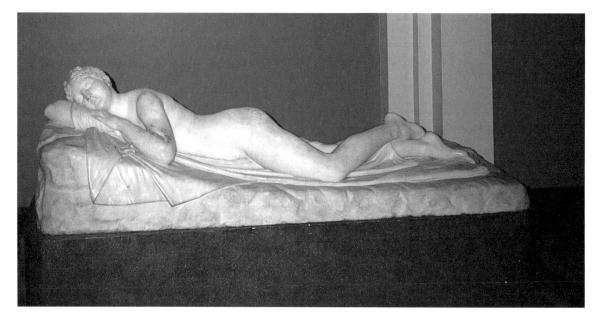

Ingres' Napoleon in the Olympian pose. Zeus was less fully robed!

Ulysses and the Sirens by Herbert Draper (1864–1920). The rowers have wax in their ears so they are not lured by the Sirens' song. In Homer the Sirens sit on a rock: Draper has reasons for bringing them on board!

able to make a living by painting feminine scenes set in ancient Greece. Jean-Léon Gérome (1824–1904) trained apprentices from the United States, Russia and Japan. In England, especially in the 1870s and 1880s, long after Greek architecture had run out of steam, Grecian sculptors and artists dominated the market. Compared with contemporary pre-Raphaelites and Impressionists, their works seem to me to be second-rate and kitsch, although more recently they have been fetching high prices in the auction rooms – Pointer's *Cave of the Storm Nymphs* went for £440,000 in November 1988. Their sentimental and suggestive works are often set, not in the austere marmoreal Greece of Winckelmann, but in one full of bright colour. It had been established in the meantime that Greek sculptures were painted – a point nicely made in Alma-Tadema's *Phidias at Work on the Parthenon*. When the Crystal Palace was reopened in 1854 the Greek Court even contained a vividly coloured cast of the Parthenon Frieze.

It is hard to deny the label 'pornographic', however soft. The erotic streak in neo-Hellenic art went right back to Winckelmann. Clinging dresses and private nakedness were made respectable by classic precedent. Elizabeth Barrett Browning persuaded herself of the 'passionless perfection' of *The Greek Slave* by the American sculptor Hiram Power, which was much admired at the Great Exhibition in 1851. T. S. R. Boase on the other hand writes of its 'sadism'. Frederic Leighton, President of the Academy and eventually in 1895 a Lord, almost avoids the titillating; but Lawrence Alma-Tadema, with the help of what have been called his 'Greco-West Kensington models', certainly does not. Many others, including Watts, Richmond and Albert Moore, turned their hands to transparent drapery and exquisite young breasts. 'We seem to have infected the Greek ages themselves with the breath of our hypocrisy', wrote Ruskin.

Classical models and subjects continued to dominate the formal study of art, at the Royal Academy or Ecole des Beaux-Arts, long after the really creative influence of ancient Greece on sculpture and painting was running out. So it is not surprising that when Modernism eventually rejected the nineteenth century it rejected Greek art along with it. In the Manifesto of 20 February 1909, in which Marinetti proclaimed the end of *Le Passéisme* and the birth of *Le Futurisme*, he singled out the Greek statue which stands prominently on the stairs of the Louvre as the symbol of the culture which the heroic new age would sweep aside. 'A roaring racing car, rattling along like a machine-gun, is more beautiful than the Winged Victory of Samothrace.' The *Victory*, found in 1865, is one of the two really famous ancient sculptures found during the nineteenth century; the other, also in the Louvre, is the Aphrodite found on Melos in 1820 (the *Venus de Milo*). Both seem to me passé.

Although classical motifs can be symbolically important in de Chirico, and mythological motifs can stand for dark forces in Braque or Dali, or even

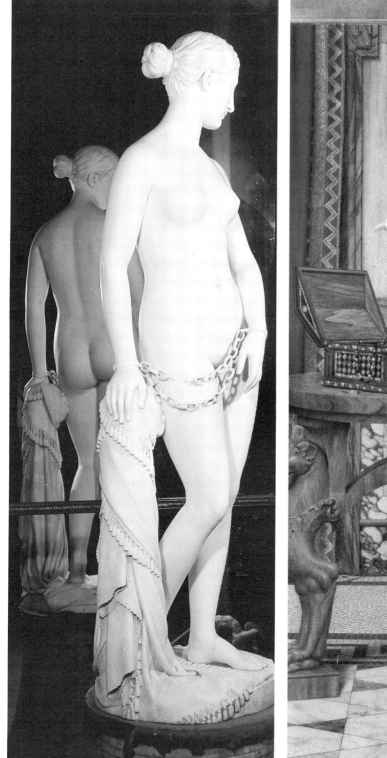

Power's *Greek Slave* (1843), bondage much admired by respectable Victorians
The New Perfume by J. W. Goddard (1861–1922), transparent antiquarianism

Picasso, on the whole modern art has little Greek Fire in it, at least until the last 15 years or so. Post-modernism is a label applied mostly to architecture, but the same eclectic return can be seen in art also. To repeat Eco's phrase: '. . . the past, since it cannot really be destroyed, because its destruction leads to silence, must be revisited: but with irony, not innocently'.

An outstanding example in sculpture is the Olympic Arch created by Robert Graham for the Los Angeles Games in 1984. The emphasis on anatomy and finish evokes Greece, and the truncation of hands and feet makes a virtue of the fragmentary, though symmetrically so. Post-modern Hellenic elements in painting are very various. In Rome, in the 1970s, Carlo Maria Mariani dreamt of an Academy presided over by Angelica Kauffman, Goethe, and – in keeping with his overt homosexuality – Winckelmann. In Scotland Ian Hamilton Finlay at 'Little Sparta' looks to a different pantheon, especially David and Flaxman. 'Apollo has migrated far from his native Greece, he is the pale Hyperborean Apollo visiting the Northern regions . . . His modern archer is the French revolutionary Saint-Just.' The Irish painter Stephen McKenna goes eclectically to Greece for myth, to museums for fragments. His *O Ilium* attempts to say something post-1945 about war (Picasso's *Guernica* was produced in 1936).

Beautiful bodies and frank nudity once again shelter behind the respectability of Greece, especially in the United States. Bruno Critico's *Danaë* (1980) gives a New England setting to Zeus' shower of gold; Thomas Cornell and Milet Andrejivic insinuate Greek myth into sexually heightened American settings. In *The Birth of Dionysus II*, Cornell has Hermes hand over the baby god to Americans who are half contemporary and half set in the days of the early settlers. The Russian émigrés Vitaly Komer and Aleksander Melamid have set up an entertaining double-act with pictures like *President Reagan as a Centaur. The Origin of Socialist Realism* (1982–3) alludes to the story told by the Roman Pliny about the origin of painting: the boyfriend of a Corinthian potter's daughter was about to go away, and as a reminder of him, she cast his shadow on the wall and drew around it. We get the sense here that the Russian Muse is more worth preserving than Stalin.

'Throwing forth beauty as a potter makes his pot'

The Greeks turned so many things into works of art that they anticipated and influenced many art forms. Their cloth and their furniture, for example, do not survive as such, yet through representation have had considerable influence. Coins, jewelry, seal-stones and gems – many of them exquisite miniature masterpieces – have made their mark. So have statuettes and utensils in bronze,

The wall painting of the *Rape of Persephone*, painted about 340 B.C. and discovered at Vergina in 1977. The horses of Pluto's chariot are also well preserved.

ivory, terracotta and glass. Unfortunately most of their *objets d'art* in precious metal, especially silver and gold, have been melted down in harder times. The lavishly ornamented fourth-century bronze urn with silver-gilt, found at Derveni in Macedonia in 1962, gives us some idea of what we are missing. Some 200 years older, the bronze urn, about five feet high, buried with a Gaulish princess and found at Vix in northern Burgundy, is stunning, especially in its incongruous setting at Châtillon-sur-Seine.

Wall painting has also been the victim of time (even more so easel-painting, of course), though the survivals at Pompeii and Herculaneum are highly derivative from Greek models. The finest Greek mural to survive was found as recently as 1977. Professor Manolis Andronikos tells in his book *Vergina* how he levelled the huge artificial tumulus at Vergina near Thessalonica, and found there the tomb of Philip of Macedon, father of Alexander the Great. Astonishingly, it remained intact and unplundered, and full of superb artefacts. A smaller tomb found next door beneath the tumulus has a dramatically fluent painting (*c.* 340 B.C.) still *in situ*, with long flowing brush strokes portraying a dishevelled Pluto in his chariot carrying off his bride Persephone, her purple robes falling from her outstretched body. In 1987–8 Andronikos dug up another superb painting in a near-contemporary tomb about a mile away. This had been robbed, except for a heavy marble throne which has painted on the back-rest another picture of Pluto and Persephone. The contrast, however, could hardly be greater, for on this throne they are reconciled as stately king and queen, and painted in a highly formal, detached, almost miniaturist style.

There remains one kind of Greek painting which survives in quantity – decorated pottery. This was a rather everyday art-form compared with sculpture or work in precious metal, but it none the less attracted talented painters and potters who were proud to sign their names on their work. Pottery painting flourished at a high level for several centuries, and it is particularly fine all the way from the first vigorous figural painting in the seventh century to the florid extravaganzas of south Italian painters in the fourth.

Athens dominated the market for some two centuries, with a transition in about 520 B.C. from 'black figure' – painting in black on the red of the clay – to 'red figure', which, in reverse, leaves the figures in red against a black background. Fifth-century Athens also produced the attractive but fragile

The 1768 title-page of the first publication of Hamilton's collection
Tischbein's engraving (1791) of the discovery of a tomb with Greek vases. Emma Hamilton stands on the right.

technique of coloured figures on a white ground. It was Winckelmann who helped to set up a chronology of the art-form, and he recognised in the style of fifth-century Athenian vase painting that very simplicity and grandeur which he so admired. He found an odd successor in Adolf Loos, the Austrian anti-ornamental architect, who wrote: 'Greek vases are as beautiful as a machine, as beautiful as a bicycle'! It was a century earlier, however, that they fired a kiln of creativity.

Greek vases had been found in Italy since the Renaissance, though not in great numbers, nor much regarded. Their discovery in Tuscany led to the assumption that they were the work of the ancient Etruscans, when in fact they had been imported by them from Greece. An Englishman with a mania for collecting antiquities plays a crucial role in the story. Sir William Hamilton was posted as Envoy at the Court of Naples in 1764, and he was much visited there during his 36 years in the office by all travellers with cultural pretensions. He quickly built up a huge collection of 'Etruscan' vases and he hoped to persuade Winckelmann, who visited him in 1766, to study them and help with their publication. Hamilton actually employed a plausible French adventurer, Pierre d'Hancarville, who might have been a good antiquary had he not also been an extravagant and dishonest pleasure-seeker. D'Hancarville and Winckelmann got on well. The first volume, with its superb engravings, came out in 1768, dedicated to King George III. In the second (1770) there is the engraving of an imaginary tomb of the recently murdered Winckelmann – though Roman rather than Greek in style. On the strength of their lavish volumes the first collection was sold in 1772 to the British Museum for 8,000 guineas – a substantial sum.

Sir William built up a second collection, which was lost on its way home when HMS *Colossus* was wrecked off the Scilly Isles. Sixteen cases were salvaged, but the rest were lost, except for some fragments recovered by diving in the 1970s. Fortunately they had already been published in engravings by Tischbein, who also painted the famous portrait of *Goethe in Campania*. Goethe had visited Hamilton in 1787, and admired, rather than his vases, his mistress Emma Hart (the daughter of a blacksmith), who was famous for dressing *à la grecque*, and for attempting a wide range of antique poses. In 1791, the year that Hamilton married Emma, Tischbein engraved a scene of the discovery of Greek vases in a tomb at Nola; the elegant woman on the right is surely her.

In Sir William's eyes, his prize exhibit was probably the vase signed by the artist Meidias, and made in Athens towards the end of the fifth century. It is indeed pretty, with its variety of figures and poses, and its delicate rippling drapery. It was so famous that the cartoonist Gillray in 1801 painted a back-view of Nelson in its shape.

Wedgwood's 'Etruscan urn' with poses inspired by Hamilton's collections

Wedgwood's Etrurian enterprise

The huge number of vases excavated in the last 40 years of the eighteenth century had considerable impact on interior design and furnishing, but above all on porcelain vessels. An outstanding example is the Sèvres collection at Marie-Antoinette's 'dairy' at Rambouillet (1785). French taste had, however, been led by the enterprising Josiah Wedgwood, whose commercial exploitation of past design is admired by Sir Terence Conran. In 1769 Wedgwood wrote in rather an excited stream of consciousness to his partner Bentley:

> And do you really think that we may make a complete conquest of France? Conquer France in Burslem? . . . Assist me, my friend, and the victory is our own. We will make them our Porcelain after their own hearts, and captivate them with the Elegance and simplicity of the ancients. But do they love simplicity? France and frippery have jingled together so long in my ideas, that I scarcely know how to separate them . . .

When their new factory opened at Etruria in Staffordshire, it had still to be established that the ancient vases were in fact Greek. Wedgwood had seen proofs of the engravings in d'Hancarville's first volume of the Hamilton collection, and on the opening day, 13 June 1769, he threw six 'Etruscan urns', while Bentley powered the wheel. These were painted by an encaustic method to produce something like Athenian red-figure. The figures and poses were taken from Sir William Hamilton's Meidias hydria. (So, rather unexpectedly, is the pose of Oedipus in Ingres' painting of the Sphinx on page 265.)

It was a small world. The young John Flaxman worked for Wedgwood from 1775 to 1787, when he went to Rome. Among his designs was a jasper plaque of *The Apotheosis of Homer*, one of which Wedgwood sent to Hamilton in Naples in 1778 as a token of their mutual benefit. Flaxman eventually carved a head of Josiah Wedgwood for his tomb in Stoke-on-Trent.

By 1819, when Keats punned 'O Attic shape! Fair attitude!', it was common knowledge that these 'urns' were in fact Grecian not Etruscan. Tastes change, and these days most people prefer the stronger style of late black-figure or early red-figure (say 580–480 B.C.), and painters such as Exekias and Euphronius, to the more sugary period of Hamilton's Meidias painter. Since the days of Keats it is hard to detect much creative influence from Greek pottery painting, though it would be strange if it all sits in museum cases without touching the post-modernism of the late twentieth century. The exquisite draftsmanship, enhanced rather than spoiled by fragmentariness, seems ripe for new inspiration.

Hamilton's Meidias Vase

Gillray's *Nelson*

Modernism brought 'the shock of the new'. When the Parthenon marbles were first displayed in Park Lane they had the full shock of the old. Post-modernism does not, however, exploit the shock of the old so much as the clever fragmentation of the old. Even such superb finds as the Euphronius vase in New York or the Vergina wall-paintings do not really seem to break out of academic interest into the world outside. Just one Greek art-form seems to have been able to escape the static security of the museum in the twentieth century: bronze sculpture. The Charioteer found at Delphi in 1896, and – much finer – the Zeus (probably not Poseidon) found in the sea off Cape Artemisium in 1928 and now in Athens – these must be the two best-known pieces of Greek art discovered in the last 100 years, the two most likely to come to life in the modern imagination. Or they were until very recently.

Brazen sexuality

On August Bank Holiday 1972 Stefano Mariottini, a chemist from Rome, was skin-diving some 300 metres off the coast of Riace down by the toe of Italy when eight metres down he saw the limbs of a statue sticking up through the sand. He told the authorities at once; and, after panic because of the danger of looting, they were raised, without any archaeological investigation, by the diving unit of the Messina Carabinieri on 21 August. People claimed that they were the local Saints, Cosmos and Damian. Some restoration work was done at the nearby provincial capital, Reggio di Calabria, but eventually in 1975 they were sent to Florence, where they finally went on public show, fully cleaned and restored,

The two Riace Bronzes

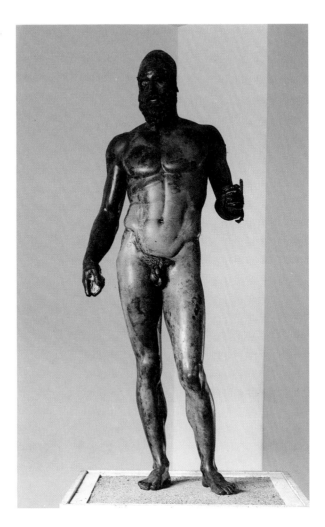

late in 1980. They were moved to the Palazzo del Quirinale in Rome before being welcomed home to a specially extended and renovated museum in Reggio in August 1981. Reggio is not the most attractive town in Italy – 120 gangland killings took place in 1986 – yet tens of thousands make the pilgrimage every year to see the Riace Bronzes.

The Bronzes emanate the shock of the old. They have been a genuinely popular cultural phenomenon, appearing on stamps and in advertisements for, among other things, perfumes and Renault cars. I know of only one scholar in the world who disputes that they are masterpieces made in the mid-fifth century, and as fine as any Greek art that we have anywhere. They will have been plundered from Greece, and were presumably on their way to furnish the villa of a wealthy Roman when they were shipwrecked, probably in the first century B.C. or A.D. Some respectable scholars believe that they can place the Riace Bronzes exactly as two of the set of thirteen dedicated by the Athenians at Delphi to celebrate their great victory over the Persians at Marathon. If so, they are the work of the Athenian master Phidias himself.

In the collection *Heroes from the Sea*, sponsored by the University of Calabria, there is an essay on 'The Popularity of the Bronzes'. This studies the sociology of their reception, including their extraordinary sexual impact on the public. Women are particularly aroused, it seems, by the rather assertive, slimmer Statue A (page 86), with his almost insolent smile and shining teeth, while homosexual men respond to the more reserved Statue B (page 87). Their palpable sexuality found extraordinary expression in the Milanese porno-comic-strip magazine *Sukia* in 1981. In the story Sukia, the glamorous and highly-sexed heroine, and a man-friend steal the statues and ship them to New York. On board there is a knock at Sukia's door, and Statue A comes to her bed with one part of his bronze anatomy enormously changed. Meanwhile her friend, who is a homosexual, is being buggered by Statue B. Here is a bizarre vulgarisation of Winckelmann's raptures over the *Apollo Belvedere* – and a curious modernisation of the Pygmalion fantasy. In its tacky way, *Sukia* shows how the Riace Bronzes have broken out of their museum to inhabit the imagination.

When Goethe was in Rome, he wrote of his mistress in his *Roman Elegies*: 'Do I not instruct myself by studying the form of her lovely bosom, and running my hands down over her hips? Not till then do I understand marble rightly . . . I see with an eye that feels and feel with a hand that sees.' Is it the way that Greek art can be 'felt' by the eye that keeps it alive? In 1807 Haydon responded to the life beneath the surface of the Parthenon marbles. In 1887 Richard Jefferies turned his eye which so closely observed the nature of Wiltshire to a Venus in the Louvre (but not the *Venus de Milo*): 'Under these folds there must be breath, there must be blood; they indicate a glowing life.' Once again there is the

A sample of the adventures of
Sukia

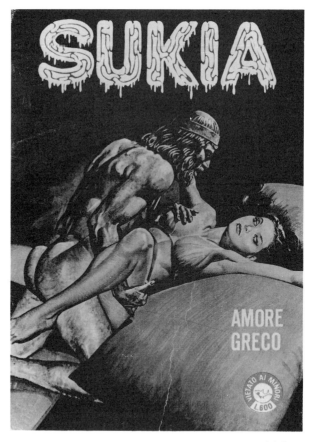

interaction of touch and imagination, stillness and movement, object and life –
even in the mausoleum of a museum. The Riace Bronzes or the *Venus de Milo*
will never (thank goodness) come to life; they will remain cold and under tight
security. We can perhaps see why Keats addressed his work of art as 'Cold
Pastoral' and as 'friend to man'.

Myth

THE CLUE OUT OF THE DARK

Myth . . . is simply a way of controlling, of ordering, of
giving a shape and a significance to the immense panorama
of futility and anarchy which is contemporary history.

T.S. Eliot

THE MODERN WEST IS IN THE HABIT of supposing that straight, objective
language is the only proper way to talk about things. The primacy of plain
prose, especially in scientific discourse, is indeed part of the Greek heritage; but
that is not the only valid mode of expression, nor can it express everything worth
expressing. Metaphor, for example, can bring together ideas and categories with
an effect which simply cannot be achieved in any other way.

It was the Greeks of the classical age, culminating in Plato, who insisted on
separating out 'myth' (*mythos*) from more rational, more objective modes of
discourse (*logos*). *Logos* may have been predominant in the twentieth century, but
mythos has far from died out – though it has sometimes resurfaced in such odd
guises as science fiction or computer games or psychological models. It may be
that myth is a way of talking about the world that can reach some parts that other
discourses cannot reach. 'Myths are good to think with,' Geoffrey Lloyd advises
me. 'Everybody lives by myth in one sense or another,' says Bernard Knox.
'Reality is too complicated, there's too much of it . . . you have to find patterns
which enable you to sort out what's important and what's not. And this whole
process of selection, so to speak, is what myths have done over the generations
. . . The pattern might not be too cheerful, might even be frightening in some
ways, but it's satisfying because it's better than chaos.'

A myth is a good story, *plus* some other special ingredient – though there is
little or no agreement over what that ingredient might be. People like myths,
even need them. All 'interacting informations systems', computers and humans
alike, need myths, according to *The Creative Computer*, a recent book on artificial
intelligence. Nearly everyone hears them as children; and poets, novelists,
dramatists, painters, composers go on to use them when they are grown up. This
adult recourse to myth may well have increased in the twentieth century, even

though it has seen modernism rejecting the past, including the classical past, in order to build anew. Not so with Greek myth, which has perhaps been a more significant ingredient in the creative cauldron since 1900 than at any other time since the first century B.C.

The Greek myths, usually mediated through Roman appropriation, especially by Ovid in his *Metamorphoses*, are *the* myths of the Western world. What, after all, has been added since? The Arthurian stories, Don Juan, Faust? These three have something of the persistence and vividness attained and retained by dozens of Greek myths; but I doubt whether there are any others to be added to the formative mythologies of the West. Unless, that is, you add the Bible or Shakespeare. Yet the Bible, quite apart from theological controversy, is quite different in that it has a definitive version – it is a sacred text – and it can only be altered or adapted as an act of daring or even blasphemy (such as in D.H. Lawrence's *The Man Who Died* or Kazantzakis's *Christ Recrucified*, basis for the recent 'blasphemous' film, *The Last Temptation of Christ*). Shakespeare also has a definitive text of near-sacred status; but it is accepted that that can be creatively adapted in such hands as Verdi and his librettist Piave.

In any case, it is a crucial feature of Greek myths that they were not and are not fixed: there is no authorised version. In ancient times they were continually open to change, development and renewal, in literature, art and presumably in oral telling. Even the *Iliad* could be altered and retold by Aeschylus in a trilogy of tragedies (lost unfortunately); even Sophocles' *Oedipus* could be recast quite differently by Euripides. You would have thought that one totally immovable 'fact' of Greek myth was that Helen eloped with Paris to Troy and thus started the Trojan War. Yet Euripides, and the poet Stesichorus before him, told a version (bitterly recalled by Seferis in his great poem *Helen*) in which the real Helen was in Egypt and only a phantom in Troy.

There must, of course, be some fixtures: there must be a Helen at Troy, even if only a phantom. Oedipus has to kill his father and mate with his mother; but there were versions in which he did not blind himself, others in which he did not go into exile, and others in which Jocasta did not kill herself. Sophocles may well have made up for the first time the story of Antigone's death for burying her brother; Euripides may well have been the first to have Medea herself kill her children – in earlier versions it seems to have been the Corinthians who did the deed.

Making the modern world possible for art

The myths have remained flexible, open to recycling, both in the details of narrative and in the significance which may be drawn from them. Their

An illustration to Hawthorne's *Tanglewood Tales*

MIDAS DAUGHTER TURNED TO GOLD

formative power has varied greatly. In the eighteenth century, when a knowledge of the myths (in Latin) was part of polite learning, they were primarily an ornament, a compliment from the author to the reader. This is what Wordsworth is talking about in 1819 (in a note to his *Ode to Lycoris*): 'No doubt the hackneyed and lifeless use into which mythology fell towards the end of the seventeenth century, and which continued throughout the eighteenth, disgusted the general reader with all allusion to it in modern verse; and though, in deference to this disgust, I abstained in my earlier writings from all introduction of pagan fable, surely even in its humble form it may ally itself with real sentiment.' In the 'romantic' period pagan fable was once again treated as raw material rather than as conventionalised ornament, and this proved liberating rather than restrictive for poets such as Shelley, Hölderlin and Mallarmé. As the nineteenth century went on Greek myth remained vital for spirits as different as Edgar Allan Poe and John Ruskin; but it tended once again to fossilise. Perhaps this was encouraged by the production of highly popular books, especially Charles Kingsley's *The Heroes* (1856), and Nathaniel Hawthorne's *Tanglewood*

94

Tales (1852–3), which I myself read spellbound as a small boy.

The transition from that era to our own coincided with important developments in anthropology and psychology, developments which gave new, hidden meanings to the myths. It was this that enabled the 'modernists' to see them as, in the words of T.S. Eliot writing in 1923 about Joyce's *Ulysses*, 'a way of controlling, of ordering, of giving a shape and a significance to the immense panorama of futility and anarchy which is contemporary history'. He goes on: 'Psychology (such as it is, and whether our reaction to it be comic or serious), ethnology, and *The Golden Bough* have concurred to make possible what was impossible only a few years ago. Instead of narrative method, we may now use the mythical method. It is, I seriously believe, a step towards making the modern world possible for art.' Joyce himself saw the story of Ulysses/Odysseus as 'the most beautiful, all-embracing theme – greater, more human, than that of Hamlet, Don Quixote, Dante, Faust'. More recently it has touched one of the best works of science fiction, Arthur C. Clarke's *2001: A Space Odyssey*, turned into a memorable film by Stanley Kubrick.

A scene on the moon from Kubrick's *2001: A Space Odyssey*

In the twentieth century myth was once more released for recycling. If we think only of poetry in English, Greek myth has had an important, varied, and far from merely ornamental, place for Yeats, Pound, Graves and Auden as well as for Eliot himself. Other far from minor beneficiaries are Conrad Aiken, George Barker, Robert Frost, Robert Lowell, Louis MacNeice, Edwin Muir and John Crowe Ransom. Philip Larkin dissented: 'to me the whole of the ancient world, the whole of classical and biblical mythology, means very little, and I think that using them today not only fills poems full of dead spots, but dodges the poet's duty to be original.' Were Larkin right (universally rather than personally speaking) Greek myth would have been finally extinguished: the whole point is that the Greek world has been used and reused *originally*. Douglas Dunn and Seamus Heaney have recently used Greek myth with their own original applications. What these poets do is to go down to the dead and to come back with new inspiration.

Looking back at Eurydice

Many myths concern a descent into the dark, the labyrinth or the underworld. Orpheus is probably the best known.

> Orpheus with his lute made trees,
> And the mountain-tops that freeze,
>   Bow themselves when he did sing
> . . . In sweet music is such art,
> Killing care and grief of heart
>   Fall asleep, or hearing die

goes the song in Shakespeare's *Henry VIII*. As ever, there was no fixed version, but the familiar story was that Orpheus was a Thracian singer of such art that the animals and even inanimate nature would be spellbound by him. His wife Eurydice is killed, and he goes down to the underworld to try to recover her. His music entrances even the powers below, and the King of the Dead allows Orpheus to take Eurydice back to the upper air, but on one condition: as they travel, he must not look back at her. He turns eventually, and so loses her for ever. In the end, the story went, he was torn to pieces by Maenads; but his head, still singing, floated across the sea to Lesbos, island of poets such as Sappho and Alcaeus.

What does the myth *mean*? Different things at different times. The myth lived transformed even during the Middle Ages. In the Byzantine East the old iconography of Orpheus surrounded by animals is found on a psalter of about

A Byzantine picture of David singing the Psalms, based on Orpheus surrounded by animals. 'Melody' sits behind David.

900 A.D. – but it is David who is the musician. In the West, in the attractive fourteenth-century Middle English verse romance *Sir Orfeo*, Orfeo manages to bring Queen Heurodys back from fairyland without losing her.

Orpheus's enchanting music can bridge the gap between the human and the animal, even the inanimate world. It can bridge the gap between life and death: love combined with music defies mortality. It is hardly surprising that poets and musicians should be attracted by the myth. The *Orfeo* of Poliziano in the 1470s, drawing on the versions of Ovid and Virgil, but in Italian not Latin, may well have been the very first secular drama of the Renaissance. The *Euridice* of Jacopo Peri was probably the first work ever performed which can be called 'opera'; a few years later, in 1607, Claudio Monteverdi's *Orfeo* was the first great

97

A production of Offenbach's *Orpheus in the Underworld* by the English National Opera

opera. The aria in which Orfeo charms the spirits of the underworld, as the orchestration of stanza after stanza becomes more and more beautiful, is unforgettable. Purcell became known as 'Orpheus Britannicus', and John Gay was nicknamed 'Orpheus of the highwaymen' for *The Beggars' Opera*. Gluck's *Orfeo ed Euridice* of 1762 was important for clearing away many of the fossilised conventions of the day and inaugurating the era that culminated in Mozart. In keeping with the tastes of the time, however, Eurydice is successfully rescued, and the opera ends with Arcadian merrymaking. Some of the themes from Gluck have become very well known, not least in the recordings of Kathleen Ferrier. This popularity was exploited by Jacques Offenbach in *Orpheus in the Underworld* (1858), a highly entertaining spoof of the classical clichés. (In the English version there is a happy set of rhymes between 'If I were king of the Boeotians' and 'notions', 'oceans', etc.)

In the twentieth century we find three very different figures fascinated to the verge of obsession by their different visions of Orpheus. Rainer Maria Rilke (1875–1926) has a very powerful poem, 'Orpheus. Eurydike. Hermes.', in his *New Poems* published when he was 32. For all Orpheus's grief, love and determination, Eurydice is dead and cannot be transplanted back to life:

G. F. Watts captures the moment when Orpheus turns round

> She was already let down like long hair
> and abandoned like fallen rain
> . . . She was already a root.
> And when suddenly
> the god [Hermes] stood still and with pain in his voice
> spoke these words: 'He has turned round' –
> She did not understand,
> and said in a low voice '*Who?*'

With the Great War and the decay of reality, this sensitive poet sought for a power, a spiritual life going beyond death, to transcend the underworld of the human condition around him. Rilke celebrated his quest, and his sense of finding, in *Sonnets to Orpheus* (1923).

Jean Cocteau (1889–1963) was a novelist, dramatist, film-maker, who collaborated with most of the great artistic figures of his age; but he liked to think of himself as above all a poet. He saw himself as a modern reincarnation of Orpheus, and he came back to the myth again and again between his play *Orphée* in 1924 (his very first had been *Antigone* in 1922), the film in 1950, and his last

One of the haunting sequences from Cocteau's film *Orphée*

Birtwistle's *The Mask of Orpheus* (English National Opera 1986), with costumes by Jocelyn Herbert

film, *Le Testament d'Orphée*, in 1960. The familiar motifs of the descent to the dead are accompanied by black motorcyclists and the erotic figure of Death in her Rolls-Royce. The poet understands, in a way that the scientist cannot; the poet is a go-between for humanity, and goes down to face the nightmares and sinister figures of this violent era. Orpheus returns with an experience which could not be gained by any other route. (Another film version, by the way, of the Orpheus myth, well worth seeing, is Marcel Camus's *Black Orpheus* (1958), set amid carnival time in Rio de Janeiro.)

Thirdly there is Harrison Birtwistle (born 1934). He was already drawn by the myth in *Nenia on the Death of Orpheus* (1970). His opera *The Mask of Orpheus* was over ten years in the making before its first performance in 1986. The story is told several times in different versions and all the main characters appear in three different forms. 'It started life as *Faust*, but Orpheus seemed a better subject for music', Birtwistle is reported to have said.

When working on 'Greek Fire', I found myself developing my own interpretation of the myth to fit the task, thus illustrating the point that Greek myths seem to have an inexhaustible capacity for reinterpretation. The music of Orpheus is the power of Greek civilisation – its art, thought and literature – a power that can still captivate the mind, and can perhaps even make some sense of the animal and inanimate world. This Orphic power can overcome death:

ancient Greece, though past, is still present, still alive. *But* we cannot turn the clock back; we cannot actually make ancient Greece happen again. And we should not want to do so. We must go by torchlight – or by the light of television – down to ancient Greece; and, having experienced the world of the dead, must then return to the contemporary world. We cannot help looking back and losing the body of Eurydice. We will have seen her but not reincarnated her.

The golden bough in the dark wood

This is just one, perhaps rather banal, interpretation of the Orpheus myth, a meaning to suit particular circumstances. It presupposes various assumptions about the relation of the mythological to the real world, or about 'mythography'. Theories of mythography have held a great fascination, reaching far beyond the academic world. George Eliot sounded a warning with Mr Casaubon in *Middlemarch*, the dry old pedant obsessed with the idea that he was on the verge of 'a key to all mythologies'. This did not, however, put off Max Müller (1823–1900), a German who was Professor of Sanskrit at Oxford for much of his life. He believed that all Indo-European myths went back to the earliest 'Aryan' race, and that they were all in some way about the sun. Müller's solar theory, with all its 'polite brilliance' (as Frank Turner puts it), managed to get behind and to neutralise everything sexual or monstrous in Greek myths, and so make them acceptable to the Victorian age. *A Manual of Mythology* written for children by Müller's disciple George Cox says: 'You may be sure that in all these tales there is nothing of which we ought to be ashamed, and that, when you have lifted the veil which conceals them, you will find only true and beautiful thoughts . . . '

By the end of the century the veil was to be lifted far more suggestively. Gladstone was once introduced in Cambridge to Jane Harrison (born 1850), who was for much of her life a Fellow of Newnham College, and he asked her which classical authors she admired. She was meant to reply 'Homer' and to be subjected to the great man's standard lecture on Homer and Christianity. Instead she could not resist answering 'Euripides', who was thought of then as a decadent iconoclast. End of conversation. Jane Harrison was one of a group, including Gilbert Murray (who enjoyed an intense Platonic relationship with her), who brought new life to Greek myth, and indeed to Greek studies. Looking back (in 1925) she reminisced: 'we Hellenists were, in truth, at that time [the 1880s] a "people who lived in darkness", but we were soon to see a great light, two great lights, archaeology, anthropology. Classics were turning in their long sleep . . . Among my own contemporaries was J.G. Frazer who was soon to light

Jane Harrison painted by Augustus John

the dark wood of savage superstition with a gleam from *The Golden Bough* . . .'
Frazer, Harrison and the others took the politeness out of myths and released
them from the tameness of mere decoration. They saw them as reflecting the
bare substructures of society and of its rituals; and they emphasised the
irrational, dark elements of myth (in keeping with the age of Nietzsche). For
them, Dionysus was not only the merry god of wine, he was the god whose
possessed followers tore living creatures into bloody fragments.

In the twelve volumes of *The Golden Bough* which appeared between 1890 and
1915 Frazer laid special emphasis on the basic myth of the doomed – or
sacrificial – king, who must die and who is to return, reborn or resurrected.
Frazer saw him as standing for the annual death of vegetation, to be reborn, we
must hope, next spring. While scholars do not have much time for Frazer any
longer, his wide learning combined with his vivid style and imagination
profoundly affected such giants as W.B. Yeats and T.S. Eliot. Eliot wrote in the
first note to *The Waste Land* (1922): 'To another work of anthropology I am
indebted in general, one which has influenced our generation profoundly; I
mean *The Golden Bough*.'

Other mythographies have come and gone since Frazer: but the enterprise keeps a broad popular fascination. Robert Graves's *Greek Myths* has been a great favourite, even though Graves's eccentric explanations of myths as garbled versions of historical events robs them of their mystery. Claude Lévi-Strauss, the anthropologist and father-figure of structuralism, put myth at the centre of his analysis of the underlying structure of the human mind. It is no coincidence, I suspect, that the two most widely read and translated classical scholars in the world today are both concerned with myth. Jean-Pierre Vernant, head of the Parisian school, sees myths as reflecting the external and internal organisation of a whole society, a key to its mental structures. Walter Burkert, Professor at Zürich, emphasises the ritual associations of myth, tracing some of them back to the concerns of early stone-age man.

Oedipus becomes intelligible?

The Golden Bough was not the only reinterpretation of Greek myth in this period. Sigmund Freud (1856–1937), who brought together the nineteenth-century developments in the life-sciences to arrive at a new model of the mind, was of course still more influential. Ever since, Greek myth has held a privileged place in psychology. James Hillman, for example, writes: 'Greek myth serves . . . more generally as a psychology, working in the soul as both the stimulus and the differentiated container for the extraordinary psychic richness of ancient Greece . . . "Greece" offers us a chance to re-vision our souls and psychology by means of imaginal places and persons . . .' George Steiner has emphasised the Greek connection with much modern psychology, especially apparent in the psychology of sexuality – narcissism, homo-eroticism and so forth. 'There is an enormous amount of Greek thinking, both very distant from us and very near, in the way it grapples with these problems.'

Freud saw myths, like dreams, as a coded expression of the unconscious; unlike dreams, however, they are shared in public. If they can be understood, he claims, we gain access to that level of the human mind which is the key to mental health. Myths are a clue to our own psychic history. He invoked the myth of Electra, who loved her father so much that she killed her mother; and of Narcissus, who loved himself so much that he turned his back on social life; in his later works he took the Greek words for love and death, *Eros* and *Thanatos*, as key terms.

Freud had studied Sophocles' *Oedipus the King* (alias *Tyrannos* alias *Rex*) at school; and as a student in Paris he saw the role played by the great actor Mounet-Sully. The play's fascination for him eventually fell into place as his psychoanalytic theories progressed. In 1897 he wrote in a letter: 'the gripping power of *Oedipus* becomes intelligible . . . every member of the audience was a budding Oedipus in fantasy'. Then, in his first major publication, *The Interpretation of Dreams*, in 1900, he refers as virtual 'proof' to the passage of Sophocles where Jocasta reassures Oedipus:

> As for this marriage with your mother,
> have no fear. Many a man before you
> in his dreams has shared his mother's bed.

Oedipus haunted Freud. The story goes that on his fiftieth birthday in 1906 his admirers presented him with a medallion with his portrait on one side and the Sphinx on the other with a line in Greek from the end of *Oedipus the King*, 'He who solved the famous riddle and was most powerful.' Freud was distressed, since as a student he had once dreamt of his bust in the courtyard of the University of Vienna with that very inscription.

Whatever one makes of Freudian psychology, 'whether our reaction to it be comic or serious', it has been taken seriously, not least in art and literature, and even in the interpretation of Sophocles. Laurence Olivier's production of *Oedipus* in London in 1946 was evidently enormously powerful: he gave Oedipus an Oedipus complex, as he had recently done with Hamlet. Pier-Paolo Pasolini's film *Edipo Re* managed to tap Freud's reading of the modern mind to make the myth new.

Before the twentieth century the Oepidus myth had not attracted particular attention – a tragedy by Kleist, a painting by Ingres – but nothing to compare with Orpheus or Prometheus or Odysseus. In this century it has been perhaps the most studied and alluded to of all Greek myths. While this must be in large part due to Freud's highlighting of it in 1900, there have been other quite different interpretations of the myth and of Sophocles' play which also plausibly and powerfully reflect contemporary preoccupations – an illustration of the inexhaustible multivalence of Greek myth.

Some have found the power of the myth in its sense of fate, of the forces that bring events to their destined conclusion, whatever humans do. The 'voice' at the beginning of Cocteau's *La Machine infernale* (1934) concludes: 'Spectator, this machine, which you see here wound up to the full in such a way that the spring will slowly unwind the whole length of a human life, is one of the most perfect ever constructed by the infernal gods for the mathematical destruction of a mortal.' Others, like Bernard Knox, have seen the myth in the play as, rather, epitomising man's urge – need, even – to go on seeking, whatever the consequences. The existentialism of such as Sartre has been influential here: the will to self-knowledge is the precondition of genuine existence and must not

Laurence Olivier as Oedipus and Sybil Thorndike as his wife/mother Jocasta in the
London production of Sophocles' tragedy in 1945–6

Oedipus after his blinding, from Pasolini's powerful film *Edipo Re*

Carl Orff's opera *Oedipus Tyrannus* performed in Athens in 1967

be compromised. So Oedipus presses on his search for his own identity despite everything. Jean-Pierre Vernant sees Oedipus' move in Sophocles' play from the extremes of good fortune, power and prosperity to their opposites as reflecting the deeper structure of the ritual of the scapegoat, who is driven from the city taking with him the plagues and evils of the world. Karl Reinhardt, under the influence of the philosophy of Heidegger, emphasises the gap between appearance and reality: Oedipus, who *seems* to be the most fortunate of men, must come to see that he is in fact the most wretched. I am inclined to develop this, under the influence, perhaps, of Kuhn's theory of revolutions of thought. Up to a certain point in his life-journey Oedipus accommodates all the – possibly conflicting – evidence to the story of his past which he takes for granted. Then there comes a terrible moment when he has to see that there is another totally different and horribly right explanation of everything, that his life journey has been a huge circle ending as husband in the womb where he was conceived.

Facing the Minotaur

Freud was, in effect, trying to take the mystery out of myth. Once it was decoded as a history of the unconscious, all was explained. As Anthony Storr put it: 'he

Picasso's cover for the first issue of *Minotaure* (1933)

G. F. Watts's Minotaur, painted in a fit of righteous indignation – and other mixed feelings?

was only happy when he was reducing things to the lowest common factor; and he did regard the unconscious as primarily the repository of bits of oneself that one couldn't accept.' A very different way of looking at the psychology of myth was developed by Freud's one-time friend and colleague Carl Gustav Jung (1875–1961). The fundamental difference between the two is immediately apparent in Jung's dictum that modern man is faced with 'the necessity of rediscovering the life of the spirit'. Jung, who was very interested in archaeology and thought of himself as excavating the mind, took myths to represent the inmost thoughts and feelings of the human race, patterns which are the product of inherited brain patterns. He called them 'archetypes of the collective unconscious', and insisted that they are not to be explained away but to be lived through. In a sense everybody has to create their own myths in order to enhance their lives. The father who is killed in the Oedipus myth is not an infantile sexual rival but the inner sense of spiritual oppression from which we must eventually break free. 'The riddle of the Sphinx', said Jung, 'was *herself* – the terrible mother-imago, which Oedipus would not take as a warning.'

Mythology was, in fact, one of the main issues which led to the break between them. For Freud there may even have been an element of his own Oedipus 'complex' about it; he wrote to Jung in 1911: 'I don't know why you are so afraid of my criticism in matters of mythology', and 'You are a dangerous rival, if one has to speak of rivalry'. Jung's wife wrote to Freud, 'Do not think of Carl with a father's feeling of "he will grow, but I must dwindle".' The great severance came finally in January 1913.

For Freud, myth presents dark irrational things that, once they are explained, lose their menace; they evaporate. For Jung these dark creatures are part of our life which we must face and subdue. It is surprising that Jung did not make more of the myth of the Minotaur, since it fits well with his notions of our all having a dark side. He merely mentions Theseus along with other heroes who encountered monsters on their way to maturity.

Theseus went into the labyrinth with the clue (or clew), a ball of thread given him by Ariadne, and there he killed the half-man half-bull, finding his way back with the thread. So, a Jungian might say, we must go down and explore the mazes of our subconscious, face the animality we find there, and return guided by the goodwill of those who love us. For Freud, on the other hand, 'the Labyrinth can be recognised as a representation of anal birth: the twisting paths are the bowels, and Ariadne's thread is the umbilical cord'. This seems to be Freud's reductionism in its 'comic' aspect: what is the Minotaur? What is Ariadne? And what about the way that the thread helps Theseus to find his way *back* out? For some interpreters the labyrinth has evoked the sense of being lost in a maze of thoughts, searching for the idea that will break out of it; for others it symbolises the creative process of looking at the dark depths before new tracks can be found.

These are fertile, strong images. W.H. Auden turned to them in 'New Year Letter', dated 1st January 1940. What man, he asks, after the horrors of the last ten years

> will not feel blind anger draw
> his thoughts toward the Minotaur?

The Minotaur and the associated myths of Daedalus, the master-craftsman who made wings for himself and his fated son Icarus, were a life-long obsession for the artist Michael Ayrton. The man-bull also preyed on Picasso's imagination. It first appears in his work in 1927, and in 1933 he drew the first cover for Albert Skira's magazine *Minotaure*. The figure recurred again and again in the next two years, finding its strongest and strangest expression in the 1935 etching *Minotauromachy*. As an image of fascism, is this hopeful or pessimistic? Can the beauty with the light and the flowers charm the beast? Is the Theseus/Christ

The Labyrinth on a coin from Knossos (about 200 B.C.)
Theseus killing the Minotaur on an amphora painted in Athens (mid-sixth century B.C.)

figure coming down the ladder or going up it? Is the Minotaur bestial or human?

Towards the end of the nineteenth century G. F. Watts, who usually spent months on painstaking detail, painted *The Minotaur* in three hours, in a fit of anger and disgust with the trade of prostitution. This Minotaur, which is crushing a bird beneath its hand, is up on the battlements waiting for the boat which will bring young Athenians to satisfy his cruel lusts. Yet monstrosity is not what the painting conveys. Most people on seeing it pity this creature, wistfully trapped inside a monstrous body. He seems to be longing for humanity and for tenderness.

If we all have within us a dark beast which threatens to consume innocence and rationality, we need to be able to go down into the labyrinth, to confront this side of our humanness, and to return. Must we kill the half-human, or can it be civilised? – or is that mere sentimentality? Whatever the answer the persistence of Greek myths may have something to do with their blending of the human and the monstrous, the heroic and the degrading, the pure and the erotic. To find our way through these coexisting elements of ourselves the clue, the guiding thread, may be myth, a way of shaping chaos and of giving significance to aspects of the human condition which cannot be reached by objective or scientific discourse.

Aphrodite

NO SEX IS SAFE SEX

Once more Eros loosener of limbs shakes me
The sweet-bitter, irresistible creeping creature . . .
Sappho

THE GREEKS DID NOT INVENT SEX. Nor were they the first, any more than they were the last, to find it bitter-sweet, or all too often first sweet, then bitter. In their attitudes to sex, as in other spheres, they were at once extraordinarily similar yet different, modern yet remote; and tracing these attitudes may illuminate some of the problems of modern sexuality. Not least of these problems is venereal disease ('venereal' derives from the Latin Venus, the Roman equivalent of Aphrodite). The World Health Organisation predicts as many as 8 million AIDS sufferers by 1994, the year that Louise Brown, the first test-tube baby, will be eighteen. So far as I know there is no evidence of any venereal disease in ancient Greece – sex was 'safe'.

Did that make it a sexual utopia, as Byron implies in his description of Don Juan coupling with the lovely Haidée?

> a group that's quite antique,
> Half naked, loving, natural and Greek.

As Thomas More saw when he coined 'Utopia' in 1516, it might be the Greek *Eutopia* meaning 'a place where all is well', or *Outopia*, 'no place'. There is no place where sex is 'safe'. Certainly not in ancient Greece, where it was regarded as exquisite, excruciating, ridiculous, maddening, obsessive – anything but safe.

According to Michel Foucault's analysis the modern West has emerged from the guilt-ridden era when sex, other than for procreation, was morally dubious; but we live now in an age of obsessive sexual anxiety instead. Apart from neuroses about performance or about disease, or about guilt (for that has certainly not gone away), there are the deceits, jealousies, broken marriages, unwanted children, rapes, pornography, child abuse, the controversies surrounding

An explicit vase – painted in Athens, fifth century B.C.

homosexuality. Despite the commercialisation of carefree sexual gratification, I wonder how many people over twenty-one have never for a moment wished sexuality away as more trouble than it is worth. Now that embryos can be fertilised *in vitro* and implanted without sexual intercourse, it is legitimate to ask whether sex is worth it. If it is not necessary for reproduction, are we not better off without it? Euripides posed that very question in 428 B.C. In his play, Hippolytus wishes that the gods had invented a cleaner, less troublesome method of reproducing the human race. For himself he will have nothing to do with it – he spurns Aphrodite.

The land of nymphs and satyrs

In popular imagination ancient Greece probably has vaguely aphrodisiac associations. The beaches of modern Greece are often sold to the holiday-makers of cold, inhibited Northern Europe on the same ticket. Some people may traipse round the archaeological sites, but many evidently prefer a visit to the sex-life of ancient Greece. Go there to discover Aphrodite, the goddess of the genitals, and her son Eros, inducer of sexual desire (even in Piccadilly Circus). Helped by sun and sea, wine and dancing, sex will have no limits and no problems – though the hoardings at the airport warn of AIDS. Greece was the land of nymphs and satyrs, and contributed the words 'satyriasis', which means

A typical kiosk in Athens (1988) selling 'dirty' postcards

perpetual male erection, and 'nymphomania', unceasing female arousal (the *Oxford Dictionary* glosses the latter but not the former as 'unhealthy'!). In modern Greece the tourist shops and kiosks sell slides and postcards of ancient Greek vases showing all sorts of romps in all sorts of positions. For some reason the undistinguished statuette in the National Museum of a satyr with an outsize cock is the best-seller.

Clearly there was a lot of erotica on view in ancient Greece, or at least representations of it. It is only recently that it has become acceptable to speak and write of such things without periphrasis and apology. The academic respectability of Sir Kenneth Dover's commentary on Aristophanes' comedy *Clouds* (1968) and his book *Greek Homosexuality* (1978) have made a great difference. In 1976 I reviewed a book on 'obscenity' in Aristophanes which, among other feats, gathered 106 ways of talking about the male genitals and 91 about the female. A venerable Professor of Philosophy warmly congratulated me on being 'surely the first Fellow of Magdalen to use the word "fuck" in print'. Aristophanes, the exuberant, fantastical creator of comedies in Athens in the late fifth century B.C., banished coyness in late twentieth-century A.D. Oxford.

Contemporary Britain draws the line short of the public representation of the ithyphallic, to use the Greek for erect penis – with odd exceptions like the Cerne Abbas giant (Arthur Mee's *Children's Guide to Dorset* says that 'all we know about him is that he is very old and very ugly'!). In Athens giant phalluses were carried through the streets on some religious occasions (as they still are in Japan), and hymns were sung to Phales, the god. Herms stood in the streets: heads of the god Hermes on a square pedestal, with phallus protruding. After the tragedies, the Athenians would watch a satyr-play, with a chorus whose erections never flagged. They are also a favourite subject for painted drinking cups. Comedy was, if anything, even more lewd. In Aristophanes' *Lysistrata*, for example, Myrrhine repeatedly brings her ithyphallic husband to the verge of penetration before frustrating him. Decorated pottery from various times and places, but especially from fifth-century Athens, shows a variety of unembarrassed scenes. 'There is no fuller record of man the lover in any other medium or period of Greek art; few to rival it in the history of art, outside Japan', writes John Boardman of Athenian fifth-century vases. In this sentence 'man' means men and women, hetero- and homosexual; and 'lover' means sexual performer. Even in our age of permissiveness and of sexually explicit photography and film, some of the ancient Greek material is rather strong stuff.

Eros welcomed and rejected

The sex on show in ancient Greece was not all of this 'hard-core' sort. Think of all those statues, male and female, without fig leaves. Their cultural

The holiday image of Greece
The best-selling satyr, a bronze statuette from the fifth century B.C.

respectability supplied many nineteenth-century artists with the excuse to paint classy soft porn. In France Gérard's painting of *Phryne Before the Jurors* took advantage of a story that Phryne, the model of Praxiteles' statue of Aphrodite ('Cnidian' because it was on the island of Cnidos), had to display her charms in court. This famous statue was regarded as so desirable that, unlike most cult-statues, it was displayed so that it could be seen from all sides. Tourists to Cnidos were also shown the stain where one man had secretly ejaculated on it in the night. W.B. Yeats may have had this story in mind when he wrote, in one of his last poems, of boys and girls who

> pressed at midnight in some public place
> Live lips upon a plummet-measured face.

The statue has the title role in the spaghetti-Hellenic film *Aphrodite, Goddess of Love* (1958), whose hero is Praxiteles.

The Olympian gods not only set no prohibitions (outside their sanctuaries), they set examples to humans for sexual indulgence. Ares and Aphrodite even commit adultery, until, as told in the *Odyssey*, the cuckolded Hephaestus traps them in the act with a kind of giant cobweb. The male gods couple with mortal women, always scoring a pregnancy first time. Zeus was especially lusty and ingenious in taking different forms to have his way. In the *Iliad*, when he wants to make love to his wife Hera, he says:

> Never before has desire for a goddess or woman
> so flooded the heart in my breast and enslaved it
> – not even when I fell in love with the wife of Ixion
> . . . or with Danae . . . or with the daughter of far-famed Phoenix
> or with Semele or Alcmene . . . or when I fell in love
> with queen Demeter or with Leto or with you yourself . . .

The amours of the gods, mostly mediated through the Latin of Ovid's *Metamorphoses*, supplied countless painters, especially in the sixteenth and seventeenth centuries, with titillating subjects which had none the less the respectable excuse of classical antiquity. Correggio's paintings for Frederic II of Mantua, for example, illustrated three of Zeus' girlfriends, Danaë, Leda and Io, and for good measure his boyfriend Ganymede.

Some goddesses also made love with mortals, such as Thetis, the mother of Achilles, with Peleus. They tended, however, to have longer relationships rather than one-night stands. Aphrodite's union with the Trojan prince Anchises, father of Aeneas, is celebrated in a hymn:

Aphrodite of Cnidos, a Roman copy of the original made by Praxiteles in about 340 B.C.
The Sculptor's Model: Sir Laurence Alma-Tadema takes advantage of the respectability of Greek sculpture

with her came grey wolves, fawning on her,
and grim-eyed lions and bears and swift panthers.
She delighted in her heart to see them
and imbued desire in their breasts. And they all
mated in pairs throughout the shady glades.

Tiepolo's eighteenth-century version of the Danaë story. Is Zeus a shower of gold or a heap of coins?

opposite 'Anon' from *Histoire Universelle* (1740): Greece used as an excuse for mere pornography. Zeus takes advantage of Leda's distraction, caused by his metamorphosis.

Mortal women, as well as goddesses, evidently enjoyed sex; they did not lie still and think of ancient Greece. It is clear from the vase paintings that they are actively enjoying themselves, and they are sometimes shown with artificial dildoes (unless of course this is all the product of male fantasy). In Aristophanes the women talk a lot about affairs, sexual positions, and so on. In *Lysistrata* the heroine puts her plan to end the war to her fellow-conspirators:

> *Lys.* Will you really do it then?
> *A.* We will, we will, even if we have to die for it.
> *Lys.* Well then, we must give up the cock.
>   Why do you turn away? Why do you bite your lips
>   and shake your heads?
> *A.* No, I won't do it. Better the war goes on.
> *B.* Anything else. Make me walk through fire;
>   but do not rob us of our favourite cock.
>   What else is there like it, dear Lysistrata?

There was an old story that Tiresias had been both male and female in his

118

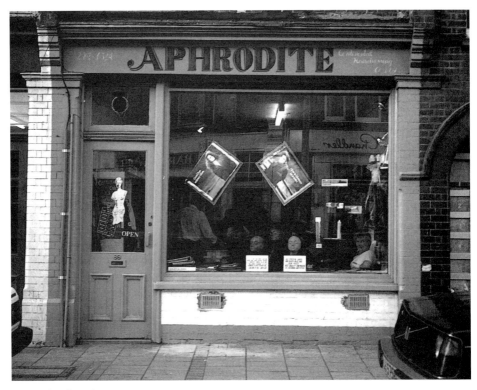

A London hairdresser

time ('old man with wrinkled dugs', Eliot calls him in *The Waste Land*). Zeus asked him which derived more pleasure from sex, and he replied that the woman won by nine to one. Hera was so angry at his revelation of this secret that she blinded him.

Last but not least, there is an abundance of Greek love poetry, from archaic times through to the end of antiquity, homosexual and heterosexual, sentimental and realist, passionate and frivolous. The finest comes from the great age of lyric poetry back in the seventh and sixth centuries B.C. Mimnermus protested:

> What would life be, what pleasure without Golden Aphrodite?
> May I die when secret love and sweet gifts and the bed
> mean nothing to me any more. Such things are the flower
> of our prime, delightful to men and women.

Sophocles hymns Eros in a famous ode from *Antigone*:

> Love, never conquered in battle . . .
> Love standing night-watch on a girl's soft cheek . . .
> Not even the deathless gods can flee your onset,
> nothing human born for a day . . .

Paris and Helen by David. They seem to have the Caryatid porch in their bedroom!

One of the most erotic pieces of Greek poetry was lost for more than 1,500 years before it was deciphered in 1974 from a papyrus acquired by the University of Cologne. I was present at the Oxford Philological Society when it was first unveiled. Professor Martin West was billed to give a paper bafflingly entitled 'Last Tango on Paros'. This turned out to be some 30 lines of poetry by Archilochus of Paros who lived in about 700–650 B.C. In the new poem he seduces an adolescent girl, younger sister of his former girlfriend. He promises that he will not 'go the whole way' – 'I will stay out in the garden grass, not force the doorway.' The poem ends:

> But I'd talked enough. I laid the girl
> down among the flowers. A soft cloak spread,
> my arms around her neck, I comforted
> her fear. The fawn soon ceased to flee.
> Over her breasts my hand moved gently,
> the new-formed girlhood she bared for me,
> and over her body, the young skin bare;
> I spilt my white force, just touching her yellow hair.

Maria Callas in Cherubini's *Médée* (Royal Opera House 1958)

Enough of this utopia, this fantasy. The young Paris had to choose between Hera, Athena and Aphrodite, and chose Aphrodite because she promised to fulfil his sexual dreams. In the world I have been painting he would live happily and erotically ever after. But that was not the story: Paris got Helen, 'the face that launched a thousand ships, and burned the topless towers of Ilium', the most fatal *femme fatale* of all time. Ancient Greece was not the playground held out by the 'Club 18–30' brochures. George Steiner was nearer the mark when he included the unpredictable word 'sexual' in. 'You have to know something of that world [ancient Greece] and of its enormous importance for us, and of the problems it has bequeathed us. For it has also, I think, left us with some very tough political and human and social and sexual problems; and to cut ourselves off from that would be a kind of zombie activity, as if memory began yesterday morning.'

Aphrodite was not all golden delight. The last lines of the stanza from Sophocles' ode say:

> Not even deathless gods can flee your onset
> nothing human born for a day –
> whoever feels your grip is driven mad.

The hymn ends:

> Irresistible Aphrodite, never conquered –
> Love, you mock us for your sport.

Aphrodite and Eros are cruel gods: they burn people up, they shake them like stormwinds, they send them mad. In ancient Greece sex is seen as madness and pain as much as, if not more than, sweet delight. At the beginning of Plato's *Republic* the aged Sophocles is (fictionally) asked about Aphrodite. 'Hush,' he replies, 'I am delighted to have left that behind me; it is as if I had escaped from some cruel and crazy taskmaster.' In Plato's *Symposium* we hear how Socrates spends a night in bed with Alcibiades, the heart-throb of every woman, and man, in Athens – and he does nothing more erotic than talk philosophy. He is putting into action his (or Plato's) doctrine that for the wise physical sexuality is merely an incentive towards the love of the truly beautiful. Hence 'Platonic love' (a phrase first coined by the Florentine philosopher Marsilio Ficino in the fifteenth century).

In Euripides' *Hippolytus* the young prince rejects Aphrodite far more vehemently. The positive choice of celibacy is not quite so unfamiliar in the Christian world. Hippolytus' attitude is, admittedly, not found often in ancient Greece; none the less Euripides thought it worth making into a play. Hippolytus devotes himself to the virgin goddess Artemis, spending his time hunting in the mountains and chariot-racing on the flats by the shore. When urged to pay homage to Aphrodite, he replies, 'I do not like any god who is admired in the dark.' Accused by his father Theseus of seducing his stepmother Phaedra he replies:

> To this day my body has been pure of the bed of love.
> I do not know this act except by what I have heard,
> and seen in pictures. And I have no desire to see these things.
> I have a virgin soul.

For all his devotion to Artemis, Aphrodite destroys him. It is fatal to spurn the goddess of the genitals. Yet Hippolytus is not merely negative: he has a positive drive towards purity (foreshadowing Christ, according to Keble), towards freedom from all those secretions and secrets.

The subdued matriarch

In the process of destroying Hippolytus Aphrodite destroys Phaedra also. She makes her fall in love with her desirable and unattainable stepson. When this shame is bound to be revealed to her husband Theseus she kills herself, leaving a suicide note accusing Hippolytus. Euripides takes care not to present her simply as possessed; she is a fully understandable portrait – one that inspired Racine – a woman whose sexuality proves stronger than all considerations of good sense and respectability. For Phaedra her good name is everything and she is prepared to die for it. This tallies with the sentiment that Thucydides attributed to Pericles in his famous 'Funeral Speech', that the highest virtue in a woman is 'to be least spoken about, for good or ill, among men'. There is a clear – and familiar – 'double standard' here: men may be promiscuous, women had to remain totally monogamous.

Ancient Greece was certainly not a utopia for most women, especially not in the great 'enlightened' age of Athens. An Athenian orator Apollodorus claimed: 'Tarts we have for pleasure, mistresses [non-citizen] for the daily refreshment of our bodies, but wives to bear us legitimate children and to look after the house.' So women had either the low status of a sex-object or the respectability of a child-bearer and producer of cloth. The vase-paintings generally reflect this deep division. This 'suppression' of women in Athens has led to a curious outbreak of Greek Fire.

Athenian women had no legal or political existence independent of their men. They could not hold public office (except some religious functions), they could not attend or speak in the assembly, nor in the law courts, they could not inherit property (though men could inherit through them). For the whole of their lives they were subject to a 'master', so that when they were married they passed, along with a dowry, from father (or closest male relative) to husband, all arranged by their men. If divorced or widowed they reverted to the men of their blood family. They were not only systematically subordinated on an official level, they were also restricted in terms of physical space. They were expected to be seen in public as little as possible, and to stay indoors with the children and the weaving. The significant exception was at religious festivals.

At the beginning of Plato's *Phaedo* Socrates has his wife Xanthippe taken home: his final day of philosophising is no place for a woman. There were rooms, the furthest away from the street, which were the women's part of the house. They did not go into the room where men held their *symposia*, parties to which they might well invite prostitutes or boyfriends. Athenian men seemed obsessed, in a city with strict qualifications for citizenship, with the thought that, if their wives or daughters were free outside for a few minutes, they would promptly beget illegitimate children. The men believed in their own strength and self-discipline, and attributed the opposite pole of irrationality and self-indulgence to women.

It has been claimed that this is not so very different from the condition of some 200 million women in the Islamic world today. The fact that Athenian women were so restricted does not necessarily mean that they were unhappy; and love and respect evidently could grow between husband and wife, as is witnessed by touching epitaphs and grave monuments. Exactly the same is said of Islam. But fifth-century Athens is not Islam; it is a time and place as much studied and emulated as any in the Western world. Was it really so utterly male-dominated, the very model of patriarchy? Such questions began to nag seriously in the mid-nineteenth century. After all, the eponymous god of Athens was female; there were powerful female Olympians (including Aphrodite); there were powerful and self-willed women in Greek myth, especially in tragedy, product of this very era in Athens.

In the *Eumenides*, third play of Aeschylus' *Oresteia* trilogy (458 B.C.), the ancient female goddesses, the Furies, are defeated by the male Apollo and the new Olympian gods, fathered by Zeus; and they are persuaded to lead a new, tamer life within the city of Athens. Moreover, the goddess Athena insists that she had no mother, but was born direct from Zeus; so Athens was dominated by the temple of a goddess whose paternal legitimacy was definitive. *Eumenides* was a central text for the Swiss proto-anthropologist J. J. Bachofen who published *Das Mutterrecht* in 1861 (eventually translated into English as *Motherright* in 1967). According to Bachofen there was once an age when women ruled and when men devoted themselves to living nobly up to the ideals of their feminine rulers (like 'She'). This age was violently overthrown by the patriarchy, epitomised by Zeus, which we still share with the Greeks. Friedrich Engels was much influenced by Bachofen, though he saw the change in more materialist terms. Through Engels this analysis of the position of women, and of their potential for contribution to society, if once liberated, has influenced the communist world, where the emancipation of women has in some respects gone further than in the West.

Although the move from matriarchy to patriarchy is these days regarded as symbolic rather than historical, the *Oresteia* has remained a key text in feminist literature, for example in Simone de Beauvoir and Kate Millet. I would go so far as to say that the 'women's movement' has brought about the single greatest social change in Western society in my lifetime. Greece is not irrelevant, so this is not a trivial repercussion. In the development of courses in 'Women's Studies' in the last 20 years, especially in the United States, the study of *Eumenides* and of women in ancient Greece has a prominent place. The similarities as well as the differences between the place of women in ancient Greece and in the contemporary world have proved a good way into these complex and unstable issues, and they continue to be so. As Mary Beard puts it: 'The second wave of feminism, as it looks at the ancient world, is not trying to say "Gosh, wasn't it dreadful!": it's trying to say "*How* was it dreadful? How were women perceived? How is gender constituted? And how did images and literature play a part in all that?"'

The tragic turning of women

The most intriguing complexity is the portrayal of women in Greek tragedy. There is an unsettled dispute whether there were even any women in the audience. There seems to be good evidence both for and against – my own view is that there was no actual prohibition, but that they were not numerous – in any case, the tragedies were made by men for men. Yet many have women as their main characters, indeed some of the most powerful women ever created by art, the most memorable, terrible and determined: Hecuba, the fallen queen of Troy, Clytemnestra who kills her husband when he is helpless in the bath, Electra devoted to vengeance, Antigone who goes to her death for burying her brother. This is nothing like Islam; these women could have held no fascination for men who were complacent about their women. The audience of Athenian men must have been well aware, at some level of consciousness, that the women they shut in their houses had potency and intelligence, the power to destroy their men and their households. These women who break out of subordination are a dramatisation of profound anxieties.

When Jason, in Euripides' *Medea* of 431 B.C., deserts Medea, his oriental conquest, for the younger, richer princess of Corinth, she hurts him in the supreme way within her grasp, by killing their sons. 'Did you see fit to kill them just because of infidelity in bed?' asks Jason at the end; and she replies, 'Do you think that is a small hurt for a woman?' There is an alarming message here for men which reads, 'If you hand your children over to your wives and yet wrong your wives, you must not be surprised to find that the children have been alienated, taken away, even destroyed.' Yet Medea, at least in the first half of the play, is presented in a far from unsympathetic light. There can be no light dismissal of the great speech which includes:

> Of all creatures that feel and think,
> we women are the unhappiest species.
> In the first place we must pay a great dowry
> to a husband who will be the tyrant of our bodies . . .
> When the man tires of the company of his wife,
> he goes outside and relieves the burden of his heart . . .
> They say that we women have a safe life at home,
> while men must go to war. Nonsense!
> I would rather fight in the battle line three times
> than go through childbirth once . . .

It is for sentiments like these that *Medea* is often just below the surface of George Eliot's novels, especially *Felix Holt*. In 1913 songs and speeches from the play were chanted at suffragette meetings. The women used the new version of Gilbert Murray, Regius Professor at Oxford from 1908 to 1936, and a great

Pasolini's *Medea*, the only film in which Maria Callas agreed to appear

left Melina Mercouri in *A Dream of Passion* (1978)   *right* A New York production of Euripides' *Medea* in 1910

supporter of women's causes (though he drew the line short of suffragettes as opposed to suffragists). The play does not lose its modernity. There were three productions of *Medea* in London in 1986 alone, though none was as good as the Japanese production by the Ninagawa company which has been put on all over the world.

It is a curious synchronism that within a year or two of 1890 Euripides had been revalued, after a long period out of favour, by the great German scholar Wilamowitz; the young Murray had chosen him for special study; Ibsen had put on *A Doll's House*, which has considerable analogies with *Medea*; and George Bernard Shaw had published *The Quintessence of Ibsenism*. Euripides was one of the bonds between Murray and Shaw, life-long friends, even though Shaw caricatured Murray's family blatantly in *Major Barbara* (1912), where Murray is Adolphus Cusins. Another playwright whose portrayal of women was influenced by the women of Greek tragedy was Eugene O'Neill, especially in *Mourning Becomes Electra*. (O'Neill's son became a professor of Greek.)

Medea has inspired operas from Cherubini (1797) to Tony Harrison's *Medea, a sex-war opera* (published 1985, though not yet performed) which incorporates quotations from many versions, including Cherubini and Euripides, in a critique of the role of parents and the misuse of women in modern society. Maria Callas, who often sang Cherubini's *Médée*, at least once at Epidaurus, only ever agreed to be in one film: Pasolini's *Medea*. Another film inspired by Euripides' play is *A Dream of Passion* (1978) directed by Jules Dassin and starring his wife Melina

Mother and daughter from Cacoyannis's fine film of Euripides' *Iphigenia*. Clytemnestra was played by Irene Papas; Tatiana Papamoschou, who played Iphigenia, was fourteen at the time.

Mercouri as an actress who is both acting the play and trying to understand a woman in prison for murdering her children. Mercouri had an earlier screen encounter with *Medea* in *Never on Sunday* (1960). As the tart with the heart of gold she cries all the way through watching Euripides' tragedy, and then at the end turns beaming to her friend: 'and then they all went to the seaside!'

A fine moment in Greek tragedy was indelibly marked on my memory by another recent film. It is a single line of great simplicity from Euripides' *Iphigenia at Aulis*, which was turned into an excellent film by Michael Cacoyannis in 1977. The manager of the New York cinema where it opened described it as a 'four-

A somewhat dated *Lysistrata* at Epidaurus

hanky movie'. Clytemnestra, played by Irene Papas, is trying to persuade her husband Agamemnon not to kill their daughter Iphigenia as a sacrifice to help the Greek fleet on its way to Troy for a war provoked by male lust for a promiscuous woman, Helen, the choice of Paris. 'Think of me at home', she pleads, 'surrounded by mementoes of our daughter. Don't, by the gods, don't force me to become a bad woman over you.' This line, as delivered by Irene Papas, became the cry of wives across the generations, wives 'forced' by the insensitivity of men into meeting wrong with wrong.

We have come a long way from aphrodisiac utopia into something more like a sex-war nightmare. What about Aristophanes, who seemed to have taken such an uninhibited and lighthearted attitude to four-letter words and four-letter activities? In *The Women at the Thesmophoria* the women of Athens plot to get Euripides because of the way he presents them in his tragedies as deceitful, highly-sexed and clever. The joke is not that they regard this picture as false, but that it gives the game away to their husbands. Aristophanes also gives them a chance to stand up for themselves and point out the inconsistency of male

Women 'embrace at the base' at the famous Greenham Common demonstration on
12 December 1982

attitudes towards them. If they are such a nuisance as men say, why are they kept
at home? And if a man sees one of these damned women at a window, why does
he hang around in the hope of seeing her again?

The sex-war comedy is, of course, *Lysistrata*. The women of Athens occupy
the Acropolis, which contains the treasury, so that the men have no funds to
continue the Peloponnesian War. All over Greece the women conspire to refuse
their husbands sex until they are reduced to making peace. Eventually
representatives of both sides arrive with unpleasantly persistent erections
(satyriasis is unhealthy!), and Lysistrata negotiates a settlement. The play ends
with a feast on the Acropolis, and all the couples go off home to bed. In the early
1980s when women were encamped outside the military bases at Comiso in
Sicily, Seneca Falls in America and Greenham Common in Britain, it was only
appropriate that there should be a feminist anti-war magazine called *Lysistrata*.
Even closer, perhaps, is the group of Finnish women led by Mago Liukkonen
who refuse to conceive until their country is free of nuclear power.

There are three ways in which *Lysistrata* is an antidote to the picture built up

131

so far. First, the plot is initiated and implemented by a woman of determination and diplomacy. Such a figure cannot have been inconceivable. Second, the satisfaction that the men want so desperately is sex with their wives. The possibility of prostitutes or slave girls is simply not raised: this suggests that wives were thought of sexually, and not merely as institutions of reproduction. Third, boys are not thought of as an alternative either. Indeed in Aristophanes homosexuality is not generally smiled on. It is mostly associated with unhealthy, city-dwelling politicians, while sound, country-dwelling blokes only go for women. 'Loose-arseholed' is Aristophanes' favourite term of abuse.

Love staining thoughts with its bloom

Aristophanes' attitude may seem surprising, since homosexuality (*amore greco* in Italian) is probably the best known fire lit by Aphrodite, following the precedent of Zeus himself, who stole the Trojan prince Ganymede to be his 'cup-bearer' on Olympus. *Homo-* is, I should add, the Greek for 'same' (not Latin for 'man'), as *hetero-* is Greek for 'other'. Even more to the point 'pederasty' is the Greek for desiring boys. It is clear, despite Aristophanes, that there was no general objection to pederasty in ancient Greece. Throughout the classical era it was regarded as quite acceptable, especially in fifth-century Athens, and even more at Sparta, where it was a regular part of the initiation of the young males. It is said that the fifteenth-century Mayan civilisation of Yucatan is the only other example of a society which has fully accepted male homosexuality.

We find evidence of homoeroticism in poetry, comedy, sculpture, vase paintings, which are often inscribed 'X is beautiful' (X is always male). Above all it surfaces in the dialogues of Plato. Plato (and Socrates) moved in a circle of wealthy Athenians who evidently regarded the courtship of good-looking boys as the finest form of sexual activity. The boys, unlike the women, whether wives or whores, could love them for themselves, and could refuse or accept them. This comes through most clearly in *Symposium* and *Phaedrus* in both of which Plato, while advocating a higher love which transcends the physical, vividly evokes the experience of more carnal passion, and explicitly for males rather than females. It is from these two works more than anywhere else that the flame has spread. George Steiner, defying Clause 28, declared: 'these are among the well-springs of all imagining and understanding in the West. If this makes us more alert to the richness and cultural complexity of a homo-erotic order of feeling, then surely its importance is still very great.'

It was no coincidence that Winckelmann was a pederast. His life and his work were indivisible: he wrote, for example, from a country villa, 'I generally live

Ref. for Life
Time/Life files on
Mexican "Lost
Civilizations"
Set - Keep
with "Mayan"
Aztecs".

there alone in August, but this year I intend having the company of a certain beautiful person since I wish to write about beauty after a model of living beauty.' His appreciation of ancient sculpture often has an unmistakably sexual element in it, whether he is admiring of the *Apollo Belvedere* or the obviously suggestive *Barberini Faun*. Walter Pater recognised in him his own proclivities: 'That his affinity with Hellenism was not merely intellectual, that the subtler threads of his temperament were inwoven in it, is proved by his romantic, fervent friendships with young men. These friendships, bringing him in contact with the pride of human form, and staining his thoughts with its bloom, perfected his reconciliation with the spirit of Greek sculpture.'

In the nineteenth century Plato provided a kind of respectability for homosexuals. Some he helped to come to terms with latent homosexuality, and following Socrates' high doctrine they did not put it into base practice. For others he gave a high antique precedent for their outlawed practices. There was a problem for those who abhorred homosexuality. Benjamin Jowett, Master of Balliol, found it a flaw in his beloved Plato, 'a great gulf fixed between us and them, which no willingness to make allowance for the differences of ages or countries would enable us to pass'. At one time Jowett wanted to write an essay arguing that Plato referred to homosexuality 'metaphorically', but he was dissuaded by his pupil John Addington Symonds. Symonds had himself discovered homosexuality when, aged seventeen, he happened to come upon a copy of the *Phaedrus* one night. He stayed up reading it, and by the time he had finished the *Symposium* as well, it was morning.

Oscar Wilde picked up the culture he fancied from any time or place. There is, however, a strong streak of the late nineteenth-century Grecian in him, especially perhaps in *The Picture of Dorian Gray* (1891). When Wotton is tempting Dorian Gray he urges him to 'forget all the maladies of medievalism, and return to the Hellenic ideal – to something finer, richer than the Hellenic idea, it may be'. André Gide (who was eventually awarded the Nobel Prize for Literature in 1947) met Oscar Wilde in 1891 when he was only twenty-two. He was captivated by his voice, his wit and his love of sensuous beauty. Wilde encouraged Gide to write his sexuality into his literature, which often turns to ancient Greece for its setting. Other modern writers whose homosexuality has drawn courage and colour from Greece include the German visionary poet Stefan George and the Alexandrian Greek Constantine Cavafy (both died in 1933). Cavafy and E. M. Forster became lifelong friends after they met in Egypt in 1917. Forster wrote his most explicitly homosexual book, *Maurice*, in 1913, when he was thirty-four, and had it circulated privately; but it was not published until 1971, the year after his death. There are several allusions in it to Greece, most tellingly when the 'autobiographical' hero Clive Durham reads Plato's

Oscar Wilde   André Gide

Peter Pears as von Aschenbach in the English Opera Group production of Benjamin Britten's *Death in Venice* (1978)

Phaedrus at school. 'He saw there his malady described . . . calmly as a passion which we can direct towards good or bad . . . He could not believe his good fortune at first . . . Then he saw that the temperate pagan really did comprehend him, and . . . was offering a new guide for life.'

Thomas Mann's *Death in Venice* was published the year before in 1912. Gustav von Aschenbach continually looks to Greece, and to myths such as that of Ganymede, as a kind of ratification for his infatuation with the beautiful, unattainable boy Tadzio. When he first sees him 'his face recalled the noblest moment of Greek sculpture . . . It was the head of Eros, with the yellowish bloom of Parian marble'. He imagines himself in dialogue with Socrates' young friend Phaedrus as he agonises over the relationship between beauty and physical passion. 'But now tell me, my dear boy, do you believe that an artist can ever attain wisdom and thus true manly worth, for whom the path to the spirit must lead through the senses?' The concern with homosexuality in *Death in Venice* is present in almost all the operas of Benjamin Britten (E.M. Forster worked on the libretto of *Billy Budd*). Britten actually turns the imaginary dialogue into an aria:

> Does beauty lead to wisdom, Phaedrus?
> Yes, but through the senses . . .

no mention in Newton Grand Opera when the essays discuss the Libretto of Billy Budd.

Intercrural impassivity

The last 25 years have seen a radical change in the acceptability of homosexuality in the West; and not only in the eyes of the law. Despite some recent reaction the gay movement has persuaded many people that it is an alternative, natural – and perhaps genetic – orientation. Jonathan Walters, a prominent campaigner, says that ancient Greece had a special interest because it was a place and time where homosexual activity was socially more acceptable than it is now. Yet contemporary gays have not particularly turned to ancient Greece for encouragement or endorsement. This is probably well-advised, since uninhibited modern research, especially by Dover, has made it clear that in Greece homosexuality was not regarded as an alternative to heterosexuality, but as an addition. As Walters points out, there was no common vocabulary for the distinction – both were Aphrodite.

Lifelong exclusive homosexuals, especially those who were effeminate and passive, were regarded with contempt. Fun is poked at an unfortunate Cleisthenes in almost every comedy of Aristophanes. The only 'normal' and acceptable activity for mature men, most of them married and enjoying sex with women, was to seek the favours of adolescent boys who had not yet reached the bearded stage. It is moreover clear that it was the courting, the present-giving, the pursuit, as much as the physical satisfaction, which was regarded as the delight. There was a social element in this – it was expedient to win the favours of the right people. It is an irony that these days heterosexual favours are liable to be used for 'getting on in the world', while homosexuality is usually regarded as 'purer' in its motivation.

It is clear that in Greece the satisfaction did not usually take the form of buggery. It was a disgrace for the boy to allow himself to be penetrated; indeed if he did so for money he could be brought to law and deprived of citizenship. The older man was fired by desire, but the younger one was not expected to return it. Dover sets out the rules: 'Refusal of payment, obdurate postponement of any bodily contact until the potential partner has proved his worth, abstention from any sensual enjoyment of such contact, insistence on an upright posture, avoidance of meeting the partner's eye during consummation, denial of true penetration.' We see this in performance in the vase paintings. The older man

Bearded lover making headway with his boyfriend (cup painted in Athens in the fifth century B.C.)

bends his knees and comes 'Intercrurally', that is by pushing his cock between the boy's thighs. The boy stands straight without even an erection. He was expected to not enjoy it. One cannot help wondering whether he anticipated the day when he would be the bearded thruster.

Where burning Sappho loved and sang

We hear much less of female homosexuality in ancient Greece. Since Aristophanes is hardly reticent about such things, that may well mean that there was less of it around, at least at Athens. There are two exceptions: Sparta, where women and girls seem to have had something equivalent to the semi-institutionalised bonds between men and boys, and Lesbos. The island of Lesbos was famous for the beauty of its women; and they were famed for their readiness to indulge in all sorts of sex, especially fellatio. The word 'lesbianism' came into modern languages only within the last 100 years, because of the poetess Sappho, the 'tenth Muse', who lived there in the seventh century B.C. The island today is a place of pilgrimage for women gays. The upper deck of the ferry in summer is sometimes littered with their double sleeping bags.

The sensuality of Sappho's poetry still draws Aphrodite to Lesbos. This invocation was found in Egypt written on a broken fragment of pottery:

> Come from Crete to me here in this shrine
> with the lovely apple grove and altars smoking with incense.
> Here cold water chatters through the apple boughs,
> the whole place is shaded with roses,
> and from the trembling leaves sleep drops down . . .

Many male classical scholars have tried to deny it, but it is clear from her poems that Sappho desired and had physical erotic dalliance with quite a number of girls. They included one called Gongula as in Ezra Pound's poem:

> PAPYRUS
> Spring . . .
> Too long . . .
> Gongula . . .

This does not entail that Sappho was gay in the modern fashion. She was married with a daughter; and there was a popular story that she threw herself off

Aphrodite riding on a goose (Athens, fifth century B.C.). Sappho calls on Aphrodite to visit her in her chariot drawn by sparrows.

the cliff of Leukas for the love of a young boatman, Phaon (inspiration of a fine poem by Leopardi and weak plays by Lyly and Lawrence Durrell). It is more than likely, it seems to me, that Sappho's homosexuality was analogous to that of men, as at Athens. The older woman courted and hoped to make love to younger unmarried girls. Sappho was famous for her wedding-hymns, and some of these may well have been composed for former girlfriends.

While Sappho may supply a figurehead for radical feminists, she has not, so far as I know, inspired any outstanding art or poetry by women – this Greek Fire may yet be lit. Up to now she has rather stimulated men who have sought to kick against the sexual world of the day. For example Algernon Swinburne:

No Sex Is Safe Sex

Lesbians kissing across their smitten
Lute with lips more sweet than the sound of lute-strings
Mouth to mouth and hand upon hand.

Her strangest descendant is surely *Les Chansons de Bilitis*. This was published in 1895 by the 25-year-old Pierre Louÿs, and dedicated to Gide. (Louÿs also wrote a best-selling novel called *Aphrodite*.) *Les Chansons de Bilitis* are prose poems which purport to be the translation of a Greek manuscript found in a tomb. They are the intimate diary of a woman who joined Sappho's circle on Lesbos and had a good time there, before going to Cyprus and a good time there as a temple prostitute. The great German classicist Ulrich von Wilamowitz-Möllendorff published ten pages of concentrated scholarship in the *Göttinger Gelehrte Anzeiger* to prove that *Bilitis* was a forgery. This did not stop it from inspiring three beautiful songs by Debussy (whose erotic piece called 'L'après-midi d'un Faune' is half-inspired by a poem of Mallarmé half-inspired by the Greek poet Theocritus). Music more directly inspired by her is *Sappho Fragments* by Harrison Birtwistle (1964).

It would be better to close with Sappho herself rather than Louÿs. There is

From the film of *Bilitis*

Sappho and her fellow-poet from Lesbos, Alcaeus (Athens, fifth century B.C.)

something essentially female about her poems, though it must be conceded that one of the most famous was translated and appropriated by the Roman poet Catullus:

> whenever I look at you even quickly
> it is no longer possible to speak,
> but my tongue fixes, and at once
> a delicate fire flickers under my skin.
>
> I no longer see with my eyes, my ears hum,
> sweat trickles down me, trembling seizes me all over,
> I am paler than grass, and I seem to be
> little short of dying.

In another fragment, found on papyrus, she does seem to be rejecting the values of male militarism when she begins:

> Some say that the most beautiful thing on this dark earth
> is a squadron of cavalry, others say
> a troop of infantry, others a fleet of ships:
> but I say that it is the one you love.

Sappho expresses as well as anyone, man or woman, the paradox that we cannot live with sex and we cannot live without it. It was for her a vital, painful, exquisite part of being human – but never safe.

Physics

HALFWAY TO EXPLAINING THE WORLD

> Give me a firm place to stand and I will
> move the whole earth.
>
> Archimedes

FERMILAB, THE HIGH-ENERGY PHYSICS RESEARCH CENTRE at Batavia near Chicago, has a circular machine for accelerating elementary particles which is four miles in circumference. At CERN, the European research centre near Geneva, there is a tunnel which runs for 27 kilometres towards the Jura Mountains; and the SSC, the Superconducting Supercollider which is planned in the US, will have a circuit of tunnel 53 miles round. Fermilab is, in effect, a non-optical microscope for looking at the smallest constituents of matter, a billion billion times more powerful than a common-or-garden microscope. Nature – *physis* in Greek – is having her most intimate parts pried into.

What is it all for? All this trouble, expense and brainpower is directed at finding out what the universe is ultimately made of. The answer, hopes Leon Lederman, Director of Fermilab and winner of a Nobel Prize in 1988, will be 'a beautifully simple formula – something we can print on a T-shirt, and students can wear it on campus. This will be the formula which explains fundamentally how the universe works, how it evolved'. He and his colleagues are driven by the unmixed desire to know: there is no evident practical application of their physics. Not, of course, that it is impossible that an application will emerge. The developments in quantum physics earlier in this century were pure science; yet modern technology is now based on them – transistors, chips, semi-conductors, lasers and masers, and indeed the particle accelerator at Fermilab.

Fire stolen from the gods

How good for mankind is this relentless and accelerating advance of science and

The punishment of Prometheus. A lithograph after the drawing by Michelangelo.

technology? The question whether human wisdom can keep up with scientific progress – or how far behind it has fallen – may be a cliché, but it remains a real one. Is 'Progress' running away out of control?

The desire for knowledge, or rather the desire to *understand*, is quintessentially Greek. The great difference is that in Greece the 'progress' was seen primarily as an advance in knowledge for its own sake, while ever-increasingly in the last two hundred years scientific progress has been regarded as the key to material and commercial advantage. To put it another way, the Greeks wanted to understand nature as an end in itself; modern science wants to understand nature in order to interfere with her and control her. Its lack of practical and technological application is always regarded as the great and puzzling failure of ancient Greek science; but perhaps the late twentieth century is a good time to reassess. After all, the criterion for the success of Lederman's T-shirt formula will not be its economic value but its beauty.

The Greeks did not have an unequivocal attitude to progress. Indeed the early Greeks had a downhill rather than uphill model of the course of the successive generations of men. This is most clearly represented by the poet Hesiod (about

145

The statue of Prometheus with fire in his hand in front of the Rockefeller Center in New York

700 B.C.) with his dire sequence of the 'Five Ages', and his agonised cry 'I wish I had not been born into the fifth age, the age of iron'. It is not until 250 years later that the upward progress of science is put forward as a rival model. Democritus is especially associated with the picture of humankind developing

from primitive savagery to a state of civilisation through growing political and technological awareness and application. It is no coincidence that Democritus was the subject of Karl Marx's doctoral dissertation (finished in 1841), because, according to his kind of philosophy, unlike that of Plato and Aristotle, science should be the starting point: if you once work out what the physical world is like, then you can go on to abstracts. Richard Jenkyns says, 'this study probably gave Marx a sort of liberation because he saw that there was a completely different way of doing philosophy; and this helped him forward to his own scientific materialism'. Democritus was also the father-figure of the 'atomic theory' that the universe is made up solely of space and of an infinite number of minute indivisible particles – 'atom' means 'uncuttable' – moving within this vacuum or void. The term 'atom' passed from Democritus to the French Jesuit Gassendi in the seventeenth century, and from him to John Dalton, founder of modern atomic theory, in the nineteenth century.

Scientific progress is allegorised in the myth of Prometheus, though perhaps with a warning. Prometheus stole fire from Zeus and gave it to mankind. Once we had fire, we developed cooking, ceramics, smelting, metalwork – technological progress. Prometheus was a Titan, an immortal, but Zeus punished him relentlessly for helping humans and betraying the gods. In the play *Prometheus Bound* (attributed to Aeschylus but more likely by an anonymous master of mid-fifth century Athens) Prometheus defies Zeus and all his tyrannical powers. It is not surprising that he became for the Romantics the symbol of man's defiance of oppression, whether human or superhuman. He had a special appeal for Goethe, Shelley, Byron, Wagner. Marx ended the Preface to his doctoral thesis by quoting Prometheus' defiance of Zeus, adding that 'Prometheus is the most eminent saint and martyr in the philosophical calendar'. Curiously, at the same time Prometheus was, thanks to chemistry, providing illumination for another great revolutionary figure. Darwin tells how on his voyages 'I carried with me some Promethean matches which I ignited by biting'. These were an early form of safety match (before the invention of 'Lucifers' and 'Vestas') with a small glass bulb of sulphuric acid surrounded by chemically treated paper.

For the twentieth century Prometheus is bound to symbolise the forward progress of science and technology: but this is related to the earlier defiance of oppressive and supernatural powers. Once man has been given the gift of 'fire', of independence, the search is unstoppable. As George Steiner has said: 'The Greeks were among the first, perhaps the very first – because this is profoundly un-Jewish, un-Hebraic – to say it is the dignity and nobility of man to pursue research wherever it will lead and at any price. And that means creating life in test-tubes, and it means creating the hydrogen bomb, and it means sending men to Mars . . . at any price because of truth.' He added this warning, 'And suddenly we are asking ourselves – we who are the children of that Greek ideal – "Is it going to be too expensive . . . if the Minotaur of self-destruction, nuclear or biogenetic – waits at the end of our search?"'

The fire stolen from the gods remains dangerous. The scientists at Fermilab induce particle collisions which produce such intense energy, such high temperatures, that they have hopes that they will come to understand the Big Bang and the creation of new matter. Some physicists also think that, if they are close to understanding that cataclysmic event when simplicity became complexity, before the familiar world of change and diversity began, then they are close to finding the fundamental laws that govern all matter. They will know the 'stuff' which everything is made of. To achieve this they have to produce temperatures of 10^5K (water boils at 373K) and a man-sized re-creation of the great creative explosion which began the universe: this might sound ominously like stealing divine fire for the satisfaction of man, his scientific curiosity and potentially his technology.

In the twentieth century, once the uncuttable atom had been split, scientists began to posit an ever-increasing number of elementary particles, each given a

Thales, from a French popular *Vies de Savants* (1866)

Particle tracks photographed at CERN, the European research centre near Geneva
Leon Lederman, Director of Fermilab, and Nobel Prize-winner for Physics in 1988

Greek letter, until the alphabet began to run out. The latest state of play has, however, reduced this proliferation to the tally of six quarks and six leptons. These have mass, charge, spin and other quantum properties, but they take up no space and have no radius. They are organised by the four forces: electromagnetic, the strong force, the weak force, and, most important and inscrutable of all, gravity. So physicists now believe that the universe is made of a limited number of irreducible particles and forces, and that beneath all the diversity there is a simplicity. The ambivalence of the Greek contribution seems to be symbolised by the combination of lepton, a Greek word meaning 'slight thing', and quark, a joke word taken from James Joyce by Murray Gell-Mann in reaction against Greek technical terms.

The first scientific question

Leon Lederman is well aware of the Greek precedent for all this. Indeed the very beginnings of Greek science and of Greek philosophy – the two are indivisible – were expressed in such terms. In the important eastern Greek city of Miletus (now on the south-west coast of Turkey) in the sixth century there was a group of thinkers who worried about why and whether the earth is stable, about the nature of the heavenly bodies and their movements. We can pin down the date of the first, Thales, because he predicted the eclipse on 28 May 585 B.C. Lederman has become an enthusiast:

> Suddenly you realise – some goosepimples in fact! – that you can actually define where it all started . . . There and then the first scientific question was asked, as far as we can tell. That is: how does the world work? We put aside mythology, superstition, magic, and we ask, 'Can we understand if there is a rational basis for the way the world works?' The Greek word *cosmos* is a word for order. Is there order to the thing? That was a tremendous breakthrough. It is also important to understand that this is not technology. A vast technology was already available by 600 B.C. But the question of *why* does this happen, what is the mechanism and what is an understanding of all these things – that is new.

The Milesians did not fall back on the gods or myths as explanations. Thunder

The earth floating on water as maintained by Thales. On it stands Archimedes. The four elements of earth, air, fire and water are all represented. From an edition of Archimedes printed in Venice in 1503.

was not the anger of Zeus, for example, but it might be wind bursting out of a cloud. Thus they began to develop a notion of *physis*, or as we would say, nature, on the premise that the world has a substance or construction which can be open to reasoned investigation. Physics is the study of *physis*, 'natural philosophy'.

So the breakthrough was one of method, the logical sequence, the process of demonstration. As Lederman insists, this is not technology, it is a way of thinking. Geoffrey Lloyd makes the point: 'Ancient science, we might say, never fully emancipated itself from philosophy: yet if it had not been part of philosophy, it would scarcely have been pursued at all.'

The power to demonstrate gave these Milesian philosopher-scientists a confidence, which led them towards the claim that there is some 'stuff' which is the foundation of the world and all that is in it, and from which, moreover, it originated. Thales said that everything derives from water, and that the earth rests on water. Anaximenes held that air surrounds and contains and constitutes the world. Anaximander was more complex: the stuff is 'the infinite' or 'the unlimited', a fundamental principle which generates such properties as hot and cold, but which cannot be pinned down materially like water or air. The modern German philosopher Heidegger regarded Anaximander's theory as one of the greatest insights.

In some ways the most modern of their attitudes was that they were not afraid to put forward theories which are counter-intuitive, which run counter to common sense. Niels Bohr, the great physicist, once said to a colleague, 'Your theory is undoubtedly crazy: the question is, is it crazy enough?' It seems crazy enough to postulate that the world with all its diversity is all made of one single substance. Yet Anaximenes' claim that stones are air at its most solid – with ice, water, vapour and fire as phases of rarefaction – is not, on second inspection, repugnant. Thales pointed out that, if you dig, you come to water, that seeds contain moisture, and that water is essential to all nourishment. Anaximander traced the origins of life to the interaction of the heat of the sun with the wet of the sea; and he postulated that humans were derived from some sort of fish. That is crazy enough to foreshadow Darwin.

These theorists, the earliest of the 'pre-Socratic philosophers' as they are conventionally labelled, took the Promethean step of jettisoning the supernatural from their explanation of the world – though that did not make them atheists. They tried to find a consistent system, or internally coherent way, of accounting for the variety of the cosmos about us. Not least, they joined in debate: the argumentativeness so characteristic of the Greeks (modern as well as ancient!) extended into science and theories of explaining nature. Dispute rather than orthodoxy was an essential attitude for them; and it has been said that belief in fact and in orthodox teaching does not make for good science, now as then.

151

Geoffrey Lloyd has emphasised a comparable turning-point in the history of medicine. Hippocrates of Cos was active in the second half of the fifth century. He became the legendary founding father of the medical profession (the Hippocratic Oath was still taken until recently in some medical schools); and some sixty written treatises became attached to his name, the so-called 'Hippocratic Corpus'. A few go back to his lifetime, if not to him, and one of these is *On the Sacred Disease*. This was epilepsy – such a strange, violent and unpredictable affliction that it was attributed to a variety of god-induced 'sacred' causes. The treatise begins, 'I do not believe that the "sacred disease" is any more divine or sacred than any other disease; but, on the contrary, it has specific characteristics and a definite cause.' The point is that Hippocrates does not favour any one supernatural explanation over the others, he rejects them *all*, and insists on physiological explanation. It is beside the point that his explanation, which has to do with a non-existent vein descending from the brain, is nowhere near the truth. It is in itself no more weird than the actual explanation that epilepsy is to do with electrical discharges between parts of the brain.

Aristotle and the four elements via Islam

When it comes to later direct influence the monistic theories of Thales and Co. are not highly significant. The system of basic materials or elements which dominated Western ideas through the Middle Ages and into the Renaissance went back to Empedocles, a colourful and versatile figure who came from Sicily in the fifth century B.C. (his probably fictional death by jumping into Etna inspired a fine poem by Matthew Arnold). Empedocles' four 'roots', as he called them, were earth, water, air and fire. He recognised that, rather as in modern particle physics, you must posit forces as well as the basic elements. The two forces of Love, which attracts, and Strife, which separates, operate, according to him, on the four elements; and this process accounts for the 'nature' of things as they are in all their diversity. Many ancient scientists took issue with this account, but, crucially, it was taken over and adapted by Aristotle, about a century later. He arranged the four elements by sets of oppositions: earth, cold and dry; water, cold and moist; air, warm and moist; fire, warm and dry. He added a fifth element, aether, to account for the heavenly bodies. Through Aristotle's unique influence, this became the orthodox model in the later Middle Ages.

It is probably in the translation of these terms into the four humours of medicine and psychology that they are most familiar. This came down through the second-century-A.D. medical polymath Galen, who took over the four-

The four humours, from a sixteenth-century edition of *The Shepheardes Calendar*. The choleric man has a lion, the sanguine an ape, the phlegmatic a sheep and the melancholic a pig.

element system, and favoured the doctrine that good health calls for a balance of opposing elements, and that illness comes from an imbalance. The four humours became canonised as blood (hence sanguine), phlegm (hence phlegmatic), choler (choleric) and black bile (melancholy). These were still popular notions in Shakespeare's day. A psychology colleague at Oxford remarked recently that, as a classification of personality types, the four humours are as good as any that has ever been offered.

The Greek who has dominated the history of science is, however, Aristotle (384–322 B.C.). Sambursky writes, 'Aristotle's physical doctrine was accepted as dogma for sixty generations. No other personality in the history of science, and very few in the whole history of human culture, has had so deep and long-lasting an influence on subsequent thought.' His father was a doctor in the relatively obscure city of Stagira in the relatively isolated north of the Aegean. He is a towering figure in almost every area of human intellectual endeavour: in a university he would have been a professor in every faculty. Gilbert Ryle once described him to me as 'the one all-round genius in human history'. In 'Greek

The modern statue of Aristotle in his home village of Stagira
Rembrandt's painting *Aristotle Contemplating the Bust of Homer*

Fire' he figures for his literary criticism, his political theory, his logic, his metaphysics and his ethical philosophy, as well as science.

The Arabic transmission of science is one of the less-known stories of Greek Fire. The scientific works of Aristotle, and indeed of other major figures such as Archimedes, Ptolemy and Galen, were known in Arabic at Baghdad and Toledo long before they were known in Latin in Florence and Paris. Indeed they mostly came into Latin translated from Arabic and not from Greek, the work of such men as Adelard of Bath, Robert of Chester, and Gerard of Cremona.

Within a few years of the death of Mohammed in 632 A.D., the Arabs had conquered Syria, Palestine and Egypt. Before long the Arab empire stretched from Samarkand to Cordoba. Constantinople itself barely survived attacks in 677 and 717 A.D. with the help of the incendiary substance known as 'Greek fire'. At the time when the Greek world had lost interest in the science, and indeed in most other achievements of ancient, pagan Greece, the Arab world showed a growing interest. This came to fruition under the Caliphs of Baghdad, who established the 'House of Wisdom' in 833, where a great number of Greek writings were translated, often through an intermediary version in Syriac. This prepared the ground for some of the most important contributors to Muslim thought, including the two great figures of Arab Spain, Ibn Sinā or 'Avicenna' in the eleventh century and Ibn Rushd, 'Averroës', in the twelfth (subject of a good short story by Jorge Luis Borges). These translations into Arabic were, however, severely limited to philosophy and science (except that *The Thousand and One Nights* is influenced by Greek romances). Islam accepted only parts of the Greek heritage, but these combined with the Arab traditions to change their whole history. The transmission of Greek science from Islam to the medieval West was, in its turn, no less influential. Above all, the Arabs revered Aristotle.

As a scientist Aristotle's greatness lies in his combination of thoroughgoing empirical investigation with a highly developed framework of theoretical explanation. He observed the phenomena and then tried to account for them. It was this combination that enabled him to prove triumphantly the counter-intuitive fact that the earth is a sphere, for example. His written works are not finished products, dressed up for publication, and, as Lindsay Judson pointed out, 'An advantage of the fact that Aristotle's surviving writings are lecture notes and research papers is that you actually see him thinking aloud, worrying about problems, trying out explanations, trying to sort out why other explanations that other people have given are no good. So you actually see a great mind at work.'

An Arabic Herbal (1334) drawing on ancient Greek botany

Of Aristotle's many fields of scientific expertise – astronomy, meteorology, chemistry, virtually every department – his favourite was probably the life sciences, particularly zoology and biology. 'To the intellect the craftsmanship of nature provides extraordinary pleasures for those who can recognise the causes in things', he said. He regarded it as the task of human intelligence to study and account for change and movement as well as to observe the static.

In the works which we have, Aristotle classifies over 500 species of animal, including about 120 species of fish and 60 different insects. This must in itself have been very demanding in careful observation; but he went beyond that. He collected the data as a basis for explaining what is going on in zoology. 'In particular', to quote Lindsay Judson, 'he thinks that the central problem of zoology is to explain why animals are different . . . And he thinks that the sort of explanations which are going to be able to explain the differences will be to do with how they manage to survive in different environments, and given different sorts of starting points.'

This leads to theories of lasting interest. Aristotle proposed, for example, a classification of 'blooded animals' (in effect vertebrates) based primarily on mode of generation: thus he makes a basic division between viviparous (giving birth to live young) and oviparous (egg laying), which is divided in its turn into creatures with perfect and imperfect eggs. This cuts interestingly across more obvious and superficial categories like land and water creatures. Similarly quadrupeds are fundamentally divided between (a) oviparous amphibians and reptiles and (b) viviparous quadrupeds, which are in their turn divided into (b i) those with solid hooves, like horses, and (b ii) those with cloven hooves and cutting teeth in the lower jaw only, such as sheep and oxen.

Aristotle also applied dissection far more thoroughly and scientifically than any predecessor. Dissection will have been familiar in a sense to everyone from animal sacrifice, but you have to know what you are looking for. Aristotle found, for example, that the mole has concealed eyes, and that the hyena does not have the genitalia of both sexes, observations which were only quite recently reconfirmed by modern science. Of course he could make mistakes. He thought that younger people had smaller children. Some of his worst errors derive from his belief that females are by nature inferior to males. He is simply wrong to say that women have fewer teeth and fewer ribs and fewer sutures in the brain – the last related to inferior brain-power. It is alleged that he claimed that bison kill their prey by farting, though I have yet to find the source for this!

Aristotle is usually given an unfairly negative place in the history of science, largely because modern science had to break free of Aristotelian orthodoxy, which stifled the higher education of the Middle Ages, in order to achieve the major breakthroughs of Galileo, Harvey and others. Some of Aristotle's science was translated from Arabic and later from Greek into Latin in the thirteenth and fourteenth centuries, and, through the dominance of his logic and rhetoric in the education of the time, everything he said came to be regarded as beyond question. He was, in Dante's phrase, 'the master of those who know'. This orthodoxy included the doctrines that health is a matter of the four humours, that the planets go round the earth, and so forth. But many of the most wrong-headed 'Aristotelian' doctrines did not go back to the master, but were the elaborations of the 'schoolmen'. Aristotle would not himself have approved of slavish orthodoxy; he was always for open dispute. Roger Bacon could call on him as authority to back his call to scholars to place less trust in authorities.

Earth, air, fire and water in a geocentric system. The Aristotelian universe outlined in a *Cosmographia* of 1539.

In any case Aristotle is by no means all wrong. Consider two of his observations on fish. We know that he spent two whole years in 344–342 with his pupil Theophrastus studying marine life in the Bay of Pyrrha on Lesbos. (Theophrastus, who became a distinguished biologist and philosopher in his own right, came from the same small town as Sappho, Eressus.) Aristotle claimed that a certain species of dog-fish (now known as *Mustelis Laevis*) carried the embryo of its young attached by a sort of navel string to a placenta in the female's womb. This was not confirmed by modern biology until 1842. He also

The Greek scientists and mathematicians at work (note Pythagoras' theorem). From *The New Royal Encyclopaedia* of 1790.

claimed that the male of a kind of sheat-fish (*Glanis aristotelis*), rather than the female, cared for and defended its young. This seemed to be disproved by modern observation in Europe until Louis Agassiz in the mid-nineteenth century found sheat-fish in America which behaved as Aristotle claimed. He then found the same phenomenon in Greece.

It is true, nevertheless, that many of the major scientific advances between 1500 and 1750 involved the rejection of Aristotle and of the other ancient Greek authorities. Yet those authorities were needed in order to reach the point at which science could move away and break new ground. It is only because Aristotle was so substantial that his rejection was so important. As Jürgen Mittelstrass puts it: 'The core of our story is this. Greek science had not only achieved the possibility of exact science . . . but had also set up a *principle of research*.'

Euclid, Archimedes, Ptolemy and Galen

Towering figure though Aristotle is, most of Greek science came after him, especially with the stimulus of the great academic centre at Alexandria in Egypt, which was founded not long after his time. Much which has activated modern developments, both positively and negatively, especially in the period 1500–1750, was contributed by other later successors. The range of subjects is enormous, as can be seen by a glance at the seven small-print pages of the 'list of contents' of *A Source Book in Greek Science* by Cohen and Drabkin. All I can do is to give four indicative glimpses.

Geometry

Euclid's *Elements* has been described as 'the most successful text book ever written'. My father was still being taught from Euclid at his Elementary School in the early 1920s. Euclid (Eukleides) was working in Alexandria in about 300 B.C., and seems to have systematised earlier work rather than innovating himself. Thus, for example, the famous proof of 'Pythagoras' Theorem' – that the square on the hypotenuse of a right-angled triangle is equal to the sum of the squares on the other two sides – is handed down by the first book of Euclid. For

A school Euclid printed in Oxford in 1806

SCHEMATA GEOMETRICA

EX EUCLIDE ET ALIIS, TABULIS ÆNEIS EXPRESSA IN USUM TIRONUM.

E TYPOGRAPHEO CLARENDONIANO. MDCCCVI.

centuries the ability to give demonstration (QED) that the two base angles of an isosceles triangle are equal was treated as the basic qualification to embark on mathematics (the so-called '*pons asinorum*'). In many ways, Euclid's method of demonstration was more significant than his content, as it supplied the model of an axiomatic deductive system. The presentation first of postulates and definitions, then of theorems to be demonstrated, can be traced throughout early modern science, not least in Newton's *Principia* (1687). Apollonius of Perge (about 200 B.C.) also deserves a mention. He did important work on conic sections, coining such terms as ellipse, hyperbola and parabola, and he directly influenced Galileo, Halley and Newton among others.

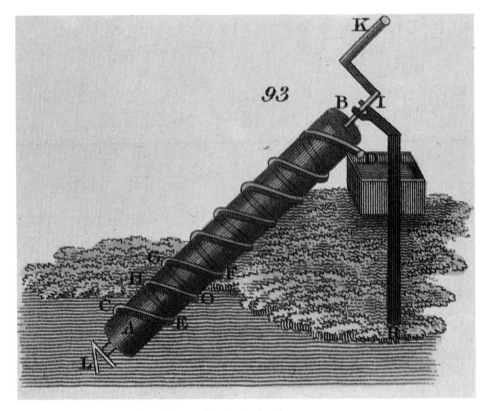

Archimedes' screw explained in an old physics book

Physics

Archimedes of Syracuse in Sicily died for science. The story is that when the Romans captured Syracuse in 212 B.C., a soldier burst into the room where Archimedes was absorbed in his calculations. 'Man, do not disturb me,' he said: the Roman simply butchered him. Like Euclid he worked on mathematics at

A device very like Archimedes' screw still in use in Egypt

Alexandria, where he did pioneer work on the geometry of indivisibles, and on number theory, where he worked out a notation for up to $10^8 \times 10^{16}$. He is most celebrated for his physics – mechanics, astronomy, and optics. He developed mirrors and lenses, and invented a water-raising device – Archimedes' screw – which is still in use in many parts of the Middle East. His work on levers led to

An eighteenth-century mosaic imitating an ancient Roman mosaic: the death of Archimedes at Syracuse in 212 B.C.

his ambitious plea for firm ground to move the earth; but it was his discovery of the science of hydrostatics which led to his most notorious exploit. Hydrostatics covers the behaviour of liquids in relation to gravity, shape of container and floating bodies. Given the task of assessing the amount of gold and/or silver in a crown, he first thought, while in the bath, of the principle of specific gravity, that the same weight of different substances will displace a different volume of water. He is said to have rushed naked through the streets to try the experiment out, shouting 'Eureka' – 'I have found the answer'.

Hero of Alexandria (first century B.C.) developed a range of complicated mechanical gadgets, which were mostly put to trivial applications such as playing one-man-bands. He invented a steam device which would revolve a ball at high speed; he also developed valves, pistons and cylinders, but he never made the connection between them. That would have to wait for over 1,500 years more. Even if he had, it is doubtful whether it would have been given any practical, let alone commercial, application.

A reconstruction of Hero's steam-driven sphere (Paris 1874)

Astronomy

Astronomy came a long way with the Greeks. It was generally supposed, for instance, that the earth is round. Eratosthenes of Cyrene (now in Libya) went further, and calculated the circumference by having shadows simultaneously observed both at Alexandria and at Syene (Aswan), a known distance apart. He arrived (probably) at 39,690 km., remarkably close to the modern figure of 40,009 km. In around 275 B.C. Aristarchus of Samos even worked out a heliocentric model of the solar system with the sun static at the centre. This was not widely accepted, however.

The most influential astronomer was Ptolemy (Claudius Ptolemaeus), who worked in Alexandria 300 years later in the second century A.D. His *Syntaxis* ('System') worked out a geocentric model of the cosmos with the earth at the centre. His complex and sophisticated system of epicycles and eccentrics seemed to account for nearly all celestial phenomena. That is why it took so long to be overthrown. Ptolemy's work is usually known as the *Almagest*, an Arabic version of the Greek for 'the greatest work'. It was indeed through the Arabic that Ptolemy arrived in a Latin West emerging from the Middle Ages, when Gerard of Cremona began to translate the *Almagest* into Latin in 1175. His *Optics* is known in Arabic and Latin but not Greek. The *Almagest* remained virtually unchallenged until Copernicus, and even then he was closely dependent on it. The decisive breaks were not made until Galileo and Kepler at the beginning of the seventeenth century. Though Kepler conclusively rejected Ptolemy, he still appealed to the mathematical cosmologies of Pythagoras and Plato. He attributed to Plato the aphorism 'God always does geometry'.

Medicine

Hippocrates (fifth century B.C.) remained and remains the father-figure of medicine; but the authority whose writings first activated modern medical studies was Galen of Pergamum (129–199 A.D.). He was a polymath, but was always in great demand as a doctor, not least to the Roman Emperor Marcus Aurelius (whose famous *Meditations* was written in Greek). We have 20,000 pages of Galen's works in Greek along with some others that survive only in Arabic. It was above all his schematic physiology and pathology of the four humours that were to be so influential.

Galen was much translated and respected in the Arab world, and his translation from Arabic into Latin, especially by Constantine the African in the eleventh century, really revived the study of medicine in Europe. So this initial momentum arrived, by way of Baghdad and Toledo, first at Salerno and not long after at Paris.

Bit by bit the orthodoxy had to be challenged; but Galen was not seriously superseded until Harvey's demonstration of the circulation of the blood (1628). Even then Harvey cites and praises Galen (along with Hippocrates and Aristotle) as models of scientific method. In 1713 it was still part of the examination of the medical faculty at Würzburg to answer questions on Hippocrates and Galen: the candidate had to select passages by inserting a knife into each book, a curious anecdote of intellectual surgery. Right up to 1833 candidates for the Doctorate of Medicine at Oxford had to give six solemn lectures on Galen!

Mathematics as language

Very little of what the Greeks had to say about the physical world remained intact, then, after about 1700. All the same, the scientific revolutions were based on Greek principles and methods. In physics proper the mechanistic world-picture built up by Galileo and Newton started from the phenomena and moved by means of demonstration to their conclusions, however counter-intuitive. By the 1920s this physics was in its turn in crisis. It became necessary to believe in objects which are in two places at once, in things which are simultaneously waves and particles, in objects which appear out of nothing. The old solid anchors of empiricism, of a mechanics based on the analogies of physical experience, the metaphors of matter, force and energy – all these lost their grip. Physicists began to talk in terms of conceptual creativity and of the harmony of mathematics. The beauty of the calculation wins over common sense, over the apparently nonsensical conclusions. 'Is your theory crazy enough?' said Bohr.

Before quantum mechanics physicists thought that if you knew where a particle was and knew how fast it was moving, you could predict where it would be in the future. 'But now we had to come to terms', says Leon Lederman, 'with the notion of virtual particles, and the notion that a particle can have a fleeting existence, but disappear when you try to measure it. Particles try to tunnel through energy barriers, and so on. All these counter-intuitive ideas were a shock, so shocking in fact that Einstein couldn't accept that one had to deal with probabilities rather than certainties.' The latest theoretical fashion is 'string'. This holds that the twelve fundamental particles, the quarks and leptons, are not points, but are vibrations in 'strings' of such incredible shortness that they cannot be detected empirically at all. Strings vibrating in many dimensions are a purely mathematical construct; and mathematicians are enormously excited by the elegance and beauty they offer. The experimentalist Lederman says wistfully, 'I hope that before long somebody connects the string theory with the world of observation. But so far it hasn't happened.'

This fundamental change in the emphasis of physics was summed up by Werner Heisenberg, one of the founders of modern physics, on 3 June 1964 in an open-air public lecture on the Pnyx at Athens. In the lecture, called 'The Law of Nature and the Structure of Material', he took Democritus, the atomist, as

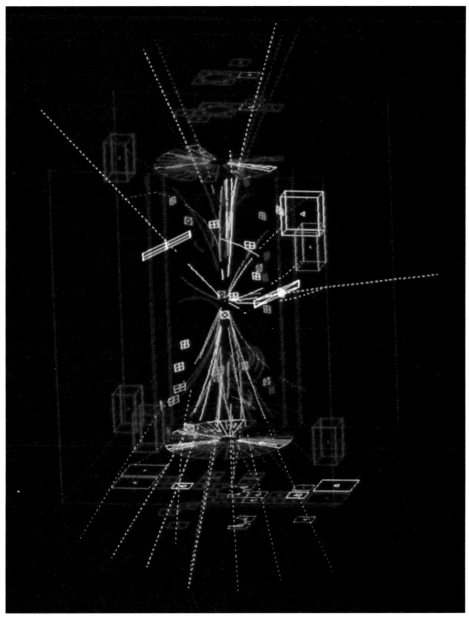

More particle tracks from CERN

epitomising the mechanical approach which dominated ancient Greek science from Aristotle onwards, and modern science from Newton. In opposition to this he set Plato (in the *Timaeus*) and Galileo, who asked not 'What are the phenomena of nature?' but 'How can we prepare the phenomena of nature so that they show their mathematical structure?' We also associate this attitude with the semi-legendary Pythagoras and his school, who developed the notion of the

165

Werner Heisenberg in 1958 commemorating the 100th birthday of Max Planck at the school in Munich where both he and Planck had been pupils

'music of the spheres', and who related mathematics and harmony as the underlying principle of the cosmos.

Heisenberg continued, '. . . we are going to a world of very remote phenomena. Either we go to the distant stars or to very small atomic particles. In these new fields our language ceases to act as a reasonable tool. We will have to rely on mathematics as the only language that remains. I really feel that it is better not to say that the elementary particles are small bits of matter: it is better to say that they are just representations of symmetries . . . The mathematical structures are actually deeper than the existence of mind or matter. Mind or matter is a consequence of mathematical structure. That of course is a very *Platonic* idea.'

The theorists of contemporary physics do not go to Plato or to ancient Greece for their inspiration – despite the way that they cover their calculations with Greek letters – they work with the novel ideas of their contemporaries. Yet Chris Hill of Fermilab reckons that we are only halfway between Democritus the atomist and the ultimate energy scale of gravity. He calculates that his equipment can 'see' particles some 10^{16} times smaller than the smallest particle visible to Democritus' naked eye. He goes on: 'It's important to realise that today we are some 16 powers of 10 away from being able to probe matter at an energy scale, the so-called gravitational energy scale, which most theoretical physicists believe would represent an ultimate understanding of the unification of all forces and all matter . . . A pessimistic view might be that it would take another 2,500 years before we're going to get there.'

Meanwhile where are science and technology taking us? Is it time to reconsider the presumption that the driving motive behind the desire to understand *physis* must necessarily be so that we can interfere with her and control her? Maybe the Greeks were not such fools when they applied their science in such limited ways.

Ideas

THE UNEASY MARRIAGE OF MINDS

The legacy of Greece to Western philosophy is Western philosophy.

Bernard Williams

Governments do not like open questions. Those who have found favour with the electorates of the West in recent years have, on the whole, appealed to the traditional fixed ideas – religion, the family, patriotism, prosperity – and they have called for a return to stable values, Victorian values even. Meanwhile 'intellectuals' compulsively question. 'It all depends what you mean by "values"'; 'It all depends what you mean by "Victorian" . . .' During the secure Reagan years the arts faculties of America have been overwhelmed by the theory of 'deconstruction' which undermines and confounds traditional categories and relentlessly exposes the 'ideology' concealed in apparently plain speaking, especially the plain speaking of politicians.

The same dispute can be put in terms of the relative versus the absolute. Is everything a matter of opinion, in the eye of the beholder? Is 'man the measure of all things', as Protagoras put it? How can I know what is true and what is merely a matter of opinion? Can I count on anything beyond appearances and the experiences of my senses? Is there anything behind or other than this material world? Are there any fixed points, ultimate truths? Put like this, these questions are clearly 'philosophy'. In so far as every thinking person shares the urge to enquire into the principles on which we found our perception of the world, the need to ungrant temporarily the things we take for granted, every thinking person can be a philosopher. The image of a modern philosopher which comes to mind may be something like the hair-splitting, unworldly, Wittgenstein-obsessed academic of Tom Stoppard's *Jumpers*; but we do talk of having 'a philosophy of life' or 'taking a philosophical view' and the multi-millionaire television evangelist is a philosopher of sorts. In ancient Greece the word *philosophia* covered a wide range of theory and investigation from logic to ethics, from scientific principles to theology. The image of the *philosophos* extended from Gorgias who would mesmerise huge audiences, and collect a lot of cash, by his speeches at the Olympic Games, to Diogenes who (so the story goes) went round in an earthenware tub instead of clothes, and, when asked by Alexander the Great what he would most like, replied, 'I would like you to get out of my sunlight.' Bernard Williams in his chapter in *The Legacy of Greece* states: 'In philosophy the Greeks initiated almost all the major fields – metaphysics, logic, the philosophy of language, the theory of knowledge, ethics, political philosophy . . . Not only did they start these areas of enquiry, but progressively distinguished what would still be recognised as many of the most basic questions in those areas.' The Greeks, as so often, raised the basic questions; and it is the formulation of these, no less than the answers, which is the inflammable contribution.

Gorgious rhetoric

It was characteristically Greek not to take things for granted. 'An unquestioned life is not worth living', said Socrates. During the second half of the fifth century

A Roman sculptured relief of Diogenes and Alexander

B.C. the inherited features, the givens of reality and knowledge, came in for interrogation. Is reality anything more than seeming? Is knowledge anything more than sensing? Are the received truths anything more than customs, habits, culturally conditioned prejudices? Once the old foundations are taken away, opinion becomes central. Persuasion controls opinion so persuasion becomes the key to success and power; truth and knowledge become irrelevancies. The skill of saying the effective thing for any given audience and occasion is – another Greek word, of course – *rhetoric*. We cannot pretend that this complex of ideas is alien to the modern world. You have only to follow an election campaign or to switch on a sequence of commercials to be subjected to persuasion, with little regard for truth, through the skilful use of words – rhetoric. There could hardly be a more subjective objectivity than the 'expert' in a TV commercial.

The Sophists are particularly associated with thinking along these lines. The Sophists were not a guild or collaborative group in any way; they were varied and colourful individuals from all over the Greek world who made a living by their wits, and by teaching young adults. They supplied in effect the higher education of the day. They held forth on a wide variety of subjects, from cosmology to literary criticism to chronology; but they all claimed to teach skills of use in public life, above all effective speech. They gravitated to Athens as the main centre of teaching. We have only tantalising fragments of their works; and we know about them mainly from an Athenian who was not at all well-disposed towards them, Plato. As a result they have been generally underrated by later ages – hence the derogatory use of 'sophistry' – yet in the last part of the twentieth century they seem in some ways extraordinarily modern.

Gorgias is often regarded as epitomising the shallow speciousness of the Sophists. He came from Leontini in East Sicily and is said to have lived to about 110 in good health and 'with the mind of a young man'. He was already sixty when he came to Athens on a diplomatic mission in 427 B.C., and scored a great hit with his speeches and showpiece lectures. He could be quite heavy going, however, to judge from what we know of his discourse 'On the nonexistent' which set out to prove that nothing exists; that even if anything did, it cannot be apprehended by men; and that even if it were apprehended, it would be incapable of being expressed or explained. (Unless this was a parody?) Gorgias was associated with a particularly flamboyant style of rhetoric with much word-play, tricks of sound and word-balance. It should not be assumed that such a style is intrinsically lightweight. He was, after all, invited one year by the Athenians to give the funeral speech for those killed in fighting in defence of the city, a grave occasion. Here is a single sentence:

For these men attained an excellence which is divine and a mortality which is human, often preferring gentle fairness to inflexible justice, often straightness of speech to exactness of law, believing that the most godlike and universal law was this: in time of duty dutifully to speak and to leave unspoken, to act and to leave undone, cultivating two needed qualities especially, judgement and strength, one for deliberating, the other for accomplishing, giving help to those unjustly afflicted and punishment to those unjustly flourishing, determined in regard to the expedient, gentle in regard to the fitting, by prudence of mind checking the irrationality of the body, insistent with the insolent, decent with the decent, fearless with the fearless, terrible among terrors.

Gorgias must have made his audience feel that this was appropriate to the occasion; that the dead were honoured and the living consoled by such virtuosity.

The main work we have by Gorgias is a defence of Helen, which he himself describes as a *jeu d'esprit*, a clever shot at making a case in favour of the great femme fatale. The arguments are not entirely frivolous, however:

If it was speech [or 'language' or 'discourse' – the Greek is *logos*] which persuaded her and deceived her heart, it is not difficult to make an answer to this and to banish blame. Speech is a powerful lord, who by means of the finest and most invisible body effects the divinest works: he can stop fear and banish grief and create joy and nurture pity . . . All who have to and do persuade people of things do so by moulding a false argument . . . So that on most subjects most men take opinion as counsellor of their soul; but since opinion is slippery and insecure, it casts those employing it into slippery and insecure successes. What cause then prevents the conclusion that Helen similarly, against her will, might have come under the influence of speech, just as if ravished by the force of the mighty?

In our world of manipulation through the media this is not easy to dismiss.

Serious Socrates

I am tempted to demonstrate the variety of the Sophists by pointing out that the antithesis of Gorgias was the one and only significant native Athenian sophist, Socrates. It is, however, highly controversial to call Socrates a sophist. He had much in common with them, and Aristophanes in his comedy *Clouds* treats him as the archetype. On the other hand the dialogues of his devoted pupil Plato are our main evidence for Socrates, who did not leave written evidence himself; and Plato, whether or not he is putting anything like Socrates' own words into his mouth, is keen to distinguish him from the Sophists. Socrates did not take money (he had rich admirers and did not need to do so, it might be argued); he did not think that the most important things could be taught; he stood outside politics; and he despised rhetoric. Plato's *Gorgias* sets up Gorgias as Socrates' victim in a scathing rejection of rhetoric, which is associated with the pursuit of power and immorality as opposed to philosophy, knowledge and virtue. Socrates would never have been the thought-provoker that he is without the (other) Sophists to react against. Yet it is true that he was fundamentally opposed to Gorgias, and to most of them, on the very question of opinion versus knowledge, of the relative versus the absolute. For Socrates (or at least for Plato's Socrates) the immediate material world is a matter of appearance, but there is a higher reality, the 'ideas', the world of true knowledge, which can and should be sought. Language and persuasion are unreliable and poorly related to the truth. Absolute truth is the goal of *philosophia*.

Behind Socrates' rejection of Gorgias and of rhetoric lies a radical difference in the whole approach to life, a division which still persists. For me this is well brought out in the first chapter of Richard A. Lanham's *The Motives of Eloquence*. Lanham opposes '*homo seriosus*', as championed by Plato, with '*homo rhetoricus*', as championed by Gorgias. 'Serious man' regards language as a means of

Socrates and Alcibiades. Plato's *Symposium* tells how Socrates was above the temptation of Alcibiades' physical charms.

A mask by the Greek artist Ghikas for Socrates in a production of Aristophanes' comedy *Clouds* in 1951

communication which should be clear and sincere and unadorned, in keeping with his emphasis on a central, irreducible self. For him words are not in themselves important, only the realities behind them. 'Rhetorical man', on the other hand, as Lanham puts it:

> is an actor; his reality is dramatic. His sense of identity, his self, depends on the reassurance of daily histrionic reenactment. . . . His motivations must be characteristically ludic, agonistic. He thinks first of winning, of mastering the rules the current game enforces . . . From birth, almost, he has dwelt not in a single value-structure but in several. He is thus committed to no single construction of the world; much rather, to the prevailing game at hand . . . He is not, like the serious man, alienated from his own language. And if he relinquishes the luxury of a central self, a soul, he gains the tolerance, and usually the sense of humour, that comes from knowing he – and others – not only may *think* differently, but may *be* differently. He pays a price for this – religious sublimity, and its reassuring, if breathtaking unities.

Lanham is not advocating one world-view over the other. 'The western self has from the beginning been composed of a drifting and perpetually uneasy combination of *homo rhetoricus* and *homo seriosus*, of a social self and a central self. It is their business to contend for supremacy. To *settle* the struggle would be to end the Greek experiment in a complex self.' Whether or not Lanham is right to extend his typology to the whole of the cultural history of the West, his Greek-based analysis certainly seems to say something interesting about the Western self in the last 20 years.

The Sophists were, then, no mere sophists. They were the Greek Enlightenment, introducing a new scepticism and empiricism, and opening up a gap of questioning in between human laws, customs and religions on the one hand and any unchanging natural order of things on the other. It was no chance that they clustered round Athens in the second half of the fifth century B.C.: there more than any other time and place in ancient Greece was the climate for a cultural revolution. The same season that produced the Sophists also nourished the historian Thucydides, the tragedian Euripides, and, by reaction, Plato.

Socrates and Plato in situ

Socrates has become a half-mythical figure because of the story of his life and death, and because we know him through the glass of the creative genius of his disciple Plato. Plato presents his philosophy in the form of dramatic dialogues, and in all the earlier dialogues Socrates is the leading participant. The dialogue form makes the reader feel that the answers are not 'given' but that you must yourself enter into the activity of the quest. 'So philosophy is an activity, not a product of learning and passive reading. This is the message of the Platonic dialogue,' said Klibansky.

It is the city of Athens that gives Socrates solidity: there he lived, and it was his fellow-citizens who condemned him to death in 399 B.C. for subverting accepted religion and corrupting the young. As Plato tells it in his *Crito*, Socrates preferred to drink the Athenian hemlock rather than escape to live elsewhere.

In the dialogue *Phaedrus* his desirable young admirer Phaedrus takes Socrates for a walk outside the city walls by the river Ilissus (now little more than a polluted ditch when it is above ground). They find an idyllic spot – plane tree, cool water, cicadas, grass to pillow the head. Socrates is lulled into making a pair of set speeches, one against Love and then one in praise of Love, which includes an account of the experience of being in love that has since spoken vividly to many in that state. Then Socrates, however, deprecates these speeches as mere playing, showpieces in the style of the Sophists who can argue for and against with equal facility. He goes on to attack first rhetoric and then writing as a means of communication. Socrates has not really been under the spell of the romantic spot; his real business is in the city talking philosophy with his fellow-citizens.

Plato was not the only disciple of Socrates who wrote dialogues inspired by him. Though not a word survives, we hear of 33 'Shoemaker's dialogues',

The foundations of Simon the cobbler's workshop at the edge of the Agora in Athens

written by one Simon: 'When Socrates came to his workshop, he used to make notes.' At one corner of the Athenian civic centre (*Agora*), by a stone saying 'I am the boundary of the Agora', the American excavators have recently found hobnails and other cobbler's paraphernalia along with a cup inscribed '*Simon's*'. This is surely one precise place where Socrates used to hold forth.

Socrates used to go the rounds; but Plato set up a sort of school at The Academy (named after the local hero, Hekademos) in a large grove a couple of miles north-west of the Agora, now a very grubby part of Athens. A school continued there after Plato's death in 347 B.C., and indeed for another 900

Nails etc. from Simon's workshop and his cup signed ΣΙΜΩΝΟΣ

years or so – as long as the oldest surviving university. Plato's successors there, while they always kept the main features of his transcendental philosophy with its ideal other world, by no means stuck slavishly to his doctrines.

In the third century A.D. there grew up (not particularly in Athens) the school now known as neo-Platonism. Its greatest exponent was the strangely rational mystic Plotinus. Neo-Platonism was far more other-worldly and overtly religious than Plato, and it was deeply influential on early Christianity, though in some ways in tension with it. Both Plato and neo-Platonism were taken up with enthusiasm by the Italian humanists of the fifteenth century. At Florence under the Medici Marsilio Ficino set up The Platonic Academy devoted to learning and contemplation. The members included the painter Botticelli. The 'Cambridge Platonists', I should add, a group of important rationalist Anglicans in the seventeenth century, were influenced as much by Plotinus as by Plato.

The schools of Athens

In the century after Plato founded The Academy various other schools of philosophy grew up in Athens, and most of them lasted hundreds of years until the sixth century A.D. Not even Alexandria could rival this. Intelligent young men would flock there to try out the various competing approaches and life-styles. The schools were usually locked in dispute over fundamental issues, and so Raphael's picture of the disputing sages in a single grand seminar room is rather far from reality. We can still go round Athens and more or less pinpoint the places where the various competing philosophies were pursued.

Thus Aristotle set up his school at The Lyceum (hence *Lycée* etc.), named after a sanctuary of Apollo Lykaios. It stood where the National Garden now is, near Syntagma Square, familiar to every tourist, and just behind the Greek Parliament building. In later centuries its members, also known as 'peripatetics', were largely devoted to science.

Aristotle himself came from the north Aegean and studied at The Academy for twenty years from 367 to 347. While he owed much to Plato, he also rejected him in many fundamental ways. As Bernard Williams puts it: 'Aristotle renounced these [Plato's] extravagant other-worldly hypotheses in favour of a more down-to-earth, classificatory, and analytic spirit, more respectful of the ordinary opinions of men – but defining a grand style for all that, since the systematic impulse was directed to producing one unified, ordered and hierarchical world-picture.' Aristotle's influence on philosophy, as in most other spheres, has been immense, not least in twentieth-century Britain. There simply is not room for me to pursue everything.

A mid-nineteenth-century photograph of Syntagma Square in Athens. Aristotle's Lyceum was just behind the (former) Royal Palace on the right.

The Painted Stoa lay beneath the building in the bottom right of this photo, which has now been demolished. One corner is already excavated here.

The Stoics took their name from a famous building in central Athens where they held their discussions. The painted Stoa (or colonnade) ran along the north side of the Agora and was decorated with huge scenes by the most famous painters of the fifth century. The Athens-Piraeus railway runs between it and the main archaeological site; and the American School has just started full excavation in 1988. This setting was chosen by Zeno, who came to Athens from Cyprus in about 310 B.C. His followers developed a philosophy according to which the wise man exercised his reason (*logos*) to be in harmony with the cosmos or inherent god. In practice this implied a life of duty and stiff upper lip. Stoicism influenced Christianity; but it was especially congenial at Rome, handed down through Cicero and Seneca among others. Through Cicero's *De Officiis* ('Tully's *Offices*') it urged generations of noble students to lives of dutiful public service.

Neglecting among others Sceptics and Cynics, I shall glance lastly at the school which proselytised the doctrines of Epicurus (341–271), an Athenian born and bred on Samos. He taught in the large garden of his house, which may have been west of Athens in the area of what is now the suburb of Kholargos. His philosophy, which is best known through the poetry of his Roman disciple Lucretius (died about 55 B.C.), is very unlike that of Plato or of the Stoics. It held that all our knowledge is based on sense-perception; that the world is entirely material, made up of atoms and void; that there is no life after death; and that the gods take no interest in our world. Epicurus held that the chief evils of

The parable of Plato's cave reconstructed for television by Transatlantic Films

Restaurant L'Epicure

human life are superstition and fear of death, and that the sole good in life is pleasure. This has led to Sir Epicure Mammon in Ben Jonson's *The Alchemist*, to 'Epicure' as a brand name for luxury foods, and so forth; but Epicurus himself advocated, and lived, a rather austere and un-self-indulgent life-style on the grounds that this gives most pleasure in the long run. Through the poetic power of Lucretius, Epicureanism has made its mark on, for example, Montaigne, Shelley and Leopardi; and its materialism has held a fascination for some twentieth-century Marxists.

The radiance of Plato

Over the centuries the transcendental idealism of Plato has, however, been far more significant than these other schools. In the middle of the *Republic*, a huge work which applies his philosophy to a political utopia, Plato tells the allegory of the cave. Prisoners are sitting manacled with their backs to the mouth of the cave and with a bonfire behind them. On the inmost wall are cast the shadows of a procession of puppets which move along a kind of conveyor-belt. This, says Plato, is the condition of unenlightened man, who takes the shadow of a cardboard cut-out by an artificial light to be reality. Think: if only his eyes and body could be released and acclimatised, what would it be like to turn, to see the fire, and to see real objects, and finally to emerge out of the cave into the sunlight? This is the journey of philosophy out from the common unenlightened state, gradually and with effort, towards the ideal world of truth and goodness. This is the only way 'to see the light'.

It is not surprising that all this should have had great appeal for the Romantic poets. The end of Goethe's *Faust*, the whole of Wordsworth's *Prelude* are infused with a Platonic sense of true and permanent beauty and goodness beyond the transient world. Shelley more than any other turns to Plato for the transcendence which he refused to find in Christianity. Take the lines from 'Adonais', his lament for Keats:

> The One remains, the many change and pass;
> Heaven's light forever shines, Earth's shadows fly;
> Life, like a dome of many-coloured glass,
> Stains the white radiance of Eternity,
> Until Death tramples it to fragments.

In the nineteenth century in Britain, Plato was made into a kind of pagan messiah with an authority second, perhaps, only to the Bible. Frank M. Turner traces this well, under the headings 'The Prophetic Plato', 'Plato the Radical Reformer', and 'Plato as Father of Idealism'. After an era in which Plato was enlisted as a patron for all good causes, it is not surprising to find Nietzsche repudiating both him and Socrates. His reason, however – that their rationalism took all the poetry and mystery out of the earlier Greek vision – seems perverse, since Plato is hardly the prototype of rationalism. In the twentieth century Martin Heidegger similarly preferred the pre-Socratic philosophers to Plato. This is also paradoxical in that Heidegger gave his support to the Nazis, and yet Plato is often regarded as a forerunner of Fascism. More recently Iris Murdoch's novels, with their search for truthful goodness, subtly incorporate her professional study of Plato. She has even written a Platonic dialogue on Art, performed at the National Theatre in 1980, and another on Religion, published as *Acastos* in 1986.

Through a glass darkly

Generally we see Greek Fire in opposition to Christianity, sinking below the surface with the rising tide of the new religion, and reviving with its ebbs. W. B. Yeats wrote:

> Odour of blood when Christ was slain
> Made all Platonic tolerance vain
> And vain all Doric discipline.

(In fact, Plato was an exception – and was tolerance his characteristic?)

In many other respects the first 500 years A.D. were a life-and-death struggle between Christianity and the pagan 'classical' world. At the time of Christ, according to a popular story, the most pagan of pagan gods, Pan, gave up the struggle. Some Greek sailors off Paxos heard a loud voice call, 'Make it clear on land that the great god Pan is dead.' Milton has a similar presentiment in his 'Hymn on the Morning of Christ's Nativity':

> The Oracles are dumm . . .
> From haunted spring, and dale
> Edg'd with poplar pale,
>   The parting Genius is with sighing sent,
> With flowre-inwov'n tresses torn
> The Nimphs in twighlight shade of tangled thickets mourn.

Yet Christianity absorbed a lot of ancient Greece as it gathered the strength to sink it. The fourth Gospel was especially aimed at Greeks: 'In the beginning was the word' – the Greek for word is '*logos*', a key concept of Greek philosophy, especially Stoicism. (There is still an evangelical magazine in America called *Logos*.) Greek words in the current Christian vocabulary – as well as Christ and Christian from *Christos*, anointed – include bible, epistle, baptise, hymn, martyr, ecumenical, evangelical, cathedral, pentecost, orthodox and catholic. A and Ω (*alpha* and *omega*), and the XP monogram are still in Christian symbolism. The fish became a symbol because the initial letters of the Greek word $IX\Theta Y\Sigma$ are an acronym of the Greek for 'Jesus Christ God's Son, Saviour': $IH\Sigma OY\Sigma$ $XPI\Sigma TO\Sigma$ ΘEOY $YIO\Sigma$ $\Sigma\Omega THP$.

St Paul in his Epistle to the Colossians was wary: 'Beware lest any man spoil you through philosophy and vain deceit, after the tradition of men after the rudiments of the world, and not after Christ.' The account of Paul's visit to Athens in Acts 17 is intriguing both for its hostility to the professional philosophers there, and for its admiration, almost in despite, for their openness to any interesting new argument.

18   Then certain philosophers of the Epicureans, and of the Stoicks, encountered him. And some said, What will this babbler say?, other some, He seemeth to be a setter forth of strange gods: because he preached unto them Jesus, and the resurrection.

19   And they took him, and brought him unto Areopagus, saying, May we know what this new doctrine, whereof thou speakest, *is*?

20   For thou bringest certain strange things to our ears: we would know therefore what these things mean.

A nineteenth-century illustration of Acts chapter 17

21   (For all the Athenians and strangers which were there spent their time in nothing else, but either to tell, or to hear some new thing.)
22   Then Paul stood in the midst of Mars' hill [the Areopagus], and said, *Ye* men of Athens, I perceive that in all things ye are too superstitious.
23   For as I passed by, and beheld your devotions, I found an altar with this inscription, TO THE UNKNOWN GOD. Whom therefore ye ignorantly worship, him declare I unto you.

Surely Paul had taken in more of Greek education and philosophy than he liked to admit. It is hard to deny the influence of Plato's doctrine of the ideal forms behind reality on this famous verse of 1 Corinthians: 'For now we see through a glass darkly; but then face to face: now I know in part; but then shall I know even as also I am known.' To know God directly is the same as to emerge from the cave into the sunlight.

Plato's influence on important early fathers of the Church such as Origen and Clement is explicit. St Augustine was converted to Platonism and to Christianity in quick succession as part of his spiritual development in 384 and 386 A.D. He wrote: 'When I read these books of the Platonists, I was taught by them to seek incorporeal truth, so that I saw your invisible things, understood by things that were made.'

In the later nineteenth and earlier twentieth century it was perfectly acceptable to be a 'Christian Platonist'. The battles fought 1,500 years earlier seemed to have been over illusory differences, and as recently as 1926 A. E. Taylor wrote in a book on Plato (which is still in print), 'Metaphysically the Form of the Good is what Christian philosophy has meant by God, and nothing else.'

Hemlock and crucifixion

A further reason for the special appeal of Plato to Christianity is Socrates: Socrates, the prophet with a divine inner voice, who was rejected by his own people, condemned, and put to death in dishonour; who taught by word of mouth and whose faithful disciples wrote down and circulated his doctrines. The description of the perfectly good man in the *Republic* seems to reflect him and to prefigure Christ. 'He must have the worst of reputations for wickedness, even though he has never been wicked, so that we can test his justice and see if it weakens in the face of unpopularity and all that goes with it. He should . . . stick to his chosen course until death. Thus we will have a proper account of his goodness.'

In excavations near to the Agora in 1977, the American School in Athens found a building which they plausibly argue is the state prison. They found there a statuette which may be Socrates, and little medicine jars which may have been for hemlock. More vivid than either of these, they found one cell with washing facilities. Two or three pages before the end of Plato's dialogue *Phaedo*, Socrates leaves Phaedo in the cell where the dialogue is set, and goes to 'another room' to bathe and to say farewell to his family, before returning to his hemlock. *Phaedo* concludes, 'Such was the end of our friend, the man who, we would say, was of all the men known then the finest, the wisest and the most good.' For Socrates, as for Christ, the vivid record of his death is an essential nutrient of his power.

Justin Martyr was a Greek born in Judaea who ended up in Rome in the mid-second century A.D. He calls Abraham and Socrates 'Christians before Christ', and argues that Socrates was hounded to death by the Athenians because he rightly perceived how corrupt the old religion was. Likewise Christians should be prepared to follow Christ to martyrdom. The parallels between Socrates and Christ encouraged Justin to assimilate Platonism to Christianity. They also helped Christian Victorians to worship Plato with a good conscience. Benjamin

Jowett, the great Master of Balliol, was moved by the *Phaedo* to write: 'There is
. . . nothing in poetry or history (with one exception) like the last hours of
Socrates in Plato.' Bishop Thirlwall refused to meet a German academic who
had attempted to stand up for the Athenians' treatment of Socrates.

Yet the famous painting of *The Death of Socrates* by David (1787, now in New
York), if set alongside a crucifixion picture, brings out a way in which Socrates'
death was quite unlike that of Christ. While his disciples are in agonies of grief,
Socrates himself remains calm and poised; his philosophy has saved him from
pain and passion. Christ, on the contrary, dies after hours of torment and doubt.
Socrates imperturbably takes the cup of hemlock: Christ in the Garden of
Gethsemane cries out, 'Take this cup from me!'

Socrates might even supply a martyr-figure to satisfy a non-Christian: he was
prepared to die for the truth, a kind of proxy Christ for one who had rejected the
inherited faith. John Stuart Mill is a clear example, speaking of Socrates in terms
that a believer would reserve for Christ: 'a man unique in history, of a kind at all
times needful, and seldom more needed than now'.

This syndrome may throw some light on a book which unexpectedly became a
best-seller in the USA in 1987, *The Closing of the American Mind* by Allan Bloom,
a professor on the Committee on Social Thought at the University of Chicago,
previously best known for his translation of Plato's *Republic*. He maintains in a
lively and combative style that American higher education, and high culture in
general, has declined into a spineless, indiscriminate, nihilistic relativism. This
shelters behind slogans like 'liberal', 'tolerant' and 'pluralist', catchwords of the
'do your own thing, man' era of the late sixties and early seventies, which
epitomised for Bloom this 'spoiling' of the young. He advocates a return to firm

The David painting of the death of Socrates

The Crucifixion by Graham Sutherland in St Matthew's Church, Northampton

values, to established truths, to giving students a sense of intellectual discipline and purpose. This is all very like Socrates versus Gorgias and the other Sophists. So it is interesting that Bloom has no recourse to the Bible or to the revealed truth and absolute faith of Christianity (or Judaism). His messiah is Socrates.

According to Bloom, Nietzsche set out to kill Socrates, and thus to subvert the scientific, the rational and the universal. This is how he expresses Nietzsche's message:

A darkness on top of a void is the condition of life and creation, and it is dispelled in the light of rational analysis. The poet, in his act of creation, knows this. The scientist and the scholar never do . . . There cannot be, as Socrates believed, the pure mind, which is trans-historical. This belief is the fundamental premise and error of science, an error which becomes manifestly fatal in dealing with human things.

Bloom's distaste now begins to emerge:

> The scholar turns away . . . to comparative religion or comparative literature, i.e. either to indifference or to a flabby ecumenism compounded out of the lowest common denominator of a variety of old and incompatible creations. The scholar cannot understand the texts that he purports to interpret and explain.

There are clear hints that Bloom believes that the aimless insecurity of our times may turn viciously on those who stand up for the truth. He for one is prepared to suffer the fate of Socrates. The chapter I have been quoting, entitled 'From Socrates' *Apology* to Heidegger's *Rektoratsrede*' ends:

> What happened to the universities in Germany in the thirties is what has happened and is happening everywhere. The essence of it all is not social, political, psychological or economic, but philosophic. And, for those who wish to see, contemplation of Socrates is our most urgent task. This is properly an academic task.

Nietzsche was not the first, however, to maintain that the Athenians had a case against Socrates; that, given their values and laws, he was guilty. Hegel, who saw the clash between Socrates and the Athenians as, like that in *Antigone*, a dialectical clash between some right on both sides, held that Socrates was guilty of the charges as brought, and that he contributed to the end of the age of independent Greek cities. The Athenians' condemnation of Socrates has, however, found in 1988 a new champion in I. F. Stone's *The Trial of Socrates*, as will be seen in the next chapter.

Phaedrus, motorcycles and deconstruction

I shall close with two other 'best-sellers' of the last twenty years which have been infused with Plato. Robert M. Pirsig's novel *Zen and the Art of Motorcycle Maintenance*, published in 1974, was a cult book for some years, much read by the young, and praised by the 'turned on' intelligentsia. It is everything that Allan Bloom despises, and it is surprising that he does not mention it, especially since Aristotle and the University of Chicago are the villains. The autobiographical narrator is motorbiking across the central plains of the USA with his son, and much of the book is the reconstruction of the spiritual and philosophical life of

'Phaedrus', who, it transpires, was the narrator himself before some kind of mental crisis. Phaedrus became obsessed with the notion of Quality, as opposed to objective factors: 'Quality, value, *creates* the subjects and objects of the world. The facts do not exist until value has created them.' He comes to despise Aristotle's smug classification of phenomena, and much prefers Plato's notion of underlying, transcendental forms. But what about Quality? Phaedrus finds out about Gorgias and the Sophists:

> The results of Socrates's martyrdom and Plato's unexcelled prose that followed are nothing less than the whole world of western man as we know it . . . The ideas of science and technology and other systematically organised efforts of man are dead-centred on it . . . And yet, Phaedrus understands, what he is saying about Quality is somehow opposed to all this. It seems to agree much more closely with the Sophists. 'Man is the measure of all things.' Yes, that's what he is saying about Quality . . . The Quality which creates the world emerges as a *relationship* between man and his experience. He is a *participant* in the creation of all things. The *measure* of all things – it fits. And they taught rhetoric – that fits.

The climax of the book is a confrontation between Phaedrus and the Chairman of the Committee on Analysis of Ideas and Study of Methods at Chicago in

The Phaedrus of the 70s

Jacques Derrida in Paris in 1986 for the publication of the book *Pour Nelson Mandela*
Friedrich Nietzsche

discussion of Plato's *Phaedrus*. The final score is 'Rhetoric 2: Dialectic 0'. So the Sophists as well as Plato, *homo rhetoricus* as well as *homo seriosus*, are central to the quest of Pirsig's book. There is a postscript: in reply to an approach to be interviewed for *Greek Fire* Pirsig accompanied his refusal with the unsigned observation: 'The opinions expressed in that book were those of an insane person.'

Allan Bloom reserves a withering paragraph near the end for 'the school of Deconstructionism'.

> It is the last, predictable stage in the suppression of reason and the denial of the possibility of truth in the name of philosophy. The interpreter's creative activity is more important than the text; there is no text, only interpretation. Thus the one thing most necessary for us, the knowledge of what these texts have to tell us, is turned over to the subjective, creative selves of these interpreters, who say that there is both no text and no reality to which the texts refer. A cheapened interpretation of Nietzsche liberates us from the objective imperatives of the texts that might have liberated us from our increasingly low and narrow horizon.
>
> The fad will pass, as it has already in Paris. This will not be the last attempt of its kind coming from the dispossessed humanities in their search for an imaginary empire, one that flatters popular democratic tastes.

The fact remains that Jacques Derrida, the single most influential deconstructionist, wrote a formative 100-page essay about Bloom's beloved Plato, 'Le Pharmacologie de Platon', first published in 1968, then in *Dissemination* (1972, English translation 1984). It is a study of the *Phaedrus* (again), and especially of Socrates' claim that the spoken word is truer, more real, than writing. Derrida rebuffs those scholars who have criticised the dialogue as incoherent or poorly constructed: he finds the whole point precisely in the ineradicable tensions and contradictions of the logic and rhetoric. Plato's attack on writing is expressed in the language of inscribing and is, in fact, written. Likewise the freedom of Athenian democracy is, he holds, indivisible from its unfree, its scapegoats. Derrida's strategy involves, as it is put by Christopher Norris, 'the dismantling of all those binary distinctions that organise Plato's text, to the point where opposition itself – the very ground of dialectical reasoning – gives way to a process where opposites merge in a constant *undecidable* exchange of attributes.'

Words have, therefore, once deconstructed, no ultimate truth, no direct relation to reality. A Platonic claim to state the truth is only one way of expressing undecidable oppositions. What words *can* do is to persuade; and the more you deconstruct the old strategies, the more you can exploit them. Such doctrines sound very like Gorgias, who could argue equally effectively for either side. 'Truth' was for him merely a rhetorical label used on behalf of whichever side you are advocating. We remain caught in the fifth-century Greek dichotomy. On one side is the security and harmony of Socrates, pulled down by its intolerance: on the other is the sparkling cleverness and relativity of the Sophist, who liberates us into the dubious benefits of uncertainty and of disabling self-consciousness.

'This fad will pass.' Whether we like it or not, deconstruction has had great appeal, especially for students, in the last 15 years, especially in the United States, where Derrida now works at Irvine near Los Angeles. In many faculties he is now orthodoxy, and he is surrounded by disciples wherever he goes. I heard him in Los Angeles in 1987 give a curiously lucid sort of autobiography in which he related his theories to his race and education. As a Jew in Algeria, and raised in the French educational system, he felt an outsider inside it. He was drawn (he said) by the need to clear a space in the centre, free of the three great alien traditions of his intellectual life: ancient Greece, Christianity, and German idealism. It may be that in the twenty-first century some thinkers will propose to add a fourth, Franco-Californian deconstruction. Whatever happens it is clear, in any case, that the absolute and the relative will continue in uneasy cohabitation in the household of Western ideas, as they have ever since Gorgias and Socrates.

THE CLOSING OF DEMOCRACY

This is true Liberty when free born men
Having to advise the public may speak free . . .
Euripides, translated by Milton

WHAT KIND OF DEMOCRACY WILL SURVIVE into the twenty-first century? We live in a world where over half the people are governed by dictators, oligarchies and military regimes; yet everyone or nearly everyone agrees that democracy is the distinguishing mark of a civilised modern society. East Germany, the Deutsche Demokratische Republik, proclaims its democracy more overtly than West Germany. Marxists expose the ways in which Western democracy is a charade: the West, in the name of democracy, resists Russian infiltration of the Third World. The word is used without asking the open questions: who rules? within what limits? for what ends? directly or indirectly? Implicit, and different, answers underlay the democratic claims of the inaugural speech of President Bush on 20 January 1989 and Mikhail Gorbachev's speech to the special Party Congress on 27 June 1988.

In those Western countries which regard themselves as the true democracies the citizens vote sporadically and carelessly. There are mighty forces militating against really concentrated participation in the state by ordinary citizens: the professionalisation of politicians, the growth of bureaucracy, the relentlessly swelling power of the multinationals, and the narcotic effect of the mass media. In Britain 'Charter 88', the call for a new constitutional settlement published in autumn 1988, has some harsh things to say of the British brand of democracy. It speaks of the breakdown of Britain's 'convention of compromise and tolerance: essential components of a free society. Instead, the inbuilt powers of the 1688 settlement have enabled the government to discipline British society to its ends, to impose its values on the civil service; to menace the independence of broadcasting; to threaten academic freedom in the universities and schools; to tolerate abuses committed in the name of national security. The break with the

194

immediate past shows how vulnerable Britain has always been to elective dictatorship.' When does a democracy become an elective dictatorship?

Bloom v. Stone

In the United States of America, if anywhere, democracy is held to be firmly and conclusively incorporate. Every immigrant must be able to answer some basic questions about democracy to qualify for entry. Yet two recent books have revealed, I suspect, the anxiety of the American educated public on this allegedly secure topic. Ancient Athenian democracy is central to both these best-sellers. In 1987 Allan Bloom published *The Closing of the American Mind*, subtitled *How higher education has failed democracy and impoverished the souls of today's students*. The first printing was presumably small, yet within a year it had sold half a million copies. Bloom's mission, with Socrates and Plato as his standard-bearers, is to restore sure values and standards in a society which has slipped into aimless and careless self-indulgence under the pretext of being liberal and tolerant. He claims that the intelligentsia, seen at its worst in the 'hippy' era, has encouraged the mass of people to believe that in a democracy anything goes; and that this has led to a general enslavement to the whims and desires of the lowest common denominator in society. He calls for some sort of maturity to resist this 'undemocratic and irrational mystique': 'some kind of authority is often necessary for most men and is necessary, at least sometimes, for all men'. Inspired by de Tocqueville's *La Démocratie en Amérique* (1835–40), he calls on the universities to turn to Socrates and to supply that lead.

Completely independently I. F. Stone was writing *The Trial of Socrates*, which takes a quite opposite point of view on many issues, all the way from the relative rights and wrongs of Socrates versus Athenian democracy down to the issues of contemporary liberty. Stone, whose broadsheet *I. F. Stone's Weekly* (sometimes *Bi-Weekly*) was highly influential between 1953 and 1971, especially against McCarthyism, taught himself Greek in retirement to prepare for the task. His study is detailed and scholarly; published six months before I wrote this, it has been in the best-seller lists on both sides of the Atlantic. His thesis – while not, of course, endorsing the death penalty like President Bush – is that the Athenians were justified in regarding Socrates as fundamentally undermining their democracy. For Stone the key principle of democracy is the equal right of *any* citizen, however poor, however untrained, to speak out in the parliament without fear of prosecution. This was the case in the Athenian assembly; and Section 6 Article 1 of the American Constitution declares that no member of the Congress can be prosecuted for anything said 'in any speech or debate in either

A fourth-century inscription with laws guaranteeing the Athenian democracy.
Democracy crowns the People.

Portrait bust of Pericles

House'. For Stone the great threat to democracy comes from people such as
Socrates, and indeed Allan Bloom, who set themselves up as having special
access to some higher, absolute values, to certainties which override the
independence of mind of ordinary citizens. Bloom proudly equates himself with
Socrates: Stone with Athenian democracy.

The self and society

For all their antipathies, these two have something vital in common. Both Bloom
and Stone think of the individual as a member of the 'democracy'. They do not
set up the self in opposition to society – the individual against the machine – but
as an entity which can only fully be an entity in relation to other people. 'The
self' only makes sense in relation, not just to immediate family or friends, but to
other people in the community as a whole. The classic statement of this priority

196

is Aristotle's 'Man is by nature a political animal' (ἄνθρωπος φύσει πολιτικὸν ζῷον).

This statement needs some expansion. First, the word for 'man' means 'human being' (it is not male). Second, Aristotle is making a quasi-zoological point: as some creatures go round in pairs and some in flocks and so on, so the human animal lives according to nature politically. Finally, political means 'in a *polis*'. *Polis*, often translated as 'city', does not mean 'conurbation', but an entire independent community – the town, sanctuaries, fields, hills, harbours, and everyone who lives there. The usual Greek *polis* was very small, with a population in thousands. Aristotle recommends as a criterion of the optimum size that it should be possible for all the citizens to be addressed by a single herald (without microphone!). Athens, the largest city in classical times (before being overtaken first by Alexandria, then Rome), had in the middle of the fifth century B.C. about 250,000 inhabitants in all, with perhaps 75,000 of them in the conurbation – about one fortieth of the population of New York City today. It is important to bear in mind this vast difference in human numbers.

The citizens, *politai*, were, as a rule, only the adult males whose fathers were citizens – at Athens (or rather Attica, the whole area of the *polis*, about 2,400 square km.) they are reckoned to have been about 40,000 out of the 250,000. It was their privilege to administer their own city, and to fight for her in war, if called for by the majority. It was their citizenship which made them fully human. According to the 'Funeral Speech' of Pericles, which, as given to us by Thucydides, is the finest eulogy of Athenian democracy, if a man does not

Participation in modern British 'democracy'

participate in the *polis*, then, far from being unobtrusive, he is useless. To withdraw yourself from political life in this view – a view endorsed by Aristotle – was to withdraw yourself from being fully human. I.F. Stone says, 'I share the Athenian view that a citizen has a duty to take part in the life of the city.' (We shall come back to women, immigrants and slaves who had no opportunity to be 'fully human' in this sense.)

This Greek view of the place of the citizen in society – of politics – is by no means the standard modern perspective. Moderns tend to define their selves in terms of their own inner beings and perhaps of a small circle of family and friends. Society, the state, is something imposed from outside, something which does not include 'us', which may actually be against us. The starting point of John Stuart Mill's *On Liberty* is a search to find the *minimum* that the state should be allowed to interfere with the private individual. George Steiner puts the contrast with the Greek perspective provocatively: 'we have swung into a very private ideal . . . the belief that the good life is the one which we live in our marriages . . . in our small circles of friendship, that the debts we owe are primarily to those circles and bonds . . . the feeling that the best of us is behind closed doors. This, the Greeks thought, would have been a scandalous failure of human maturity. They clearly foretold our own fate, which is that, when you do this, the mafiosi, the thugs and the third-rate move into the seats of power. And we have very little right, then, to complain.'

The mafiosi, the thugs and the third-rate are presumably the bosses of the multinationals and the people who come under the rough heading 'politicians'. In Athens every citizen was a politician. Plato criticised the amateurism and said that government should be handed over to experts. We have done just that, and relinquished the role to a small number of professionals who are overtly in power and to other small groups who operate behind the scenes. We have thus come to a much more narrow sense of 'political' than in 'man is by nature a political animal'. When a figure such as the Bishop of Durham speaks out, he is told to keep politics out of religion; when sportsmen who have participated in South Africa are threatened with disqualification, we are told that this is muddling sport up with politics. The very idea of religion or sport being divisible from politics would have been incomprehensible to an ancient Greek, whether or not a democrat.

The professional politicians wish to mark off an area as their terrain. This is true of all modern 'democracies', east, west, far east, capitalist and socialist alike. Election is the key to power. But in ancient Greece election was generally regarded as an un-democratic procedure, promoting rule by a few. In ancient Athens *all* qualified citizens were encouraged to participate in the decision-making process in the parliament, indeed they were sometimes literally roped in.

All those touched by a red-dyed rope swung around by an official in the civic centre were obliged to attend. The non-politician citizens of modern democracies are not positively encouraged towards open political expression, and have no occasion (like the Athenian assembly) where they can say anything they want without fear of redress. The nearest experience to this now is serving on a jury, perhaps the most truly democratic of our institutions. In British democracy, at least, there is, as Charter 88 points out, discouragement. How often, after all, do we actually participate in a substantive political *decision*? In a representative democracy there are a few seconds every four or five years when the citizens have power over the politicians; and even then we are not voting directly on the issues. Hardly any government in Britain since the war has been put into power by over fifty per cent of those voting (let alone of those qualified to vote), and forty-two per cent is constantly called 'an overwhelming popular mandate'. In the last election seventy-five per cent of the electorate voted; in the U.S. Presidential election of 1988 the proportion was forty-eight per cent. An ancient Athenian would be totally baffled to hear this called democracy.

The mixed Republic of the Founding Fathers

It is the Greek legacy of *political theory* rather than actual practice which gave birth to the modern kind of democracy. Much Greek political theory was based on the observation that in practice almost all Greek societies from earliest times had three levels of power: a very small number of kings or magistrates; a council of the most powerful men, which generally meant the big landowners; and then a gathering or assembly of all the other citizens. In most places at most times in ancient Greece power lay with the first of these two groups, sometimes in collaboration and sometimes in rivalry, while the third level, the masses, merely rubber-stamped by acclamation. This tripartite analysis is already found in the fifth-century historian Herodotus. In the next century it was more fully explored and theorised by Plato, especially in his *Republic*, and then by Aristotle in his *Politics*, the two foundation works of political science. In their terms, if the 'kings' were dominant you had 'monarchy' or 'tyranny' (the word was not originally derogatory); if the 'knights' dominated, you had 'aristocracy' or 'oligarchy'; if the popular assembly, the many – *hoi polloi* – managed to appropriate the power, then that was 'democracy'. The Greek word actually means 'power in the hands of the common people' (*dēmos*). Different cities came up with different combinations and emphases. Aristotle's school of political science compiled accounts of 158 different constitutions from all over the Greek world.

Aristotle regarded rule by the many (i.e. democracy) as irresponsibly self-interested and unstable. Characteristically he advocated a compromise, an attempt to have the best of all three types of political system, in other words a *mixed* constitution. When the Greek Polybius was held under house-arrest in Rome for 20 years in the middle of the second century B.C., he analysed the Roman constitution in Greek terms and praised the resilience of its mixture. The three levels – consuls, senate and people – regulated each other by having control of certain crucial spheres of influence (though in fact the popular meetings had little power).

There has been much study of how far this Greek political theory actually influenced the Founding Fathers in the United States, who in 1787 drew up the Constitution which has lasted so remarkably well and been so influential in the rest of the world. There can be no doubt of the recourse to ancient precedent; Richard R. Johnson finds that 'in retrospect, and judging simply by the frequency of citations made and parallels drawn, the influence of the Greek past reached an unprecedented peak in American political discourse around 1787'. John Corbin said, for example, 'The theory of our constitution derives from Aristotle, and was put into successful practice in Rome . . .' and John Adams that 'it is manifest that the best form of government is that which is compounded of all three forms'.

So the Founding Fathers thought of themselves as establishing a Republic, as in Rome, not a Democracy as in fifth-century Athens. Indeed Athens was a negative model. As Meyer Reinhold says, 'One of the prime lessons adduced from antiquity by the Founding Fathers was the unsuitability of direct assembly government, because of the instances known of instability and capriciousness of decisions in ancient republics.' The shift to the positive model of Athens was a late nineteenth-century phenomenon. Earlier in the century the great theorists de Tocqueville and Mill thought that ever-increasing popular participation in the United States would come closer and closer to ancient Athens. The irony is that in our times, when the paradigm of Athens is universally paid lip-service, democracy has moved away from, rather than towards, real participation by the many. The nearest that the *dēmos* of our era gets to power is a television screen.

'Who wishes to speak?'

Everyone may know that 'the Greeks invented democracy' and that 'Athens was the cradle of democracy', but few have any notion how very different Athenian democracy was from democracy as we know it, or realise that most Greeks, including Plato and Aristotle, strongly disapproved of it. Though many have

left An Athenian water clock used to limit the length of public speeches; below are voting ballots for the law courts   *right* 'Ostraka': broken pots inscribed with votes for the exile of a prominent citizen. The annual ostracism vote was a kind of safety-valve for the Athenian democracy.

maintained that it was unstable and short-lived, there was, in fact, democracy at Athens from the great reforms of Cleisthenes in 508 B.C., which set up a political organisation that cut across the old clan and local groupings, until 338 B.C. when Philip of Macedon took over. That timespan is not far short of the time that the American Constitution has lasted. Indeed democratic structures and procedures continued at Athens down into the Roman period, though in a rather empty way. The golden age, however, during which many other Greek cities became democracies under the influence of Athens, lasted roughly from the 460s to the 420s, the period when Pericles was the most influential individual. And this golden age of democracy was also a golden age in many other spheres of activity.

There were, as ever, the three centres of power. There was a small number of state officers, the most important of these being the ten military commanders-in-chief who were elected annually by the citizens. Election was not really a democratic method of choice, but they were subject to a rigorous scrutiny after their period in office. The element of the council was supplied by a body of 500. They were appointed for one year from volunteers spread among the groups of community, and the final selection was by an elaborate system of lot. No-one was allowed to serve more than twice in a lifetime, so a large proportion of citizens would serve on the council at some time. It met in a special building on the west side of the Agora, where it prepared all the business for the popular assembly, and was the day-to-day executive government. Every month (there were 10 in a year) 50 of the 500 lived at public expense in the round *tholos* next door, and were on emergency call to deal with urgent business. Their chairman was chosen daily by lot – so the person whose role was nearest to that of the President or the Prime Minister changed *every day*.

Sovereign, finally, was the people's assembly, the *ekklesia*. All matters of principle or substance were settled here by majority vote. Its decisions were final, and there was in effect no party system or opposition. The assembly met in the morning four times a month on the hill called the Pnyx, which was artificially banked to make an auditorium large enough to hold getting on for 10,000 people. The Herald would ask, 'Who wishes to speak?' No doubt a limited number of individuals tended to dominate business, but the fact remains that in principle any citizen whosoever could respond to this call. It has been calculated that at a normal meeting of the *ekklesia* 4,000–5,000, or ten per cent of the citizen body, used to attend, and there was hardly ever more than twenty per cent present. Before taking this to undermine the claims of Athenian democracy, it is worth asking how often ten per cent of a modern community gathers in one place for any occasion, let alone a serious one, let alone forty times a year. Ten per cent of the adult population of New York City would amount to more than half a million people. Do ten thousand New Yorkers know what is going on in Congress in any given month? Only fifty per cent of the electorate turns out for the one opportunity they have every four years to choose their chief executive.

Athenian democracy actually involved an extraordinarily high proportion of all those qualified in its government. It was truly participatory. Fortunately, the historian Thucydides decided to write out the speech, or his version of the speech, which Pericles delivered in the winter of 430 B.C. in honour of the Athenians killed in the first year of the Peloponnesian War. Thucydides, writing 15 or 20 years later, was aware that this marked the beginning of the end of the golden age, and that Pericles was himself soon to die of the terrible plague. His 'Funeral Speech' was revolutionary then, and in many ways still is. Students have been arrested in Greece under modern dictatorships for distributing it.

We are called a democracy, for the administration is in the hands of the many and not of the few. But while the law secures equal justice for all alike in their private disputes, the claim of excellence is also recognised; and when a citizen is in any way distinguished he is preferred to the public service, not as a matter of privilege, but as the reward of merit. Neither is

The title-page of Milton's *Areopagitica*

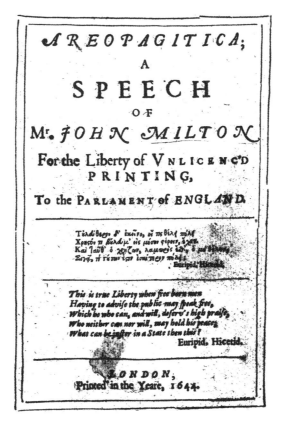

AREOPAGITICA;

A

SPEECH

OF

Mr. *JOHN MILTON*

For the Liberty of VNLICENC'D
PRINTING,

To the PARLAMENT of ENGLAND.

Τὸνδ ιθερν δ᾽ ἐκεῖνο, ὅ τις θέλει πόλει
Χρηστόν τι βούλευμ᾽ εἰς μέσον φέρειν, ἔχων.
Καὶ ταῦθ᾽ ὁ χρήζων, λαμπρός ἐσθ᾽, ὁ μὴ θέλων,
Σιγᾷ, τί τούτων ἐστιν ἰσαίτερον πόλει;

Euripid. Hicetid.

*This is true Liberty when free born men
Having to advise the public may speak free,
Which he who can, and will, deserv's high praise,
Who neither can nor will, may hold his peace;
What can be juster in a State then this?*

Euripid. Hicetid.

LONDON,
Printed in the Yeare, 1644.

poverty a bar, but a man may benefit his country whatever be the obscurity
of his condition. There is no exclusiveness in our public life . . .

Does any modern democracy genuinely aspire to this manifesto?

Liberty for the people or tyranny by the people?

Another proud declaration of the ideals of democratic Athens is put in the
mouth of the legendary King Theseus in Euripides' play *Suppliants* (420s). John
Milton translated some lines on the title-page of *Areopagitica*, his rousing call to
parliament for freedom of expression in print in 1644 (named after the
Areopagus rock near the Acropolis in Athens):

> This is true Liberty when free born men
> Having to advise the public may speak free,
> Which he who can, and will, deserv's high praise,
> Who neither can nor will, may hold his peace;
> What can be juster in a State than this?

Some Levellers in the 1640s also pointed to ancient Athens for popular participation in power, but they were long before their time. Marchamont Nedham changed his views with the times, but in the *Excellencie of a Free State* (1656) he is full of favour for Athens. During the sixteenth, seventeenth and eighteenth centuries democracy was normally regarded as unstable mob rule, as Plato and Aristotle taught. The great political theorists such as Machiavelli, Harrington and Montesquieu, even Rousseau, looked upon democracy as acceptable only if incorporated into a mixed constitution. Montesquieu (*De l'esprit des lois* 1748) put Athens back on the map as a live force in political thought, but the revolutions in France and America still did not, as a rule, use 'Athens' or 'democracy' as positive terms in their rhetoric.

In a Britain alarmed by events across the Channel and across the Atlantic, the Tory landowner William Mitford wrote a highly influential history of Greece (published between 1784 and 1810) which utterly condemned Athenian democracy as nothing less than 'a tyranny in the hands of the people'. This remained the standard view for 50 years, and was not properly challenged until George Grote, the reforming radical and former MP, went to the other extreme in his *History of Greece* (1846–56) and made Athens sound much more stable and British than it really was. Frank M. Turner's account sums up the issue well:

> Grote's strategy [was to make] Athens an object lesson in the dangers posed by conservative forces in a democracy. Previous anti-democratic writers, such as Mitford, had argued that a modern liberal democratic state would resemble lawless Athens. Reversing the analogy, Grote presented ancient democratic Athens as almost a mirror image of the stable, liberal mid-Victorian polity.

Athens now became idealised. John Stuart Mill had maintained that the Athenian system 'raised the intellectual standard of an average Athenian citizen far beyond anything of which there is yet an example in any other age of men, ancient or modern . . .' E. A. Freeman, Professor of History at Oxford, went further: 'The average Athenian citizen was, in political intelligence, above the average English member of Parliament'! In fifty years Athens shifted from an awful example to an inspiration. In 1915 extracts from Pericles' *Funeral Speech* were put up in London buses as part of the recruiting campaign for the armed forces against the enemy which threatened freedom and democracy. There was a similar shift in France, traced by Pierre Vidal-Naquet and Nicole Loreaux, by which Athens was transformed from a terrible warning to a shining model during the course of the nineteenth century, above all by the *Histoire Grecque* of Victor Duruy (1851).

Women, slaves and self-righteousness

So democracy won the nineteenth-century debate, though it was not the participatory democracy of Athens. In practice it was the representative democracy of the United States and of de Tocqueville. Indeed during the twentieth century any allusion to Athenian participatory democracy has, as often as not, been accompanied by qualification, disclaimer and even scorn. The modern reservation has not been the old horror of mob rule, but the complaint that Athenian democracy *excluded* so many people from its privileged circle of citizens. 'How can it be called democracy when women and slaves were without political rights?' There may be a hint of self-righteousness and even of resentment in the standard depreciation. What hides behind this?

First some approximate facts about Athens. Within the round-figure calculation of 250,000 inhabitants of Attica, there would have been some 40,000 *politai*, i.e., participant citizens comprised about sixteen per cent of the total. This reckoning supposes 100,000 women and children of citizen families. There were also some 20,000 or so resident immigrants, called 'metics', who were free but without citizen rights, and up to 100,000 slaves, who were owned by citizens and who had virtually no rights, not even the right to have a family. Some led quite pleasant lives, but many, especially those who worked in the silver mines of Laurion in the south of Attica, lived and died under horrific conditions. Surely this justifies the twentieth-century self-righteousness?

There is something hypocritical in treating the exclusion of women from politics let alone suffrage as a primitive inhumanity. Women got the vote in the United States in 1918, in Britain in 1919 (with limitations), in Italy and France in 1945. In Quebec and Switzerland they had to wait until 1971. In some respects the mass meetings of the small Swiss canton are the nearest modern analogy to the Athenian *ekklesia*. It is amusing, then, to find that in the canton of Appenzell, not only must men wear their swords to a meeting but women still do not have the vote at that level of government. The treatment of women in enlightened fifth-century Athens is a disturbing story (traced in the 'Aphrodite' Chapter), but we are hardly in a position to be too superior about it. In the British parliament there are at present 41 women MPs in a total of 650; and in the United States House of Representatives the proportion is even smaller.

Slavery is now of course an abhorred institution; these days we have machines instead. Yet a number of those who signed the Declaration of Independence in 1776 owned slaves, and there are still many countries throughout the world where sections of the labour force are so constrained as to be in a condition very close to slavery – *Gastarbeiter* for instance. The gold mines of South Africa have

The citizens of the Swiss canton of Appenzell-Ausserhoden meet annually for the canton parliament on the last Sunday in April

much in common with the silver mines of Laurion.

All the same, the standard indictment of Athenian democracy is not so much that it excluded slaves as that it *depended on* slave labour. It was only the economic exploitation, it is claimed, that freed ordinary Athenians for politics. The Tory Mitford was the first to put forward this argument in the 1790s, as he warned Britain of the dangers: democracy means that the workers will stop working and devote themselves to power-seeking instead. Ironically, the doctrine has since then been taken over by very different political ideologies. Engels wrote in 1884: 'the downfall of Athens was not caused by democracy, as the European lickspittle historians assert to flatter their princes, but by slavery, which banned the labour of free citizens'. Either way, recent research, for example by Ellen Meiksens Wood in her *Peasant, Citizen and Slave*, suggests that this is a myth, and that the great majority of Athenian citizens did work most of the time, especially on the land. Wealthier citizens, who could afford a suit of bronze armour and who constituted the land army, did not need to work. The larger number who manned the ships in time of war were neither wealthy nor

206

Idle, and they constituted the backbone of a peasant democracy.

It is curious that in the first century which has ever taken 'democracy' to be by definition a word of approval, the twentieth century A.D., there has also been a widespread tendency to run down the Athenian achievement. There are, I suggest, reasons why modern democracies, communist and capitalist alike, might wish to divert admiration away from ancient Athens. The elected powers do not want their citizens to participate too actively, not even the middle-class men, let alone the women and the menial labourers.

The Spartan antithesis

Democracy is by no means the only Greek model which has been evoked over the centuries. Plato and Aristotle both deplored it. The influence of Aristotle's *Politics* has been immense: Karl Marx, among his admirers, called him 'a giant thinker'. It is not surprising that Aristotle, who based his theories on the observation of practice, disapproved of democracy as unbalanced and unstable. He was not an Athenian, after all, and by the time he arrived in Athens the golden age was over half a century in the past. Plato, on the other hand, was an Athenian and so subject to the law which said, 'If any man overthrow the democracy at Athens . . . he shall be held an enemy of the Athenians and may be killed without penalty to his killer.' Yet Plato went much further than Aristotle in his rejection of the system which condemned Socrates. He equated the people (*dēmos*) with the lowest, emotional, unthinking part of man's three-level soul. The city should be run by the 'guardians', the 'philosopher-kings', who have perfected the highest, rational level of their souls. That is according to his utopian *Republic*. Later in life he worked out a 'second-best state' in the *Laws* which is so repressive and conservative that even children's games are to be stabilised and regulated. All the work is to be done by slaves and disenfranchised people, since the citizens are to concentrate, not on politics, but on military training. Ultimate power lies with an exclusive and sinister body, the Nocturnal Council.

Plato was one of a group of Athenians who thought that Sparta was great. Much in the *Laws* is Plato's own brainchild, but he was clearly influenced by the practice of the city whose politics he so much admired. Sparta (the whole area was called Lacedaemon), well inland in the southern Peloponnese, was Athens' great enemy, and was in many ways about as unlike Athens as could be. The contrast is still apparent to the modern visitor. Thucydides made a remarkable prediction: 'Suppose the city of Sparta to be deserted, and nothing left but the temples and the ground plan, distant ages would be very unwilling to believe that

A symbolic monument in
Sparta, Wisconsin

the power of the Lacedaemonians was at all equal to their fame . . . whereas, if
the same fate befell the Athenians, the ruins of Athens would strike the eye, and
we should infer their power to have been twice as great as it really is.' The grand
monuments of Athens are gathered round the majestic Acropolis: the site of
ancient Sparta, which was in effect a group of villages without a defensive wall, is
now a group of hillocks covered in olive trees, surrounded by the fertile valley of
the river Eurotas.

The political system at Sparta was attributed to the semi-legendary legislator
Lycurgus. As everywhere there were the three levels of power among the
citizens; but the relative distribution could hardly have been more different from
that at Athens. At the top were two hereditary kings, and five annually elected
magistrates called *ephors*, who had substantial executive powers. Next, the
council, called the *gerousia*, had 28 members, all aged over sixty and all
appointed for life. The *gerousia* made decisions of war and peace, and was the
centre of legislation and judicial power. Finally, there was the popular meeting
of all citizens over thirty, known as the *Spartiates*. They numbered fewer than
10,000, met rarely and irregularly, and even then did little more than

208

Sparta as predicted by Thucydides (the new town of 1834 is in the background)

Athens as predicted by Thucydides

The ruins of Mistra with a view of the plain of Laconia

rubber-stamp the proposals which emanated from the 35 people with the real power. Non-citizens were divided into the free-born inhabitants of the villages, and the *helots*, Greeks who were in effect serfs. The whole Spartan system depended on this large subject population which provided for the élite.

The life of the Spartiate was devoted to military fitness. All weak babies were exposed in the gorges of Mount Taygetus, a practice applauded by Hitler. From the age of seven until thirty every young male lived a life of harsh military training, first as a cub then as a pack-leader. A folk-lore about their way of life had already grown up in ancient times. It claimed, for instance, that every boy was allowed one cloak a year, and slept on rushes which he gathered for himself from the river. Drill exercises and violent competitive games were kept on the move by the whip; there were competitions to endure the lash without crying out. On special occasions they were let loose and allowed to lynch a few helots. At the age of thirty the new Spartiates were expected to marry and were allotted land, though they did not farm it themselves – that was what the helots were for.

They spent their days not at home but in messes, where they ate together with the members of their 'battalion' (the black broth was famous). Their purpose in life was to be one of ten thousand identical component parts in a war machine.

However repulsive this may sound, a myth was built up over the centuries of Sparta as the model of a stable, patriotic society – the 'Spartan Mirage' as it is sometimes known. Plato's admiration was significant, but the most important idealisation was that of the biographer Plutarch (about 100 A.D.), especially in his *Life of Lycurgus*. Plutarch was taken very seriously during the Renaissance, and there was a fine sixteenth-century translation into French by Amyot. In the nineteenth century Mary Garth, we are told in the finale of *Middlemarch*, 'wrote a little book for her boys, called *Stories of Great Men taken from Plutarch*'. So it is that many towns in the United States are called Sparta; and this is why in 1834, very soon after Greek independence, a new *Sparti* was laid out on the edge of the ancient site. This rectangular symbol of the rebirth of Greece went inextricably hand in hand with the end of the town of Mistra, some 8 kilometres away. Mistra was founded by the Francs in 1247, and was one of the great cities of late Byzantine Greece – indeed Gemistos Plethon even established a Platonic academy there during 1400–42. Yet this centre of orthodox religion and learning was deserted to refound militaristic and patriotic Sparta. (Comparably the last Christian service to be held in the temple of Hephaestus at Athens – a

Cruikshank's version of Spartan customs in a Victorian schoolroom

George Cruikshank

In 480 B.C. 300 Spartans under King Leonidas held up the might of the Persian army at Thermopylae. This is David's celebration of their stand for liberty (1814).

church for over 1,000 years – was to welcome King Otto on his arrival in Athens on 13 December 1834.)

The story of Sparta in later ages has been well studied by Elizabeth Rawson in *The Spartan Tradition in European Thought*. Those who have nominated Sparta and Lycurgus with enthusiastic approval include most of the great names of political science, even Machiavelli and Montesquieu. James Harrington in *The Commonwealth of Oceana* (1656) urged Cromwell to imitate Lycurgus, and cited Sparta's stability as second only to Venice. Rousseau, often seen as the founder of the Western democratic tradition, praised the Spartan system (as given by Plutarch) unreservedly in *Du contrat social* (1762). 'American leaders', writes Meyer Reinhold, 'judged Sparta [as opposed to Athens] as a model of freedom and order, a stable, long-lived commonwealth, its people distinguished by virtue, simple life-style, patriotism, vigour.' John Dickson in 1769 reckoned the Spartans 'as brave and as free a people as ever existed', and Samuel Adams looked forward to Boston becoming 'a Christian Sparta'.

It is hard to pin down a turning-point, but the reflections of the great French romantic Chateaubriand on 18 August 1806 are on the dividing line. On that day he visited the site of Sparta (no new town as yet) and wrote: 'even if I loathe the manners of the ancient Spartans, I am not blind to the greatness of a free people, and it was not without emotion that I trampled on their noble dust'. In the course of the nineteenth century, as Athens took over as the model to be admired, Sparta was forgotten more than actively condemned. I am aware of only one outburst of enthusiasm for Sparta in the second half of the century: Walter Pater's essay 'Lacedaemon'. He muses on the 'half-military, half-monastic spirit which prevailed in this gravely beautiful place', and he compares ancient Sparta explicitly, and with sentimental affection, with the English public schools. There were indeed similarities, not least the dormitory homosexuality and the obsessive fascination with beating. Richard Jenkyns has found a poignant pendant to this parallel. The Baron de Charlus in Proust is led by the struggles of the First World War to muse: 'Those English soldiers who at the beginning I dismissed as mere football-players . . . well, they are the young men of Plato, or rather they are Spartiates.'

Spartan boys and girls at exercise. Degas seems to envisage them as noble savages.

Hitler's review of 40,000 men at Nuremberg in 1938

Plato, Lenin, Hitler

The fire of Plato and of Sparta has continued to flare even in the twentieth century – perhaps at its most dangerous. The resemblances between the education of Spartan boys and the *Gioventù fascista* or the *Hitlerjugend* are no coincidence. As early as 1933 there was a book *Hitlers Kampf und Platons Staat* by Joachim Bannes. An education committee set up to oversee the Adolf Hitler-

Schule compiled a textbook about Sparta, emphasising its communal training, its toughness and spirit of *Kameradschaft*. 'Many of the plans and ground rules which the Spartans had about how to build a state and how to train its ruling class are of relevance to us . . . we want to help the Führer to build a great Reich. Sparta should be a rousing example to us.' One Hans Bogner, in a book on education published in 1937, recommends that German teachers should pay special attention to Plato's 'Guardians'. 'Germany of the New Spirit has the special destiny, on account of its historical situation, to acknowledge Plato as a living force.' Plato is cited in support of the censorship of the theatre, the promotion of gymnastics, and of the doctrine that a democracy ceases to be a democracy when it fails to pick the right leaders. (And who decides who is right?) Hitler himself, according to his *Table Talk*, often praised the Spartans, and their subjugation of the helots. He even claimed that the peasant soup in Schleswig-Holstein bore a significant resemblance to black broth!

In 1937 Richard Crossman, a future Labour minister, then an Oxford don, published a series of talks he had been giving on BBC Radio as *Plato Today*. He attacked Plato as the greatest ever enemy of liberal ideas and as an inspirer of fascism. Arnold Toynbee voiced similar sentiments, and so did Bertrand Russell, who described Lenin and Hitler as Plato's greatest disciples. The heaviest attack on Plato came later, in 1945, from Karl Popper, who had fled his native Austria when in his mid-thirties, and who established himself at the London School of Economics after the Second World War. Volume I of *The Open Society and Its Enemies* is directed against Plato, volume II against Hegel and Marx. Popper's central point is that in politics (as in science) it is a fundamental error to ask 'How can we be certain?' and 'How can we secure perfect rulers?': what we must ask is 'How can we detect and remedy our mistakes as quickly as possible?' and 'How can we minimise the damage that our rulers may do?' It is curious to find no mention of Popper in *The Closing of the American Mind*, nor any kind of defence against Popper's far from lightweight attack. In fact Bloom does not allude at all to Sparta, or to Plato's admiration for that impersonally patriotic regime. It is an intriguing, and perhaps frightening, twist of Greek Fire that in 1987 Plato can be offered as a champion of American Democracy. When does democracy become an elective dictatorship?

ATLANTIS NEW TOWN

May the days of Greece be revived in the woods of America,
and Philadelphia become the Athens of the western world!

Benjamin Latrobe

A CITY IS A REFLECTION of the people who inhabit it. The shaping, the construction, the design – in a (Greek) word, the architecture – express the values and priorities of the society; and in turn they influence that society. Of course there are social and economic forces beyond the reach of architects (there can be little aesthetic coherence in the expansion of Mexico City to contain over 35 million people by the year 2000), but the fact that they are paramount is in its turn a reflection on the society.

Nearly all the buildings of our cities have been put up in the twentieth century, most of them in the last forty years. So what do they say about the state of our civilisation? Western cities are zoned into areas for commerce, for shopping, for industry, for housing and so forth; they are significantly shaped by roads and by transport; their centres are dominated by clusters of tower-blocks made of concrete and glass. Some tower-blocks are for housing, but most, especially at the core, are for business. It surely says something about modern Britain that the City of London, which used to be dominated by St Paul's, is now overtowered by offices, the highest of all being the National Westminster Bank headquarters right by the Stock Exchange. From the outside it is nothing but another very high tower block. Its only distinctive design is a secret hidden from the human perspective: the ground-plan forms the Bank's logo.

The architect Leon Krier insists on thinking in terms of the city as a whole. His plans have hardly ever been put into practice since they demand a whole social context, something which cannot usually be supplied. So most of his work has been utopian, like his plans (1985) to 'complete' Washington DC by dividing it into four 'cities' in which the now isolated monuments would be given surrounding communities. Krier holds that 'instead of just building more

The Nat West Tower in the City of London under construction – 'an abuse of the silhouette of a town'

suburbs, we have again to build new centres, where there are places to live, but also places to work and places to meet, which have value, which are symbolically important, which are cherished . . .' He is scathing about the Nat West Tower: 'it is symbolically meaningless, because it is merely an addition of functions, small functions, rather pedestrian functions, of interest to few people. It is not a place where a lot of people go. It is a place where a lot of people *work*, but the value is a very private one, it is not shared by society at large. And therefore its size is in a way an abuse of the silhouette of a town, because it oversteps its function and its symbolic value.'

Old Ithaca with new eyes

Most twentieth-century urban architecture has been 'modernist' and has had nothing to do with ancient Greece; on the contrary it has implied a positive rejection of 'classical' styles. The architects invoke the creative figures like Le Corbusier, Mies van der Rohe and Gropius, but often they are using them merely as cover for routine and shoddy work. The last 15 years or so have seen a notable, and ever-increasingly visible, reaction, commonly labelled 'the post-modernism movement'. This tag in fact covers a variety of movements, and no doubt also covers plenty of routine and shoddy work. Sir Terence Conran complains of 'Toytown architecture with odd bits of column and pediment appearing on rather dull concrete buildings' and of 'Bricks with façades to jolly them up'. Nevertheless there is a new awareness in the air. People are freshly taking notice of architecture, and they are shedding their former passivity. Prince Charles has played a significant part, insisting that architecture is not a 'given' beyond control, but an opportunity: 'We have an opportunity therefore to do three things – to create a new renaissance in architecture: to launch a major campaign to save our heritage, and to stimulate a whole host of local activities to promote community and economic development.'

Prince Charles, like most of those who have had enough of modernism and its offspring brutalism, is in favour, at least to some extent, of classical architecture. This implies pediments, cornices, but above all it means the column, or rather the three Greek orders of column: Doric (solid and plain), Ionic (graceful with its spiral volutes), and Corinthian (smooth, crowned with florid leaves).

Symmetry is also an important association of the rough category 'classical'. Even deeper, there may be some underlying sense of *proportion*, of the translation of mathematics, of absolutes, into artefacts. This may be a delusion, but it has been a powerful one and has attracted a good deal of mathematical ingenuity since the Renaissance. To take a well-known example, when a line is divided so that the shorter section has the same proportion to the longer as the longer to the whole, you have a 'golden section'. Turn this into a rectangle, and you have a shape which most people find highly satisfying. Draw a spiral within a diminishing series of golden rectangles, and you can map the volute of an Ionic column. Does Greek architecture turn mathematics into aesthetic satisfaction?

Some claim that, at an even deeper level, the proportions of the human body underlie our instinctive aesthetic sense. The fifth-century sculptor Polyclitus wrote a book on *symmetria*, the commensurability of the parts of the body, exemplified by his statue of the 'spear-carrier' (*doryphorus*), also known as his *canon*, or rule. Can there be anything to this Greek notion that the most

A Renaissance diagram of the classical orders
The porch of Highpoint II (1939) – post-modernism before its time

satisfying buildings somehow reflect the relations of the parts of the bodies of
the people who inhabit them?

Over the centuries Greek architecture has been revived and rejected, and it
will no doubt continue to rise and fall with the times. Here as much as anywhere
Greece has been open to constant reinterpretation, forever shifting and reforming. Until recently it had been out of favour for over a hundred years. It has,
of course, been imitated for banks, town halls, and similar public buildings, but
that is part and parcel of the very association with hierarchical tradition and with
the conservative establishment which led to its rejection. In small-town
Wisconsin a wooden shack was transformed into the Security Marine Bank by
the addition of the name and some Ionic columns painted on a screen!

The reinfiltration of the classical into modern architecture has been long and
devious. In Britain, for example, Lubetkin designed the first-ever high-rise
block, Highpoint I in Hampstead, in 1934, the antithesis of the classical, and
praised by Le Corbusier himself. Yet Highpoint II, five years later, has a porch
held up by Caryatids like those from the Erechtheion on the Acropolis. They, as
Joe Mordaunt Crook puts it, 'turned out to be a long-distance sign-post marked
post-Modernism'.

The Great Peristyle Garden of the J. Paul Getty Museum at Malibu (1974). The car park is underneath.

Some post-modernism, like reproduction furniture, is in effect high-quality copying of the achievements of earlier ages. A museum in California is an early example. In 1970, J. Paul Getty, despairing of modern architecture, commissioned a scholar, Dr Norman Neuerberg, to advise his architects on how to reconstruct a Roman villa from Herculaneum on the bay of Naples to house his collection of antiquities on the Pacific at Malibu. The Villa dei Papyri (named after a collection of Greek philosophy on papyrus discovered in it) was a rich man's mansion, a Roman extravagance in the Greek style, which was buried in the eruption of Vesuvius in 79 A.D. It was rediscovered by tunnels in the lava made in the 1750s. The excavations were reopened in 1987 after being left abandoned for more than 200 years.

When it was unveiled in 1974, the Getty Museum was ridiculed – 'a camp folly in the tradition of Disneyland', 'the First Real Plastic Museum'. This is not fair: the materials are solid and of genuinely high quality. People have come round to it, not least because the solid stonework, the open arcades, greenery and water suit its purpose in the Southern Californian climate. In any case, it is not a pure antiquarian reconstruction. It has lifts and lavatories, and above all, or rather below all, a huge car park. The exquisite Great Peristyle Garden, pond and all, is on the roof of the car park – something which has a touch of post-modernist irony about it.

The Italian architect Aldo Rossi was already advocating the coexistence of the 'ordine Greco' with modern architecture in 1959. A key moment is often pinned down, however, to the architecture section at the Venice Biennale in 1980. This was called 'The Presence of the Past', and was organised by the architect Paolo Portoghesi. He is himself highly quotable on the subject: 'The Past now represents, for the first time in 40 years, a seriously articulate challenge to the Modern Movement, and puts a distance between the first and second half of the twentieth century – the first half representing the dissatisfaction with the failure of the Modern Movement, and the second half the excitement of newly aroused possibilities.' The image of Ithaca, the island of Odysseus' return, is a favourite for him. Instead of developing into a futuristic style, architecture is, he says, 'steering its course towards Ithaca . . . having rediscovered, through history, through refound familiarity with its craft, the green eternity of Ithaca'. He is keen to make it clear that this return to Ithaca is not merely childish regression, a return to safe models; it has a self-conscious, selective, sometimes ironic, even

The 'Street' of architectures at the Venice Biennale in 1980
'Les Espaces d'Abraxas' near Paris by Ricardo Bofill: the glass Corinthian columns end with a Doric column

The theatrical shape of the space inside 'Les Espaces d'Abraxas'

estranged, relationship with the past and with the Greeks. 'The return to Ithaca is a definitive estrangement, because Odysseus is no longer the same . . . he sees a different Ithaca with new eyes that his long experience has filled with images.'

This allusive self-conscious relation to the past in architecture is lavishly illustrated in Charles Jencks's book *Post-modernism*. Take, for instance, 'Les Espaces d'Abraxas', a huge development of 600 apartments at Marne-la-Vallée, near Paris, built in 1978–82 to designs by Ricardo Bofill and his Taller de Arquitectura. From the road outside it is a machined-concrete front formed round gigantic Doric columns ten storeys high. Inside, the stacks of sitting-rooms form curious glass columns, crowned by roof-top cyprus trees, alluding perhaps to the leafy Corinthian order. They face a stepped grass area clearly reminiscent of an ancient Greek or Roman theatre. By putting up system-built mass housing Bofill is in the modernist tradition. Krier does not approve. Yet however oddly, this architecture is trying to say things about outside and inside, about living in communities, the relation of housing to nature, and indeed about the presence of the past in modern culture.

Stirling's Staatsgalerie at Stuttgart (1979–84) with the Doric 'porch'

The 'locus classicus' of post-modernism, James Stirling's Neuę Staatsgalerie at Stuttgart (1979–84) seems to be quite a different phenomenon again in that it is a public building. It manages, even better than Stirling's Clore gallery at the Tate, to be an integrated collection of architectures. Like the Getty it is built over a car park, and, like Abraxas, it has echoes of Greek and Roman architecture. Within the 'domeless dome', reminiscent of the Colosseum at Rome and of Hadrian's Villa at Tivoli, is a massy Doric portico which alludes to early Greece and to an earlier Hellenic revival.

Uncompromising Doric

The Villa dei Papyri was excavated in the mid-eighteenth century, not the mid-twentieth, and it is an instructive curiosity in the history of culture that there had not been many imitations before that at Malibu. Of course the excavations of Pompeii and Herculaneum had an impact on taste, though on interior

Piranesi's attempt to make the Doric temple at Paestum look elegant is only half successful

design more than external, coming as they did when there was a growing disillusionment with ancient Rome, its grandeur and ostentation. The time was ripe for something simpler, more sublime, more free – for Greece. Paradoxical as it may seem, neo-Hellenic architecture went hand in hand with Romanticism, which was in many ways a rebellion against the classical tradition in literature and in arts. The movement in architecture was not originally a going back to the Greeks so much as a going forward with them away from the 'classical' in the search for 'Nature'.

The Renaissance, in architecture as in everything else, was inspired by the rediscovery of Rome. Alberti, Palladio, all the great figures, turned to the remains of ancient Italy and to the books of Vitruvius, written in Latin in the Rome of Augustus in the late first century B.C. Vitruvius is founded on Greek architectural theory, but with Roman colouring and application. Many features that are Roman rather than Greek became standard in Renaissance and in 'Palladian' architecture. If I make a bald catalogue, there will inevitably be over-simplifications, but a list will give some idea of familiar features of classical architecture that are Roman rather than Greek. These include the decorative rather than functional use of columns, including pilasters; columns on pedestals; the mixing of orders; the predominance of the Corinthian order; triumphal arches; extensive use of arches, vaulting and domes. Those un-Greek features characterise much of the classical architecture of the sixteenth, seventeenth and eighteenth centuries.

By the middle of the eighteenth century we are in an age of architecture for aristocrats, grand and opulent. In Britain Robert Adam (overtly influenced by Pompeii) is ornate on a grand and on a small scale; in France Ange-Jacques Gabriel designs the Petit Trianon at Versailles and the Place de la Concorde in Paris. Building of this style and scale can be seen from Stuttgart to St Petersburg, from Warsaw to Boston.

The crisis is caught on paper by Giovanni Battista Piranesi, who published in Rome immensely influential (and now collectable) illustrations of his vision of ancient Roman architecture. He was working at the same time and in the same city as Winckelmann, who was reaching beyond towards a Greek simplicity to transcend Roman *Magnificenza*. The temples at Paestum, the ancient Greek city of Poseidonia south of Naples, had long stood disregarded in shallow sea-water; they then became overgrown with woods and were used for cattle and cheese-making. They were eventually made accessible after they had been discovered by chance by surveyors planning a new road for the King of Naples. In his

James 'Athenian' Stuart's watercolour of himself drawing the Erechtheum on the Acropolis in 1751

Stuart's painting of the 'Tower of the Winds' with the Acropolis behind. Only about two-thirds of the building was above ground in the eighteenth century.

left The 'Tower of the Winds' at Shugborough, Staffs (1765)

right The Radcliffe Observatory in Oxford (now part of Green College)

engravings of 1778 Piranesi elongated the columns to make them more elegant in an attempt to Romanise these very Greek structures. The squat Doric columns refuse to be made polite, however. Three years later Goethe was at first shocked by the 'crowded masses of stumpy pillars; but', he goes on, 'in less than an hour I found myself reconciled'.

Although there were Paestum and other relics of Greek architecture scattered through Magna Graecia (the former Greek cities of South Italy and Sicily), the turning-point in taste followed from an expedition from London to 'Turkey in Europe'. In 1751, when the Parthenon was still a mosque and the Doric columns of the Propylaia were half-buried, the Society of Dilettanti put up the funds for James 'Athenian' Stuart (as he became known) and Nicholas Revett to go to the town of Setines – Athens – to make really fine, detailed architectural drawings and to publish them in proper style. Their *Antiquities of Athens* (volume I published in 1762) remained definitive for a hundred years, and not only inspired buildings throughout the Western world but supplied architectural details for countless structures large and small.

In 1765 Stuart first translated his drawings of the 'Tower of the Winds' from the street of Turkish Athens (built in the first century B.C. and now known more precisely as the waterclock of Andronikos) into a replica in the middle of a lake in Lord Shugborough's park in Staffordshire. The Monument of Lysicrates was another favourite model; it was known then as the 'Lantern of Demosthenes' and used as a summer house in the garden of the Capuchin monastery. Once you know these two monuments, you will find them incorporated in neo-Hellenic buildings all over the world, from St Pancras New Church, London

The spire of St Pancras New Church (1817) incorporates the 'Tower of the Winds' and the 'Lantern of Demosthenes'. It also has two Caryatid porches.

The Monument of Lysicrates in 1988 (formerly the 'Lantern of Demosthenes')

(1817), to the Merchants' Exchange, Philadelphia (1832–4), and from the Radcliffe Observatory in Oxford to the porch of the Old Bull Hotel in Cambridge.

These elegant ornaments were relatively easily accommodated by conventional eighteenth-century taste. The central symbol of the revolution in taste was, however, the Doric column, whose uncompromising solidity and utility is the contradiction of an era of lightweight gentility. One reason why the Doric column took a long time to become acceptable was that the second volume of *Antiquities of Athens*, which included the Parthenon and Propylaia, did not appear until 1787; but by then taste was ready for it. In 1804 William Wilkins won the competition to design Downing College, Cambridge, with his Greek design defeating the Roman-style entry by James Wyatt. The recently constructed Howard Building at Downing is a prize example of post-modernist 'reproduction' architecture. Carl August Ehrenvärd's stocky model for a dockyard gate at Karlskrona in Sweden was, on the other hand, ahead of its time in 1785. It may at last have emerged, however, in James Stirling's Doric portico in Stuttgart.

Athenses of the North

The great age of creative Hellenic architecture came finally between 1790 and 1830. It was an age of turmoil and revolution, with new ideals of freedom and democracy – and even of new nations, above all the Germans seeking to establish their unity in opposition to the oppressive Roman classicism of France. The 1796 designs by Friedrich Gilly for a monument to Frederick the Great in

Gilly's plan for the Monument of Frederick the Great

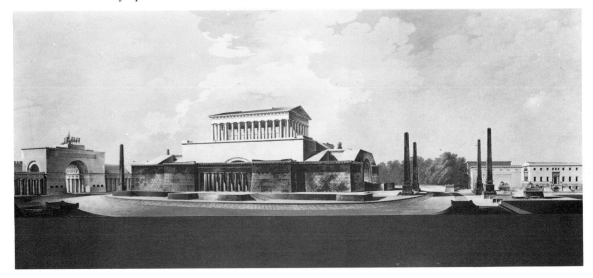

The Walhalla by von Klenze

the form of a Doric temple crowning a man-made acropolis, even though they were never carried through, were an inspiration to many in Germany. These included Leo von Klenze, who was chosen in 1816 by Ludwig, Prince of Bavaria, to design a central space for his capital, Munich, to include a Propylaia, as at Athens, and a home for his collection of Greek sculptures, the Glyptothek. The Königsplatz (Ludwig later became king) is still a central symbol of the cultural aspirations of the capital of Bavaria.

Another building commissioned by Ludwig from von Klenze was the Walhalla, above the Danube near Regensburg (1830–40). It is disturbing to find this Greek temple to German nationalism. 'The Walhalla was erected', said Ludwig, 'so that the German might depart from it more German and better than when he arrived.'

In England 'Grecian' architecture by no means won the day, and there was a fierce reaction well before the middle of the nineteenth century. Pugin hated it, and Ruskin in *The Stones of Venice* (1851) condemns it as 'base, unnatural, unfruitful, unenjoyable and impious . . . invented to make plagiarists of its architects, slaves of its workmen . . .' There may well be an element of national

The National Monument on Calton Hill, Edinburgh, left unfinished in 1830

pride, however, in the neo-Hellenic architecture of Edinburgh, 'Athens of the North', which is far more prominent and striking than that of London. Much of central Edinburgh was turned into a Greek city in the years 1820–60. The area around Calton Hill became a Caledonian Acropolis, including the National Monument, a life-size reproduction of the Parthenon, but in dour Scots granite, which was left unfinished in 1830, when the money ran out. Its duplicate in Tennessee, as seen in the film *Nashville*, is painted concrete, but complete.

The new Greek architecture made a special impact in Scandinavia and today

The New Stadium at Nuremberg by Albert Speer (1935). Hitler stands in front of this building in the illustration on page 214.

dominates the public buildings of Oslo and Helsinki. In Denmark Christian Frederick Hansen turned Copenhagen from a medieval and baroque town into a neo-classical capital. Two other Danish Hansens were responsible for much of the revival architecture in central Athens, above all the University and National Library. It is ironic that architects had to be imported from the far north to turn the newly independent home of the Parthenon into a Westernised capital city. After Athens, Theophilus Hansen went on to design the Parliament House in Vienna (1874–84); and this may well be one of the buildings which gave the young Adolf Hitler the ambition to be an architect. Later Hitler had his own architect, Albert Speer, draw up plans for a huge acropolis for his palace, neo-Classical rather than specifically Greek. None the less the Nazi 'Thingplätze', huge open areas built on the outskirts of cities for ceremonial occasions, are quite clearly based on the ancient Greek theatre. Some still survive, overgrown reminders of the sinister side of the tyranny of Greece over Germany.

Latrobe to Le Corbusier

All these European efflorescences must, however, take second place to the flowering of neo-Hellenic architecture in the United States. Throughout the eighteenth century it was Rome that was the real model for the emerging nation, in public building as in other spheres (as has been fully shown by Meyer Reinhold in *Classica Americana*). Jefferson's Monticello, though simple rather than ornate, was inspired by Roman building and ideals; the same goes for the main work on the Capitol (Roman name) which was initiated in 1792. The architect there who was most in sympathy with the Greeks – and who became Jefferson's favourite – was Benjamin Latrobe, a Yorkshireman who emigrated in 1796. The Supreme Court Chamber (rebuilt 1815–17) is explicitly Hellenic, with its squat Doric columns of sandstone; so is the House of Representatives, remodelled after the damage inflicted by the British in August 1814. Nearby, in the staircase vestibule, Latrobe designed corn-cob capitals to create a national variant on the acanthus of traditional Corinthian. In a letter to Latrobe, Jefferson calls the Capitol 'the first temple dedicated to the sovereignty of the people, embellishing with Athenian taste the cause of a nation looking far beyond the range of Athenian destinies'.

In America, as nowhere else, neo-Hellenic became a kind of national style. Greece as opposed to Rome stood for American independence as opposed to the imperial powers of the old world. In public buildings, not only Doric and Ionic columns but whole compositions based on Stuart and Revett were put up throughout the country. They outlasted the nineteenth century, long after they

The Jefferson Memorial in Washington D.C.

had become outmoded in Europe. Even in the present century of modernism two central Washington monuments – the Lincoln Memorial (1911–22, based on the Parthenon) and the Jefferson Memorial (1934–43) – are overtly Greek, though of that chaste white marmoreal style that never really existed. Yet, as any visitor to Washington knows, they are not ineffective. On a domestic scale as well neo-Hellenic extended from the mansions of the South to the cottages of New England, spread by manuals such as Asher Benjamin's *The American Builder's Companion* and *The Practical Home Carpenter*.

It might be a mistake, however, to overemphasise the moribundity of Greek revival architecture in Europe as opposed to America in the later nineteenth century. Two stories, both only recently rediscovered, strike out in different directions from the fascinating question of the extent of colour in ancient Greek buildings. Within a year of the invention of photography in 1839, N.-M. Lerebours sent daguerrotypists to Athens and quickly published *Excursions daguerriennes. Vues des monuments les plus remarquables du globe*. These and similar collections perpetuated the old picture of austere black and white. On the other

234

hand, the École des Beaux-Arts in Paris established in 1845 a 'Prix de Rome en Grèce' which inspired budding students over the next sixty years to produce plans and reconstructions of ancient Greek buildings and indeed of whole sites and cities. These were virtually unknown until they were shown in an amazing exhibition 'Paris–Rome–Athènes' in Paris in 1982, and later in Athens, Houston and New York. This revealed an exotically polychrome world conjured from the developing imaginations of young architects in counteraction to the cliché of pure white simplicity. While Stuart and Revett had observed evidence of coloured decoration, it was not until the middle of the nineteenth century that the polychromatists, led by the colourful character J.-I. Hitorff, won the day.

It was quite likely these exotic prize-pieces that the young Charles-Edouard Jeanneret was attacking when he inveighed against 'hot houses where blue hortensias and green chrysanthemums are forced and unclean orchids are cultivated'. He was better known as Le Corbusier, who more than anyone else epitomises the modern rejection of the classical. Yet throughout *Vers une*

A nineteenth-century French reconstruction of the colouring of the Parthenon

A mid-nineteenth-century photograph of the Parthenon by Stillman. Various Philhellenes had carved their names (long since cleaned up).

Architecture (1921) he constantly refers to the Parthenon as a measure of perfection, comparing and contrasting it, for example, with the design of a motor car. In 1933 he asserted that 'it is the Acropolis that made a rebel of me. One clear image will stand in my mind for ever; the Parthenon, stark, stripped, economical, violent, a clamorous outcry against a landscape of grace and terror – all strength and purity.' Le Corbusier returned, furthermore, to some sort of system of proportion based on that of the human body. He called his version of Polyclitus' *Canon* 'Le Modulor', made out of 'module' and 'section d'or'.

The new Atlantis?

Le Corbusier's constant reference to the Parthenon, and to no other Greek building, is a reminder that there are relatively few whose total architecture we know with any confidence. Nearly all of them are variations on the same few basic forms, and most of the great exemplars are temples, though there are some theatres, colonnades (stoas) and gymnasia. Greek architecture was never grandiose and huge as it was sometimes in Egypt, for example, as well as Rome. Domestic building was on an even smaller scale (contrast the Villa dei Papyri), and it contrasts strikingly with Les Espaces d'Abraxas and with the huge mass-housing products of modernism.

It was only towards the end of the nineteenth century, after the age of the Grecian revival was over, that archaeologists worked sufficiently slowly and systematically to establish the shape of whole cities, including their domestic housing. In the light of this Leon Krier says, 'I would find it enormously inspiring to reconstruct a Hellenistic town as it was. I think that would contain more lessons than any school of architecture in the last 300 years would have been able to teach – the way the buildings related, the way they are dimensioned . . .'

An outstanding example is Pergamum, near the central west coast of Turkey, described by Krier as 'probably the most beautiful place ever erected in the Western hemisphere'. Created in the third century B.C. by a dynasty of kings in the age after Alexander, its great public buildings were erected below the summit of a steep hill, evidently recalling the Acropolis at Athens – and even striving to outdo it. At the very top stood the royal palace, but the centrepiece of the layout as a whole is the theatre, symbol of civilisation and civic coherence. The building immediately above the theatre, the centrepiece, is The Library, which set out to rival that at Alexandria.

The most revealing scientific excavation for politically significant architecture has been the Agora at Athens. ('Agora' means simply 'gathering-place'.) In the

A reconstruction of the Acropolis of Pergamum. The Library stands above the theatre.
The remains of the great Altar of Zeus on the right are now in Berlin.

age of Stuart and Revett this whole area was covered by the streets of the
modern town and there was little to record other than the temple of Hephaestus,
known then as the Theseum. The American School at Athens bought the whole
site and since 1931 has excavated it with exemplary care. It has emerged that
around the main open space were the council chamber and other administrative
buildings, the records office, shops, stoas, along with important altars and
statues. The Agora really was a civic centre, and must have been thronged by
people on political, legal, commercial, religious and social business. It reflected
and underpinned the values of its society, just as the downtown banks and
shopping-centres do today.

A plan of the Agora at Athens

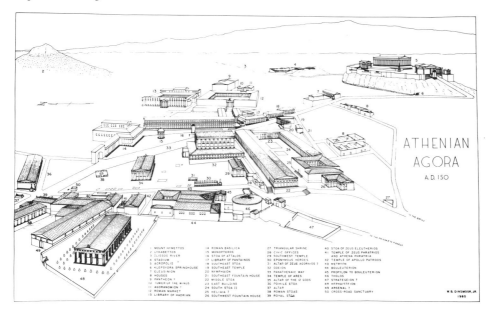

The inauguration of Atlantis in 1987, painted by Carl Laubin

Our greater understanding of the political dimension of Greek architecture might not have come too late to affect twentieth-century architecture, even though on an intimate scale inapplicable to the commercially-dominated centres of our vast modern conurbations. This is the view of Leon Krier. He has recently been working on a real rather than a utopian scheme, a hundred-acre site at Seaside Town, in Florida. This is an attempt to return to a human scale and to foster a community which is both architecturally and socially integrated. There is no zoning of work, housing, commerce, culture and so forth, and everything is in walking distance. The citizens of Seaside are not forced to abandon their cars, they simply do not need them. They are not forced to talk to each other across the fence, but, given the architecture, it is hard to resist.

Krier's latest project is the most interesting outbreak of Greek Fire in contemporary architecture. He has plans to build a city called Atlantis, named after the ideal community lost beneath the ocean, as told in Plato's *Timaeus*. It is to be completed by the year 2000 on Tenerife in the Canary Islands in the Atlantic. Atlantis is conceived as an integrated city with more than 100 separate buildings. The site is the slope of a hill rising to some 635 metres above sea level. The topmost part, to be called the Acropolis, will have as its centrepiece the art museum – not unlike The Library at Pergamum.

Even more significant is the civic centre on the next level down, with a long stoa dominating the main part of the city below, the Greek-shaped open-air theatre, and the surrounding landscape. This civic space Krier calls 'the Agora', openly declaring his roots. 'To build a town which is no longer just housing or an office block, or an industrial zone, but is a real town – that is an unbelievably inspiring thought.'

Coherent cities would reflect a coherent society. What the Greeks have to offer the city-builders of the next century is not Toytown bits of columns, but the prompting that architecture is worth thinking about, that the placing and grouping of a city centre declares the values of the society which uses it.

War

INSPIRATION AND DANGER

> Many people say: 'Yesterday's rain can't wet
> us now.' It is this insensitivity which we have
> to fight. Its most extreme form is death.
>
> Bertolt Brecht (1952)

IS MAN CAPABLE OF LIVING without war? History is against us. As long as memory goes back, there has always been war. The destruction of Troy is virtually the first recording of Western literacy. Troy has become the archetype of the city in flames. A city is a centre of humanity; it not only contains government and commerce, it also protects the storehouses of memory – archives, museums, libraries. Yet paper, film, discs, like people, burn.

Col Paul Tibbetts, pilot of the B-29 bomber Enola Gay, recalled 6 August 1945: 'I saw a perfectly outlined city, clear in every detail, coming in . . . the navigator came up, and looking over my shoulder he said "Yes, that's Hiroshima" . . . the bombadier says "It's just sitting there . . ."' The books of Hiroshima, like the people, were vapourised by the heat, they vanished into thin air. One person left a kind of reverse shadow, recorded on the granite steps of a bank as a lighter patch in human shape when he or she eclipsed the full blast of the heat. With these words he or she is recalled. Similarly the recollection of Troy is kept alive by the very flames that destroyed it. At the end of Euripides' tragedy *Trojan Women* the conquered city is set alight, and the women, about to set sail to a life of slavery, lament and call on Troy herself:

> you soon will fall to the earth and lose your name . . .
> The very name of the country will be obliterated.
> Everything is dispersed, and Troy no longer exists.

Yet every time these words are read or performed, they are falsified.

242

Hiroshima, August 1945

The holocaust of memory

If there is an all-out Third World War it is unlikely that the memory even of ancient Greece, let alone Troy, will survive. There are underground silos deep in the soil of Greece itself, waiting like the Trojan Horse to release their destruction. Man now has at his disposal over 12,000 megatons, a million times the Hiroshima bomb – the equivalent of 2.5 *tons* of TNT for every person in the world. Up to half the human race, it is reckoned, would be immediate victims of a full nuclear war, without speculating on longer-term effects. Tony Harrison has compared the picture of women dancing on top of a nuclear silo at Greenham Common with the Muses dancing on Mount Helicon: 'This is a mountain where our extinction is stored, where even Memory, the mother of the Muses, won't survive to make a story of our sufferings like that of Hecuba and the women of Troy – an extinction that will mean no going back to civilisation even for one learned in Classics. There will be no emphasis, no significance in life, no dance, no Helicon, no Muses.'

The very word 'war' in 'nuclear war' means something quite different from anything that has gone before. 'Everything is changed,' said Einstein in 1945, 'except our way of thinking.' War still conjures up images of individual fighters face to face, of the opportunity for personal bravery, of the opportunity for a noble death that will be personally remembered. War is the means to glory.

Indeed ancient Greek attitudes contribute to the persistence of this image:

> Some talk of Alexander and some of Hercules
> Of Hector and Lysander, and such great men as these . . .

William Blake burst out against Homer, 'The Classics! It is the Classics . . . that desolate Europe with wars!'

The Trojan prince Hector is immortalised, even for the British Grenadiers, thanks to Homer's epic poem, the *Iliad*. Homer was a bard in Asia Minor in about 700 B.C. He may have learned the new art of writing himself, or he may have dictated his poem, or disciples may have preserved it by re-performing it – whatever happened, what is certain is that the poem was somehow written down. The *Iliad* is to all intents and purposes our earliest Greek record in writing; it is also arguably the greatest work of all Greek literature.

The *Iliad* is a poem of war, although through its similes, its glimpses of domestic life and of the past and the future, it is about much else in human life as well. Battle is narrated for hour after hour; men are killed by the score in gory detail. The horrific physicality of death is personal. 'Achilles struck Demoleon on the temple, through his bronze-cheeked helmet. The bronze of the helmet

Stephen McKenna's *O Ilium* (1982): the fragmentation of the violence of war

could not hold, but the spear point pushed on through it and smashed the bone, and all his brains were spattered inside.' The horror is balanced by the glory. When Andromache, wife of Hector, begs him not to return to battle, he replies:

> I would feel terrible shame before the men of Troy and the women with their trailing dresses if like a coward I skulk away from the fighting. Nor is that what my own heart urges, because I have learned always to be brave and to fight in the forefront of the Trojans, winning great glory for my father and for myself

And when he eventually faces death at the hands of Achilles, he says: 'Even so, let me not die ingloriously, without a fight, but with some great deed done that future men will hear of.'

This is not a war of chivalric single combat or of professional soldiers well away from civilians. Hector's death means that Troy will go up in flames, her men and boys will be killed, and her women taken off into slavery. This was the fate of a Greek city defeated in war. We are now once again back in an era of total war involving soldier and civilian alike.

The violent teacher

Many, many ancient Greeks died in battle, like Hector, like Achilles. They were not good at coexisting in peace, at least not during the great creative era of between 700 and 150 B.C. (the next 500 years, under Roman rule, were comparatively peaceful and unenterprising). The fiercely independent city-states found it hard to tolerate each other without coming to blows, so that the history of Greece is largely a history of war, mostly of Greek against Greek. Most wars are fought along national or racial lines, but the ancient Greeks, despite all that they had in common, fought wars among themselves.

It is true that some of the cities united to meet the westward expansion of the Persian empire, and their panhellenic victory was indeed a turning-point in world history. The glory of that struggle is stirringly recorded by Herodotus, the man who first called his narrative 'history' (*historia* meant 'enquiries'). Just as Homer recorded the glories of Troy, so Herodotus was determined that his great war should not go unrecorded. Yet less than 50 years later Athens and Sparta, the two most powerful cities, embarked along with their allies on a long and bloody war against each other. It is terrible to think how this drained the energy of Athens in the great age which produced tragedy, Socrates and the buildings of the Acropolis. It is reckoned that she lost over half of all her citizens in the 30 years between 432 and 403 B.C.

The history of the Peloponnesian War finds an appropriately severe and penetrating recorder in the exiled Athenian Thucydides, unquestionably one of the great historians of all time. George Marshall said that no-one could understand the Second World War in our own time unless they had read him. Thucydides too wished to record great events; but he had no illusions about war: 'In peace and prosperity both states and individuals are activated by higher motives because they do not fall under the dominion of imperious necessities. But war, which takes away the comfortable provision of daily life, is a violent teacher and assimilates men's characters to their conditions . . .' War, Thucydides believed like Homer, was a prerequisite of human society – 'the ultimate constraint by which all settled societies protect themselves', as John Keegan puts it. He also believed that human nature will under necessity use ultimate force. The Athenians liked to think of themselves as the most humane of the Greeks; yet under the stress of this violent teacher they voted in 416 B.C., after full democratic debate, to massacre the men and enslave the women of the

Ingres' first important painting (1801) illustrates the ninth book of the *Iliad*, when three representatives of the Greeks come to plead with Achilles to return to the field

weak island of Melos because it remained neutral. The Athenians, Thucydides warns us, pushed the button.

Thucydides also goes on to observe what happens to language under political stress, especially the stress of conflict. 'The meanings of words have no longer the same relation to things but are changed. Reckless daring is held to be loyal courage; prudent delay is the excuse of a coward; moderation is the disguise of weakness; to know everything is to do nothing. Frantic energy is the true quality of a man; the lover of violence is always trusted and his opponent suspected.' This is a forerunner of George Orwell's 'Newspeak', and of contemporary 'Nukespeak'. This passage is regarded as so subversive, even now, in Czechoslovakia, that it is circulated in *samizdat* form by dissidents. It is typical of Greece to have produced *both* the terrible war *and* Thucydides' analysis. It leaves us, however, with the frightening question of whether the creative energy could have existed – can exist – without the war.

The original genius

Are vitality and creativity somehow connected with bellicosity? Could there have been Greek civilisation without this restless obsession with fighting? The place of Homer, especially the *Iliad*, in Greek culture accentuates these disturbing questions. While the cliché that Homer was 'the Bible of the Greeks' is misleading – his was in no way a sacred or unquestionable text – he was central to their basic education, and at least as familiar as Shakespeare is to us, if not more so.

The two great poems, the *Iliad* and the *Odyssey*, seem to have gained this centrality in the middle of the sixth century B.C., about 100 to 150 years after their composition; and they retained it for the rest of the classical era. For over 1,000 years 'The Poet', as he was known, remained a constant point of reference for poetry and for painting, cited and discussed, almost automatically, by philosophers, critics and historians. Greek tragedy could never have flowered without Homer as its pioneer. He is also the direct and explicit model for another of the world's most significant works of literature, the *Aeneid* of Virgil, written in Rome in the 20s B.C. Colin Macleod claimed that Virgil was Homer's greatest literary critic. In the *Aeneid* Troy is rebuilt at Rome, but only out of the ashes of violence and of compromised principles. Her foundation is glorious but tragic.

The reception of Homer – the submersion and re-emergence of his flame in various forms, some dark, some bright, some dangerous, some benign – is an epic worth telling. From A.D. 500 to the fifteenth century he was read only by

Achilles tries in vain to grasp the dream of the dead Patroclus. One of several striking paintings and drawings which Homer inspired from Henry Fuseli.

the educated élite in the Byzantine East. In the West there were, however, romances set in Troy: the most popular, the *Roman de Troie* by Benoît de Sainte-Maure (*circa* 1160), was imitated and plagiarised in almost every European language, including eventually Greek.

The Renaissance rediscovered the huge esteem in which Homer had been held, and duly paid homage, or at least lip service. While the first experiments in translating the *Iliad* into English by George Chapman influenced Shakespeare's *Troilus and Cressida*, it is more a Roman play than Greek. The scholar and critic J. C. Scaliger was at least honest when, idolising Virgil by constantly comparing Homer unfavourably with him, he said in 1561: 'It is ridiculous, it is stupid, it is Homeric.' Dryden had to insist that Aeneas is a far more admirable model than any in Homer; and in 1714 La Motte published in French an improved *Iliad*, purged of barbarisms like the impropriety of the Gods, the discourtesy of Achilles, and the heroes' self-catering.

By the beginning of 'La Querelle des anciens et des modernes', or the Battle of the Books, in the late seventeenth century, it was openly recognised that Homer was too rough and direct for refined taste, and he supplied the prime example of the outmoded primitiveness of the ancient world. Yet one hundred years later Homer is almost universally heroised – even apotheosised in Wedgwood's pottery and in Ingres' painting. Pope's translations into rhymed couplets (1720 and 1725) were in many ways the last glimmering of the Latinate

Flaxman's design of *The Apotheosis of Homer* on a Wedgwood urn

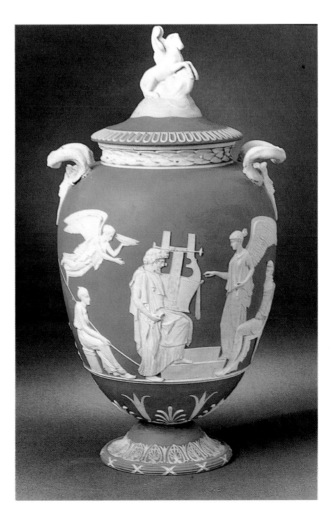

Homer, with Athena still Minerva, and with a Roman triumphal arch on the title-page (contrast the purely Greek title-page printed in Oxford in 1800). By 1781 the great German translation of Johann Heinrich Voss (he also translated Shakespeare in later life) into what have been called 'megalithic hexameters' could hardly be more different from Pope. Similarly Keats in 1816 rejects Pope for the unsweetened bluntness of Chapman:

> Yet never did I breathe its pure serene
> Till I heard Chapman speak out loud and bold.

Homer is at the core of the Greek Renaissance. As Winckelmann catalysed the great change in art and Stuart and Revett the change in architecture so the key figure for Homer was Robert Wood. Though he visited Turkey and the Troad in the 1740s, he did not publish *An Essay on the Original Genius of Homer* until 1767 (and then only privately; posthumous public edition in 1775). Wood regarded as virtues the very features of Homer that polite criticism had condemned, and in keeping with this he criticises Pope for obscuring Homer's direct simplicity. Above all he commended Homer for his *truth*: he lived and worked in reality, in a certain time and place. 'The *Iliad* has new beauties on the banks of the Scamander', he claimed.

Wood's work was extraordinarily influential, especially in Germany (or what would become Germany). At this very time Herder was advocating the primitive and natural, standing up for Shakespeare (as opposed to Racine), for folk song, and for Ossian, that brilliant forgery of primitive Scots epic by James Macpherson. It was Herder who persuaded Goethe to embark on reading Homer in 1770. 'The Sun of Homer dawned for us afresh,' Goethe wrote later, 'very much in keeping with the spirit of the times.' He even embarked on an epic, *Achilleis*, picking up from the last line of the *Iliad*. After centuries of condescension Homer was regarded as the sublime archetype for a new age of direct honesty without laboured moralising, 'naive' rather than 'sentimental' in Schiller's terms.

Once the nineteenth century settled down to respectability, Homer was assimilated in the system and became an idol of orthodox education. He sits in the centre of the poetry frieze on the Albert Memorial, even more prominent than Shakespeare, Milton and Dante. As education in Britain was more gentlemanly and amateur than in Germany, so it produced a more curious collection of Homeric followers. For George Grote, the influential radical, Homer was an ally against the Christian establishment. Gladstone, on the other hand, wrote seven books devoted in the main to showing how the bard was in effect a Christian. It must be said that many at the time regarded Gladstone's Homeric lucubrations as loony. Matthew Arnold, as first Professor of Poetry at

Oxford in 1860, gave his lectures 'On Translating Homer', offering the *Iliad* and *Odyssey* as the touchstone of the grand style, 'when a noble nature, poetically gifted, treats with simplicity and with severity a serious subject'. His scapegoat was F. W. Newman (brother of the future Cardinal) who, still stuck in the mode of Ossian, had written a quaint, ballad-like version. That anti-Victorian Victorian Samuel Butler (author of *Erewhon* and *The Way of All Flesh*) not only translated the poems, but argued in *The Authoress of the Odyssey* (a book which James Joyce liked) that the *Odyssey* had been composed by a woman.

O hell of ships and cities

Homer was deeply entrenched in the Victorian public schools, the world of the competitive spirit and of Tom Brown's schooldays, as is entertainingly illustrated by Richard Jenkyns. This complacent glow was, however, suddenly to break into lurid flame in 1915. For nearly a year the Allies fought a desperate and unsuccessful campaign – 'Gallipoli' – to capture the Dardanelles from the Turks

A trench during the Gallipoli campaign in 1915

and to open up the route to Russia. Troy stood near the mouth of the Dardanelles (or Hellespont) – anyone travelling there from modern Çanakkale will have seen the series of military cemeteries along the shore. This locality was not lost on the English public school men who sailed with Sir Ian Hamilton taking Homer in their kitbags.

Rupert Brooke began to write on the voyage:

> They say Achilles in the darkness stirred . . .
> And Priam and his fifty sons
> Wake all amazed, and hear the guns,
> And shake for Troy again.

He died of blood poisoning on 23 April, and was buried on Skyros, the island where Achilles was lurking when the Greeks came to fetch him to Troy. There are ironies in his never reaching Lemnos, where the British Fleet anchored on 25 April before the final assault. Lemnos is where the Greek hero Philoctetes was abandoned, suffering from a poisoned foot, when Agamemnon sailed for Troy; and Lemnos is where the Turks signed the armistice on 30 October 1918 on board the *HMS Agamemnon*.

Patrick Shaw-Stewart, a brilliant Etonian, turned to the *Iliad* to face his own impending death at Gallipoli:

> O hell of ships and cities
> Hell of men like me
> Fatal second Helen
> Why must I follow thee?
>
> Achilles came to Troyland
> And I to Chersonese:
> He turned from wrath to battle,
> And I from three days' peace.
>
> Was it so hard, Achilles,
> So very hard to die?
> Thou knowest and I know not –
> So much the happier I.
>
> I will go back this morning
> From Imbros over the sea;
> Stand in the trench, Achilles,
> Flame-capped, and fight for me.

The ballistics of the mortar-shell and the machine-gun with the mathematics of conic sections (first established by the Greeks) gave war a different dimension. Increased accuracy and firepower led to a war of industrial production, a war on both the Home Front and the Western Front which was moved 10 yards at the incredible loss of 10,000 lives. I believe that in *Strange Meeting* Wilfred Owen's 'I am the enemy you killed, my friend' echoes Achilles to Lycaon in *Iliad* 21, 'So die, friend, you also'. As the First World War dragged on however, Homer became less and less appropriate. Trench warfare was too far away from the 'trench' where Achilles stood 'flame-capped' in the *Iliad*. John Buchan recalled that 'to speak of glory seemed a horrid impiety. That was perhaps why I could not open Homer'.

All too soon after 1918 the Third Reich was happy to invoke the precedent of Greece when it served a purpose, and to remodel the idea of the heroic warrior and of Alexander the Great, who impressed both Hitler and his would-be assassin von Stauffenberg. 'Some talk of Alexander . . .'

If Homer was behind Hitler's troops as they went into battle, he was also to hand in defeat. George Steiner pointed out: 'Every time we destroy a city, every time we see people under burning roofs fleeing for their lives, Homer becomes immediate. In the first production on a Berlin stage in 1945 against a photo-background of the great gutted city and of fire bombs, they read from the *Iliad* because there was no contemporary text even half as contemporary. So in that sense he is at the beginning both of our sense of war as a constant central masculine activity and of the horror and tragedy which it visits upon other human beings.' This may help to explain why Moses Finley's *The World of Odysseus* (1954) regarded Homer as an inhuman and pre-moral poet, and why the great historian Arnaldo Momigliano described the *Iliad* as number one of the world's most dangerous books. Both were Jews with good reason to be aware of Germany's formative influences.

An intriguing difference or imbalance in the interpretation of the *Iliad* has grown up in recent times. The most potent representative of one side is Simone Weil, the French-Jewish socialist and religious thinker who died aged 34 in Kent in 1943 (a few miles and a few days distant from the place and time that I was born). *L'Iliade ou le Poème de la Force* was published in Marseilles in 1940 and in Mary McCarthy's translation in New York in 1945. It is not the sentimental apology of a scholar but the direct response of a passionate activist to Hitler's invasion of France.

Weil claims in her opening sentence, 'The true hero, the true subject, the centre of the *Iliad* is force', and yet also maintains that 'as the gospels are the last marvellous expression of the Greek genius, so the *Iliad* is the first'. She reconciles these claims by arguing that the *Iliad* is always aware of the victim as much as the victor, so that force does not triumph. 'Subjection to force is the

Berlin in July 1945 (with the neo-Hellenic Brandenburg Gate still standing)

common lot . . . no-one in the *Iliad* is spared by it, as no-one on earth is. No-one who succumbs to it is by virtue of this regarded with contempt.' The poem does not spell out any anti-war, let alone pacifist, message; it is rather its lack of sententiousness, its balance, that leaves the lesson implicit. Simone Weil concludes her essay: 'Nothing the peoples of Europe have produced is worth the first known poem that appeared among them. Perhaps they will yet rediscover the epic genius, when they learn that there is no refuge from fate, learn not to admire force, not to hate the enemy, nor to scorn the unfortunate. How soon this will happen is another question.' It has not happened yet.

In my view her words are needed as much now as in 1940; yet Weil's essay has also attracted patronising and even hostile reactions. Some regard it as a high priority to avoid sentimentality and the self-righteous 'liberal humanism' that Weil typifies. This attitude is epitomised by Christopher Logue's *War Music* (subtitled 'An account of books 16 to 19 of Homer's *Iliad*') which has been performed to several settings over the last 10 years, most powerfully by Alan

Howard. It is vivid, gripping stuff, evoking a terrifying life-force which is hungry for death, and which glories in the physiology of fatal wounds. George Steiner shares Logue's attitude: 'There is something in the descriptions of battle, the sheer beauty of combat, the sheer choreography of a great swordsman or javelin man or a man leaping from his chariot, the marvellous supple beauty of a young body in mortal encounter . . . of Nürnberg Stadium marching under Hitler – the sheer maddening, very Greek beauty of that occasion, with the great torches in the night – a very Greek moment, that. It embarrasses us, yet we have to face it in order to read Homer rightly.' The open question is whether the *Iliad* relishes them as Logue does or regrets them as Weil does.

The burning memory of Achilles

No-one who has actually read the *Iliad* could claim that it is a poem of chauvinistic triumph in which admirable Greeks triumph over monstrous barbarians, to live gloriously ever after. The two finest things in the *Iliad* are both doomed: while not actually narrated within the poem, the death of Achilles and the sack of Troy are repeatedly and vividly foreshadowed. Their glory is indivisible from their destruction, the waste of all that valuable humanity.

Achilles is the most effective killer in the *Iliad*. 'As monstrous fire rages through the deep valleys on a parched mountainside, and the thick forest burns as the wind drives the flames billowing all over, so Achilles stormed with his spear all over the field like some inhuman being, driving men on and killing them: and the black earth ran with blood.' It is this side of him which led the East German writer Christa Wolf to pick on Achilles in her novel *Kassandra* (1983) to epitomise the hatefulness and hatred of war. Near the beginning Cassandra, the Trojan princess, about to die as a slave at Mycene, thinks, 'O yes it is gone, my plump juicy hatred. I know one name that could awaken it, but I prefer to leave that name unthought as yet. If only I could. If only I could wipe out the name not only from my memory, but from the memory of all men living. If I could burn it out of our heads – I would not have lived in vain. Achilles.'

Yet the Achilles of the *Iliad* ends on a note of reconciliation, sharing some insight into the human condition with Priam, the King of Troy, and teaching the old man how to live with bereavement. Homer's Achilles (as opposed to the stereotype) has a special maturity and penetration which are indivisible from his knowledge of his early death.

So there was a partial appropriateness in Alexander's veneration for Achilles. When he crossed the Hellespont to the Troad in 334 B.C., he paid homage at the (supposed) tomb of Achilles; and he is said to have carried a copy of the *Iliad*

The Trojan Horse was the star attraction at Astley's Theatre in 1833

with him in the King of Persia's casket on his conquering path through Samarkand, the Hindu Kush, and the Punjab as far as the Oxus and the Indus. Alexander died at Babylon in 323 B.C., aged 32. If we look for a contemporary Achilles we might think of Rambo. 'So he stormed all over the field like some inhuman being, drawing men on and killing them. And the black earth ran with blood.' But Rambo does not die young; and he does not weep and eat with Priam.

Homer's Troy is a fine and civilised city; Hector, Aeneas, Priam are admirable men; Zeus himself admits that it is his favourite city. The gods will destroy it, none the less, and will exterminate Priam's line because of the crime of Paris who stole Helen under cover of hospitality in Menelaus' house. Over the centuries the Trojans have, indeed, been more widely perceived as sympathetic or kindred than the Greeks. Several cities in Italy claimed fugitive Trojans as their founders, above all Rome and Aeneas. There was even a story, which finds its way into Spenser's *Faerie Queene*, that the ancient British kings were descended from Brute, a descendant of Aeneas who founded London or New

Troy, Troynovant (an echo of the ancient British tribe Trinovantes). Similarly Theodoric, King of the Ostrogoths, was given Trojan ancestors back in the sixth century, and later the Francs claimed descent from Francus the Trojan. So Christa Wolf is heir to a long tradition, including Virgil, when she tells her novel from a Trojan perspective.

The sack of Troy in the *Iliad* is vividly foreseen, especially in association with the death of Hector. When the lamentation for him goes through the city 'it was just exactly as if all of beetling Ilium was glowing with fire from top to bottom'. The stories surrounding the event reverberate through art and literature: the Trojan Horse, Laocoön wreathed with serpents, Aeneas' escape with Anchises on his shoulders, Andromache captured and her boy Astyanax thrown from the walls, Helen's mollification of Menelaus by baring her peerless breasts. There were also the two worst acts of sacrilege: the rape (or attempted rape) of Cassandra by Ajax (not the great Ajax), even though she clung to the statue of Athena, is retold on the penultimate page of *Kassandra*; and Priam was slaughtered by Achilles' son Neoptolemus, alias Pyrrhus, despite his refuge at the altar of Zeus. Of the many paintings inspired by the sack of Troy in ancient

A superb evocation of the sack of Troy by Adam Elsheimer. In the foreground Aeneas escapes with his father Anchises on his shoulders.

Though fragmentary, this cup decorated with scenes of the sack of Troy is still very striking (painted in Athens in about 500 B.C.). At the bottom Eros hovers between Helen and Menelaus as he drops his sword. (By kind permission of the Getty Museum, this is the first publication of this painting.)

times, possibly the most powerful to survive is on a huge cup, painted in about 500 B.C., and acquired by the J. Paul Getty Museum in Malibu. It is, I suggest, no coincidence that the rape of Cassandra, the death of Priam and the charming of Helen are all aligned on the vertical axis. It is worth remembering that neither Ajax nor Neoptolemus saw old age, indeed not many of the victorious Greeks died in their beds.

The death of Priam inspired one of the most memorable passages in Virgil's *Aeneid*, culminating:

> to the very altar stones Pyrrhus drew Priam, trembling and slipping in his own son's streaming blood, and wound his left hand in his hair while with the right he raised high the flashing sword and buried it to the hilt in his

side. Such was the close of Priam's fortunes; such the doom that by fate befell him – to see Troy in flames, he once lord of so many tribes and lands, the monarch of Asia. He lies a trunk upon the shore, a head severed from the shoulders, a nameless corpse.

By the time of the player king in *Hamlet* the scene can be used as a showpiece for old-fashioned ham acting:

> First Player   *When she saw Pyrrhus make malicious sport*
>   *In mincing with his sword her husband's limbs,*
>   *The instant burst of clamour that she made –*
>   *Unless things mortal move them not at all –*
>   *Would have made milch the burning eyes of heaven,*
>   *And passion in the gods.*
> Polonius   Look! wh'er he has not turned his colour and has tears in's eyes.

This provokes the famous question from Hamlet:

> What's Hecuba to him or he to Hecuba
> That he should weep for her?

Yesterday's rain: from *The Trojans* of Berlioz to Tippett's *King Priam* we go on weeping for Hecuba.

Where Troy Town stood

The obliteration of Troy exerted a special fascination even in ancient times. In Shakespeare's day there was a popular ballad with the refrain:

> Waste lie those walls that were so good
> And corn now grows where Troy Town stood

This is perhaps echoed in Cressida's lines:

> When time is old and hath forgot itself,
> When water drops have worn the stones of Troy,
> And blind oblivion swallow'd cities up . . .

The same conceit appealed to Byron:

> High barrows, without marble or a name
> A vast untill'd and mountain-skirted plain
> And Ida in the distance still the same
> And old Scamander (if 'tis he), remain:

> The situation seems still form'd for fame –
> A hundred thousand men might fight again
> With ease; but where I sought for Ilion's walls
> The quiet sheep feeds, and the tortoise crawls.

Ever since the first Western explorer of Greece in modern times, Cyriac of Ancona in 1444, there has been an obsession with pinning down the actual site of Troy. This fascination with the historicity of the Trojan war has continued from Robert Wood in the eighteenth century right down to Michael Wood's television series *In Search of the Trojan War* which attracted huge audiences in 1984. The travellers and scholars disputed for 400 years and more after Cyriac, most of them thinking that the substantial ruins of the much later city of Alexandria Troas were the city of Priam. In the nineteenth century attention turned to the great mound of Hissarlik. Heinrich Schliemann, banker, enthusiast, egoist and fantasist, began his excavation in 1870, and wrote in 1872:

> In conclusion, I flatter myself with the hope that, as a reward for my enormous expenses and all my privations, annoyances and sufferings in this wilderness, the civilised world will acknowledge my right to re-christen this sacred locality. In the name of divine Homer I baptise it with that name of immortal renown, which fills the heart of everyone with joy and enthusiasm: I give it the name of TROY and ILIUM, and I call the acropolis, where I am writing these lines, by the name of *Pergamus of Troy*.

Schliemann's excavations of Troy in progress. The Dardanelles can just be seen in the distance.

Schliemann dug too fast and greedily, destroying much important evidence and making huge errors of chronology; he made such a mess that it is not easy now to distinguish bits of Troy from his throw-away tips. None the less, it is a numinous and powerful spot. Its power lies, surely, in the imagination not the reality: despite Michael Wood, it would not matter if in reality there never was a Trojan War. Troy, with its almost constant breeze, as in 'windy Ilium', has a palpable aura, not because of what did or did not actually take place there, but because of what has been imagined of it and made out of it over the centuries.

'Since 1945 past and present are the same'

Why should Christa Wolf, a writer in East Berlin in the 1980s, turn to Troy? Part of the answer emerges from the essays 'Conditions of a Narrative: Cassandra' which accompany her novel. She lives in a city divided by a military wall, a city which might ignite the Third World War. She lives in a world where, as in Thucydides' analysis, words can be used upside-down: 'cold war', 'military intelligence', 'mutually assured destruction'. In a world run by realists who are obsessed by defence and with victory, she asks when all this started: the answer is that it has been like this ever since Homer. Searching for a woman's mode of expression, she finds her voice in the dispossessed and possessed prophetess Cassandra, Cassandra who has to tell her story before she dies. 'Real history is unsuited to memory, myths are not', she writes. If we are to enjoy memory, if there is to be anything to remember, then we must turn away from those masculine ways of thinking which lead to war.

Everything has changed except our ways of thinking. Is there any way that we – especially we men – can change ways of thinking that are first recorded in Homer? The paradox is that our best lead may be not contemporary science or modern history, but myth – Troy and Troy's women, whose lamentations close the *Iliad*. Euripides' play *Trojan Women* (first performed in 415 B.C.) dramatises the fates of Cassandra, Andromache, and above all of Hecuba, when they are about to be shipped off to slavery. It is a grim two hours which paints a poor picture of the conquering Greeks. It is, in effect, an indictment of male assertion and of the cult of victory.

Trojan Women was given no special attention before this century. It is hardly a coincidence that in 1915 it was being put on in the German version by the young Franz Werfel (set as an opera by Aribert Reimann in 1986), in London in Gilbert Murray's translation; and by travelling players in the American Midwest in support of the women's peace movement. The version by Jean-Paul Sartre, which cut out the Greek gods, made a big impact in Paris in 1964, where it was

Euripides' *Trojan Women* by the Schwerin State Theatre from East Germany

Trojan Women by the Japanese Suzuki company. The baby Astyanax is about to be taken from Hecuba.

directed by Michael Cacoyannis, who went on to make a film in 1971 (with Katharine Hepburn as Hecuba) at the height of the Vietnam war. Sartre had Algeria in mind; but when the Japanese director Tadashi Suzuki staged a version of the play in 1977 (since performed world-wide, including at the 1984 Los Angeles Olympics), it was inevitable that the gutted city of Troy should be equated with Hiroshima. It would have been a kind of betrayal had it not been.

I saw that unforgettable Suzuki *Trojan Women* at the Delphi Festival in 1985. In the same year there was a Greek production in modern dress designed and directed by the painter Iannis Tsarouchis, and an East German production (of Sartre's version) by the Schwerin State Theatre, part of their 'Discoveries of Antiquity' project. In this staging the Trojan women were inside a huge wire-mesh cage like animals at a zoo; and the Greeks came with the keys to take them away. It was at that very performance on Thursday 13 June 1985 that Tony Harrison had a crucial idea for his version of the *Trojan Women* (one half of *The*

Common Chorus). The set is to be divided by a single wire fence, the fence of a nuclear missile base such as Greenham Common. But the women are *outside* the fence: it is the warders hurling obscene abuse at them who are the prisoners. The women put on versions of *Trojan Women* and of Aristophanes' comedy *Lysistrata* in an attempt to induce a new way of thinking, to keep memory alive. Yesterday's rain, yesterday's tears.

In Harrison's *Lysistrata* the heroine, to be played by Glenda Jackson (it is hoped), supplies the thought, the blending of the real and the imaginary, with a special charge of power.

> Since Hiroshima what we've done
> paradoxically's to make the whole earth one.
> We all look down the barrel of the same cocked gun.
> One target, in one united fate
> nuked together in some hyperstate.
> So Greece is Greenham, Greenham Greece,
> Poseidon is Poseidon, not just for this piece.
> Not just all places, all human ages too
> are dependent on the likes of us and you.

The women outside the fence at Greenham Common

In the Third World War we'll destroy
not only modern cities but the memory of Troy.
Stories that shaped the spirit of our race
are held in the balance in this missile base.
Remember, if you can, that with man goes the mind
that might have made sense of the Hist'ry of Mankind.
It's a simple thing to grasp, when we're all dead
there'll be no further pages to be read.
Not even leaflets, and no peace plays like these
no post-holocaust Aristophanes.
So if occasionally some names are new
just think of the ground that's under you.
If we're destroyed then we
take with us Athens 411 B.C.
The world till now up to the last minute
and every creature who was ever in it,
go when we go, everything men did or thought
never to be remembered, absolutely nought.
No war memorials with the names of dead on
because memory won't survive your Armageddon.
So Lysistrata, Glenda Jackson, it's one name.
Since 1945 past and present are the same.
And it doesn't matter if it's 'real' or a play –
Imagination and reality both go the same way.
So don't say it's just a bunch of ancient Greeks.
It's *their* tears that will be flowing down *your* cheeks.

In his similes Homer sometimes compares the most terrible and violent things with scenes of beauty and tranquillity. When Achilles' spear point glints as it is about to be driven through Hector's throat, it is like the Evening Star on its path among the stars in the darkness of the night, the loveliest star set in the sky. It was Homer's genius to see both sides of everything, even war.

Fire is ambivalent. It can burn whole cities, it could even incinerate memory. Fire also burns on the hearth: it can light, warm, cook, keep the monsters at bay. The meaning of ancient Greece is ambivalent. From it we can derive inspiration and wisdom or over-confidence and danger. We find signs, fragmentary inscriptions which lead us, like Clearchus of Aï Khanoum, to copy down the words

ΓΝΩΘΙ ΣΕΑΥΤΟΝ.

'Know Thyself': *Oedipus and the Sphinx* by Ingres. The solution to the riddle is 'Man'.

BIBLIOGRAPHY

Manolis Andronikos, *Vergina: The Royal Tombs*, Athens: Ekdotike Athenon, 1984

W. H. Auden, 'The Greeks and Us', *Forewords and Afterwords*, London: Faber, 1973

Jonathan Barnes, *Early Greek Philosophy*, Harmondsworth: Penguin, 1987

Martin Bernal, *Black Athena: The Afro-asiatic Roots of Classical Civilization*, London: Free Association Books, 1987

Allan Bloom, *The Closing of the American Mind*, New York: Simon and Schuster, 1987

J. Boardman, *Greek Art*, revised edn, London: Thames and Hudson, 1985

J. Boardman, J. Griffin and O. Murray (eds), *The Oxford History of the Classical World*, Oxford: OUP, 1986

V. Bogdanov (ed.), *Encyclopedia of Political Institutions*, Oxford: Blackwell, 1987

R. Browning (ed.), *The Greek World*, London: Thames and Hudson, 1985

E. M. Butler, *The Tyranny of Greece over Germany*, Cambridge: CUP, 1935

J. M. Camp, *The Athenian Agora*, London: Thames and Hudson, 1986

W. M. Calder III (ed.), 'The Nineteenth-Century Rediscovery of Euripides', *Greek, Roman and Byzantine Studies* 27, no. 4, 1986

Anne Carson, *Eros the Bitter-sweet*, Princeton University Press, 1981

P. Cartledge et al., *The World of Athens*, Cambridge: CUP, 1984

H. Chadwick, *The Early Church*, Harmondsworth: Penguin, 1967

Howard Clarke, *Homer's Readers*, University of Delaware Press, 1981

M. R. Cohen and I. E. Drabkin, *A Source Book in Greek Science*, Cambridge, Massachusetts: Harvard University Press, 1958

David Constantine, *Early Greek Travellers and the Hellenic Ideal*, Cambridge: CUP, 1984

B. F. Cook, *The Elgin Marbles*, London: British Museum, 1984

J. J. Coulton, *Greek Architects at Work*, London: Elek, 1977

Jan Čulík, *Orpheus through the Ages*, London: Channel Four, 1985

G. E. M. de Ste Croix, *The Class Struggle in the Ancient Greek World*, London: Duckworth, 1981

J. Derrida, *Dissemination*, tr. B. Johnson, Chicago University Press, 1981

M. Detienne, *The Creation of Mythology*, tr. M. Cook, Chicago University Press, 1986

Deutsches Archäologisches Institut, *Berlin und die Antike*, Berlin: Wasmuth, 1978

W. B. Dinsmoor, *The Architecture of Ancient Greece*, 3rd edn, London: Batsford, 1950

E. R. Dodds, *The Greeks and the Irrational*, Cambridge: CUP, 1951

K. J. Dover, *Greek Homosexuality*, London: Duckworth, 1978

P. Easterling and B. Knox (eds), *The Cambridge History of Classical Literature: I Greek Literature*, Cambridge: CUP, 1985

Ecole nationale supérieure des Beaux-Arts, *Paris, Athens, Rome*, exhibition catalogue, Paris: 1982

Mark Edwards, *Homer: Poet of the Iliad*, Baltimore: The Johns Hopkins University Press, 1987

L. Eitner (ed.), *Neo-classicism and Romanticism 1750–1850*, Englewood Cliffs, New Jersey: Prentice Hall, 1971

European Cultural Centre of Delphi, *International Meeting of Ancient Greek Drama* (1985), Athens: ECCD, 1987

Lillian Feder, *Ancient Myth in Modern Poetry*, Princeton University Press, 1971

M. I. Finley, *Democracy Ancient and Modern*, London: Chatto & Windus, 2nd edn, 1984

M. I. Finley (ed.), *The Legacy of Greece: A new appraisal*, Oxford: OUP, 1981

W. G. Forrest, *The Emergence of Greek Democracy*, London: Weidenfeld, 1966

M. Foucault, *The History of Sexuality II: The Uses of Pleasure*, tr. R. Hurley, New York: Pantheon, 1986

William Gaunt, *Victorian Olympus*, London: Jonathan Cape, 1952

S. Goldhill, *Reading Greek Tragedy*, chs 2 and 5, Cambridge: CUP, 1986

Fritz Graf, *Griechische Mythologie*, Munich and Zürich: Artemis Verlag, 1985

Greek Centre of the International Theatre Institute, *Thespis: Number 4–5* (photographs of productions of Greek Drama), Athens: GCITI, June 1966

Michael Greenhalgh, *The Classical Tradition in Art*, London: Duckworth, 1978

G. Grigson, *The Goddess of Love*, London: Constable, 1970

Pierre Grimal, *The Dictionary of Classical Mythology*, tr. A. R. Maxwell-Hyslop, Oxford: Blackwell, 1986

W. K. C. Guthrie, *A History of Greek Philosophy III: Sophists and Socrates* and *IV: Plato*, Cambridge: CUP, 1969, 1975

Tony Harrison, 'Facing up to the Muses', lecture to the Classical Association in Bristol, April 1988, published in *Proceedings of the Classical Association* for 1988

Tony Harrison, *The Common Chorus: Part I Lysistrata*, first published in *AGNI* 27, 1988

M. H. Hansen, *The Athenian Assembly*, Oxford: Blackwell, 1987

Francis Haskell & Nicholas Penny, *Taste and the Antique*, New Haven, Connecticut: Yale University Press, 1981

G. Highet, *The Classical Tradition*, Oxford: OUP, 1949

James Hillman, *Re-Visioning Psychology*, New York: Harper and Row, 1975

Arthur Holmberg, 'Greek Tragedy in a New Mask Speaks to Today's Audiences', *New York Times*, 1 March 1987

Hugh Honour, *Neo-classicism*, Harmondsworth: Penguin, 1968

David Irwin, *English Neo-classical Art*, London: Faber, 1966

Charles Jencks, *Post-modernism: The New Classicism in Art and Architecture*, London: Academy Editions, 1987

Richard Jenkyns, *The Victorians and Ancient Greece*, Oxford: Blackwell, 1980

John Keegan, *The Mask of Command*, London: Jonathan Cape, 1987

Eva Keuls, *The Reign of the Phallus*, New York: Harper and Row, 1985

Katherine Callen King, *Achilles*, California University Press, 1987

G. S. Kirk, *The Nature of Greek Myth*, Harmondsworth: Penguin, 1974

P. O. Kristeller, *Renaissance Thought*, Cambridge, Massachusetts: Harvard University Press, 1955

R. A. Lanham, *The Motives of Eloquence*, New Haven, Connecticut: Yale University Press, 1976

Roger Ling, *The Greek World*, Oxford: Elsevier Phaidon, 1976

G. E. R. Lloyd, *Early Greek Science, Thales to Aristotle*, London: Chatto & Windus, 1970

G. E. R. Lloyd, *Greek Science after Aristotle*, London: Chatto & Windus, 1973

H. Lloyd-Jones, *Blood for the Ghosts*, London: Duckworth, 1982

N. Loraux and P. Vidal-Naquet, 'La formation de l'Athènes bourgeoise: essai d'historiographie 1750–1850', in *Classical Influences on Western Thought A.D. 1650–1870*, ed. R. Bolgar, Cambridge: CUP, 1979

Kenneth Mackinnon, *Greek Tragedy into Film*, London: Croom Helm, 1986

Colin Macleod, *Homer: Iliad Book XXIV*, Cambridge: CUP, 1982

Ellen Meiksens Wood, *Peasant, Citizen and Slave*, London: Verso, 1988

S. Miles (ed.), *Simone Weil: An Anthology*, London: Virago, 1986

D. Miller (ed.), *Encyclopedia of Political Thought*, Oxford: Blackwell, 1987

H. H. Miller, *Greece through the Ages*, London: Dent, 1972

J. Mittelstrass, '*Phaenomena bene fundata*: from saving the appearances to the mechanization of the world-picture', in *Classical Influences on Western Thought A.D. 1650–1870*, ed. R. Bolgar, Cambridge: CUP, 1979

J. Mordaunt Crook, *The Greek Revival*, London: John Murray, 1972

J. Mordaunt Crook, *The Dilemma of Style*, London: John Murray, 1987

Sandra Knudsen Morgan, *The J. Paul Getty Museum: Handbook of the Collections*, Malibu: 1986

De L. O'Leary, *How Greek Science Passed to the Arabs*, 2nd edn, London: Routledge, 1951

E. Panofsky, *Renaissance and Renascences in Western Art*, Stockholm: Uppsala University Press, 1960

Jeffrey Perl, *The Tradition of Return*, Princeton University Press, 1984

A. W. Pickard-Cambridge, *The Dramatic Festivals of Athens*, rev. J. Gould and D. Lewis, Oxford: OUP, 1988

Robert M. Pirsig, *Zen and the Art of Motorcycle Maintenance*, London: Bodley Head, 1974

J. J. Pollitt, *Art and Experience in Classical Greece*, Cambridge: CUP, 1972

Sarah Pomeroy, *Goddesses, Whores, Wives, and Slaves*, London: Hale, 1975

K. R. Popper, *The Open Society and Its Enemies*, 5th edn, London: Routledge, 1966

Elizabeth Rawson, *The Spartan Tradition in European Thought*, Oxford: OUP, 1969

Meyer Reinhold, *Classica Americana: The Greek and Roman Heritage in the United States*, Detroit: Wayne State University Press, 1984

Martin Robertson, *A Shorter History of Greek Art*, Cambridge: CUP, 1981

S. Sambursky, *The Physical World of the Greeks*, London: Routledge, 1956

L. M. Lombardi Satriani and M. Paoletti (eds), *Heroes from the Sea*, Rome: Gangemi editore and Casa del libro

M. R. Scherer, *The Legends of Troy in Art and Literature*, London: Phaidon, 1963

M. S. Silk and J. P. Stern, *Nietzsche on Tragedy*, Cambridge: CUP, 1981

Michael Silk, *The Iliad*, Cambridge: CUP, 1987

Kirsti Simonsuuri, *Homer's Original Genius*, Cambridge: CUP, 1979

C. Singer, *A Short History of Scientific Ideas*, Oxford: OUP, 1959

Terence Spencer, *Fair Greece, Sad Relic*, London: Weidenfeld, 1954; repr. Athens: Denise Harvey, 1986

W. B. Stanford, *The Ulysses Theme*, 2nd edn, Oxford: Blackwell, 1968

George Steiner, *The Death of Tragedy*, London: Faber, 1961

George Steiner, *Antigones*, Oxford: OUP, 1984

I. F. Stone, *The Trial of Socrates*, London: Jonathan Cape, 1988

Richard Stoneman (ed.), *A Literary Companion to Travel in Greece*, Harmondsworth: Penguin, 1984

Bibliography

R. Stoneman, *Land of Lost Gods*, London: Hutchinson, 1987

John Summerson, *The Classical Language of Architecture*, London: Thames and Hudson, 1963

O. Taplin, *Greek Tragedy in Action*, London: Methuen, 1978

Carol G. Thomas (ed.), *Paths From Ancient Greece*, Leiden: E. J. Brill, 1988

J. Travlos, *A Pictorial Dictionary of Athens*, London: Thames and Hudson, 1971

Fani-Maria Tsigakou, *The Rediscovery of Greece*, London: Thames and Hudson, 1981

Frank M. Turner, *The Greek Heritage in Victorian Britain*, New Haven, Connecticut: Yale University Press, 1981

J.-P. Vernant, *Myth and Society in Ancient Greece*, tr. J. Lloyd, London: Methuen, 1980

Brian Vickers, *In Defence of Rhetoric*, Oxford: OUP, 1988

Michael Vickers, 'Value and simplicity: eighteenth-century taste and the study of Greek vases', *Past and Present*, 116, 1987

A. G. Ward (ed.), *The Quest for Theseus*, London: Pall Mall Press, 1970

David Watkin, *A History of Architecture*, London: Barrie and Jenkins, 1986

David Watkin and T. Mellinghof, *German Architecture and the Classical Ideal 1740–1840*, London: Thames and Hudson, 1987

Christa Wolf, *Cassandra*, tr. J. Van Heurch, London: Virago, 1984

Michael Wood, *In Search of the Trojan War*, London: BBC, 1985

D. C. Young, *The Olympic Myth of Greek Amateur Athletics*, Chicago: Ares, 1984

PICTURE CREDITS

INDEX

Page numbers in italic refer to illustrations